INTIMATE PARTNER VIOLENCE

Since the 1970s the issue of intimate partner violence (IPV) has been explained through the patriarchal desire of men to control and dominate women, but this gendered perspective limits both our understanding of IPV and its treatment. *Intimate Partner Violence: New Perspectives in Research and Practice* is the first book of its kind to present a detailed and rigorous critique of current domestic violence research and practice within the same volume.

In this challenging new text, with contributions from the UK, the US, and Canada, the subject is assessed from a more holistic position. It provides a critical analysis of the issue of domestic violence including issues that are often not part of the mainstream discussion. Each of the chapters tackles a different area of research or practice, from a critical review of contemporary topics in domestic violence research, including a critical review of men's use of violence in relationships, a consideration of male victims, IPV within the LGBTQ+ community, perceptions of perpetrators and victims, and IPV within adolescent populations. The second half of the book examines challenges and opportunities for professionals working in the field and includes an analysis of an evidence informed perpetrator programme, the challenges faced working with male victims, and a discussion of the impact of domestic violence on children.

Culminating with a series of evidence-based recommendations to bridge the divide between academic and practitioner stakeholders and to inform future working practices, this is an essential resource for students and practitioners alike.

Dr Elizabeth A. Bates is a Senior Lecturer in Psychology at the University of Cumbria. Key areas of interest include intimate partner violence with a specific focus on exploring male victims' experiences.

Dr Julie C. Taylor is a Principal Lecturer responsible for Psychology and allied subjects at the University of Cumbria. Her current research projects include: children and young people's experiences of domestic violence and young people's experiences of technology assisted harmful sexual behaviour.

INTIMATE PARTNER VIOLENCE

New Perspectives in Research and Practice

Edited by Elizabeth A. Bates and Julie C. Taylor

Routledge
Taylor & Francis Group

LONDON AND NEW YORK

First published 2019
by Routledge
2 Park Square, Milton Park, Abingdon, Oxon OX14 4RN

and by Routledge
52 Vanderbilt Avenue, New York, NY 10017

Routledge is an imprint of the Taylor & Francis Group, an informa business

British Library Cataloguing in Publication Data
A catalogue record for this book is available from the British Library

Library of Congress Cataloging-in-Publication Data
A catalog record has been requested for this book

ISBN: 978-1-138-04899-7 (hbk)
ISBN: 978-1-138-04900-0 (pbk)
ISBN: 978-1-315-16984-2 (ebk)

Typeset in Bembo
by Taylor & Francis Books

CONTENTS

List of illustrations   *vii*
List of contributors   *viii*

1 Introduction: Why change current practice?   1
   Elizabeth A. Bates & Julie C. Taylor

PART I
Research   9

2 Challenging the gendered approach to men's violence towards
   women   11
   Elizabeth A. Bates

3 "Victim cast as perpetrator": Men's experiences of the Criminal
   Justice System following female-perpetrated intimate partner
   violence   26
   Jessica McCarrick

4 "It can't be that bad, I mean, he's a guy": Exploring judgements
   towards domestic violence scenarios varying on perpetrator and
   victim gender, and abuse type   43
   Benjamin A. Hine

5 Distinctions in adolescent dating violence: An exploration of
   etiology, scope, and prevention strategies of intimate partner
   violence in adolescence   58
   Katherine Maurer

6 Barriers to support in LGBTQ+ populations 73
Phillippa Laskey & Lauren T. Bolam

PART II
Practice **87**

7 The evolution of evidence-based treatment for domestic
violence perpetrators 89
John Hamel

8 Using research in practice: Up2U an innovative approach to
tackling domestic abuse 107
Amy Ford

9 Towards evidence-based treatment of female perpetrated
intimate partner violence and abuse 123
Erica Bowen & Jenny Mackay

10 Raising awareness and improving services for male victims of
abuse: Reflections on a three-year development project in
Scotland 139
Nick Smithers

11 Childhood experiences of domestic violence and adult
outcomes: Where are we now: challenges, debates, and
interventions? 154
Julie C. Taylor

12 Conclusions and recommendations: Why change current
practice? 172
Julie C. Taylor & Elizabeth A. Bates

Index 179

ILLUSTRATIONS

Figures

3.1 Main themes from analysis   30
3.2 Sub-themes   32
3.3 Sub-themes   34
3.4 Sub-themes   37

Tables

3.1 Participants   30
9.1 Summary of evidence-based risk factors for IPVA across
    research syntheses   132
9.2 Summary of global intervention methods for women IPVA
    perpetrators (summarised from Dowd & Leisring, 2008)   133

CONTRIBUTORS

Lauren Bolam, BSc (Hons), MSc is a doctoral student exploring aggression, control and bullying within men and women's violence in both intimate and non-intimate opposite sex and same-sex relationships. Lauren completed her BSc (Hons) Applied Psychology degree and MSc Psychological Research Methods at the University of Cumbria where she continues to complete her PhD

Prof Erica Bowen is a BPS Chartered Psychologist, HCPC registered Forensic Psychologist and Associate Fellow of the BPS. In the past 19 years Erica has published extensively on the topic of the rehabilitation of adults who are abusive and violent in their relationships. In addition, Erica has led teams to develop innovative interventions for this population in the criminal justice system and the community, and primary prevention programmes for adolescents within education. Erica is currently a Director of Research and Knowledge Exchange at the University of Worcester.

Amy Ford graduated with a BSc Psychology from The Open University in 2001. During this time she developed a keen interest in working in offender rehabilitation which led to her completing an MSc Forensic Psychology from The University of Portsmouth in 2004. Amy started working at Portsmouth City Council in 2014 where she was tasked with developing and writing a programme for people who use abusive and violent behaviours towards their intimate partners. Using the knowledge and skills she had developed during her education and career, she wrote the Up2U: Creating Health Relationships programme. Up2U has been delivered in Portsmouth since May 2014 and is now delivered in Renfrewshire Criminal Justice Area, Poole, Bournemouth & Dorset Local Authority areas, in the Rotherham area and is currently being rolled out in East Dunbartonshire Criminal Justice area.

Dr John Hamel, Ph.D., LCSW, has provided treatment for perpetrators of family violence since 1992 in his private practice in the San Francisco Bay Area, and is also a researcher, currently Editor-in-Chief of the peer-reviewed scholarly journal, Partner Abuse. Dr. Hamel regularly conducts trainings in the field of domestic violence, and serves as an expert witness in forensic cases.

Dr Benjamin A. Hine, CPsychol is a Senior Lecturer in Psychology at University of West London. Since joining UWL in 2014, Ben has worked on numerous projects and collaborations in the areas of domestic and sexual violence, focusing specifically on how gender norms and stereotypes influence the judgement and investigation of such crimes. This work includes research conducted with the Metropolitan Police, the Mayor's Office for Policing and Crime (MOPAC), various sexual violence charities including Survivors Manchester, and SafeLives. He has a particular interest in 'invisible' or 'hidden' populations, such as male victims, which are the focus of the results outlined in this book.

Philippa Laskey BSc (Hons), MSc is a lecturer in psychology at the University of Cumbria. She has a BSc(Hons) in Applied Psychology and an MSc in Applied Forensic Psychology. Her research is mainly focused on gender and sexuality in intimate partner violence, and she is particularly interested in how trans people experience intimate partner violence victimisation.

Jenny Mackay is currently completing her PhD at Coventry University, researching the treatment needs of women who perpetrate intimate partner violence. Jenny previously completed her MSc in Applied Forensic Psychology. Since then, she has predominantly worked as a practitioner in a range of forensic and health settings, including prisons, secure children's homes and inpatient units for adults with intellectual disabilities and behaviours that challenge. She has previously contributed to research projects in the areas of adult education and child sexual exploitation.

Dr Katherine Maurer, Ph.D., LMSW is an Assistant Professor in the School of Social Work at McGill University where she is also a faculty member of the McGill Centre for Child and Family Research. She obtained her Ph.D. in Social Work at New York University Silver School of Social Work and a Master of Social Work from Hunter College School of Social Work, New York. Dr. Maurer practiced in New York City as a clinical social worker and a trauma therapist. Her interdisciplinary research focuses on adolescent mental and behavioral health during the transition to adulthood. Particularly, Dr. Maurer studies the physiological impact of exposure to extreme stressors, such as interpersonal violence and poverty, on the development of self-regulation capacities in adolescence and adults.

Dr Jessica McCarrick is registered as a Counselling Psychologist with the Health and Care Professions Council and a Chartered Psychologist with the British Psychological Society. She works in private practice as well as the Tees, Esk and Wear

Valley NHS Foundation Trust (her chapter was written independently of the Tees, Esk and Wear Valley NHS Trust). In her NHS clinical practice she works within a secondary care mental health team, providing psychological assessment and therapy for adults experiencing a range of complex and enduring mental health problems. Dr McCarrick has published research exploring male survivor's experiences of domestic violence. Her specialist interests include social justice, men's mental health and complex trauma.

Nick Smithers graduated with an MA Hons anthropology from the University of Aberdeen in 2003. Following a spell working as a project worker in a residential unit for adults with enduring and significant mental health problems, he completed a MA in Social Work at University of Edinburgh. Nick went on to work for five years as a father's worker in Muirhouse, Edinburgh where he completed practitioner research into fathers' experience of child protection. This research garnered significant media attention as it highlighted iniquities in the child protection system affecting some men and their children. He then moved on to become the National Development Officer for Abused Men in Scotland which is described in this publication. Currently Nick is a children and families social worker and practice educator in the Scottish Borders.

1

INTRODUCTION

Why change current practice?

Elizabeth A. Bates & Julie C. Taylor

In the introduction to their edited book "Family Interventions in Domestic Violence: A Handbook of Gender-Inclusive Theory and Treatment", Hamel and Nicholls (2007) describe the changes that were occurring within the field of intimate partner violence (IPV) research and practice; specifically, they said a "Revolution is taking place in the field of domestic violence" (p. xxxix). The authors go on to describe the increased attention paid to women's violence, the dynamics of violence within couples and families, and the ineffectiveness of current intervention models, all of which presented challenges to the dominant narratives that rendered IPV as an issue of women's inequality as a consequence of male privilege and power. Over ten years later, we find ourselves in a similar position. There is a wealth of literature that has developed over the last four decades that evidences IPV as a complex, multifarious issue; but policy, treatment provision and practice does not reflect the evidence base that exists.

Dobash and Dobash (1979) in their book "Violence against Wives" detail some important milestones in the 1970s that led to more public awareness of violence against women and IPV. In 1971 the first women's aid was opened in Chiswick, England. It was originally opened as a place for women to gather and socialise, but it soon became apparent that there were women in their community who were being beaten by their husbands. This led Erin Pizzey to open the first Battered Women's Shelter in England in the same year (Dutton, 2006). These events, and the feminist movement that originated around the same time, can be credited with raising awareness of domestic violence more widely. Indeed, prior to this in practice, violence within the family was routinely ignored in Britain, the United States, and Canada unless it had escalated to homicide. This continued into the first half of the 20th Century where both the English and American suffragettes took it up as an issue (Dobash & Dobash, 1979), although it became side-lined by the issue of votes for women. From this point, its seriousness diminished, and the perception reverted back to an attitudinal model that valued family privacy; violence that occurred within the home should be dealt with there and not aired publically (Dutton, 2006). Dutton labelled this the "Age of Denial" and during this time, until around the early 1980s, the police were reluctant to get involved in domestic disturbances as the sanctity of the family was valued so highly.

From the 1970s onwards, as social awareness grew, so did a body of research that explored and tried to understand violence against women. This research, and the models that evolved from it, presented IPV as an issue of gendered violence meaning specifically: "Gender-based violence against women shall mean violence that is directed against a woman because she is a woman or that affects women disproportionately" (European Institute for Gender Equality, 2018). Feminist researchers such as Dobash and Dobash (1979, 2004) believe that the cause of IPV is gender, and that it should always be studied in the context of gender (e.g. McHugh, Livingston, & Ford, 2005). Proponents of this model suggest that men use violence as one mechanism to control and dominate women; this control is of a social and historically constructed origin, arising out of gender inequality and male privilege. As a model for understanding IPV, it has provided the framework for a wealth of research that worked with women as victims, and men (often in prison or mandated to programmes) as perpetrators to try and understand the abuse and reduce its impact on women.

The Duluth Model was established in the United States in 1981 as an intervention programme derived from the Duluth Domestic Abuse Intervention Project (Pence & Paymar, 1993). It was designed to protect women from the tyranny of abusive men. The programme's curriculum is founded upon the concept of male power and control within relationships. The central feature of the model is a "Power and Control Wheel" which has become their signature symbol. Their treatment of aggression within a relationship was based on the assumption that men's violence was always driven by power and control and that any aggression perpetrated by a female partner must be self-defensive. The empirical basis of their model came from a sample of nine clients made up of men who had perpetrated IPV, and women who had been victim of it. The authors of the model omitted to acknowledge the problems that are associated with generalising from such a small and unrepresentative sample (Dutton & Corvo, 2006); yet one of the authors did later acknowledge:

> By determining that the need or desire for power was the motivating force behind battering, we created a conceptual framework that, in fact, did not fit the lived experience of many of the men and women we were working with…Speaking for myself, I found that many of the men I interviewed did not seem to articulate a desire for power over their partner. Although I relentlessly took every opportunity to point out to men in the groups that they were so motivated and merely in denial, the fact that few men ever articulated such a desire went unnoticed by me and many of my co-workers. Eventually, we realized that we were finding what we had already predetermined to find.
>
> *(Pence, 1999; pp. 29–30).*

Since the 1980s, this model has become the dominant way of understanding IPV, and has been influential in research, policy, and practice, and despite Pence's (1999) comments, the Duluth Model, and its derivatives, remains the most prevalent approach to perpetrator treatment in many Western countries. Despite this dominance, there is a body of literature that has undermined this approach from a theoretical and practical standpoint. For example, research has demonstrated that this approach ignores many factors known to influence men's and women's IPV such as: emotional dysregulation (Birkley & Eckhardt, 2015), the overlap between IPV and general aggression (e.g. Bates, Graham-Kevan, & Archer, 2014), and relationship dynamics such as bidirectional IPV (Langhinrichsen-Rohling, Misra, Selwyn, & Rohling, 2012). From an intervention perspective, studies that have explored the effectiveness of Duluth-based interventions have largely found them to be unsuccessful. For example, Babcock, Green, and Robie (2004) performed a meta-analysis of 22 studies and found minimal effects, concluding that the current interventions are inadequate in reducing recidivism much beyond the effect of arrest and other criminal justice sanctions. Despite this evidence, it remains the dominant curriculum within the US, the UK, and Canada. It is a political model, and we see public policy being dictated by politically motivated activists rather than by academics, researchers, and psychologists (Dutton & Corvo, 2006; Bates, Graham-Kevan, Bolam, & Thornton, 2017). Indeed, this model experiences an "immunity" from having to answer to methodologically rigorous, external, and empirical evaluation with political concerns taking precedence over science and a strong evidence base (Corvo, Dutton, & Chen, 2008; p. 112).

Mounting evidence suggests that current interventions are not effective; a significant number of studies demonstrate that the perpetrators are not always men or the victims women, therefore it is clear that a volume that pulls together this evidence and provides a useful tool for researchers and practitioners is long overdue. The aim of this book is to challenge some current, gendered practices of IPV. Specifically, it presents challenges and offers alternatives that ensure research and practice is effectively serving all those affected by IPV. Each of the proposed chapters tackles a different key area in either research or practice. The book is original in several ways; firstly, it brings together a detailed, rigorous critique of current practice in a way not seen before, to give the reader an awareness of the key issues being debated in this area. Secondly, both research and practice are critically examined within the same volume. Finally, the book culminates with a series of evidence-based recommendations to bridge the divide between academic and practitioner stakeholders and to inform practice. There exists a polarisation in the field, an academic divide that pits women's advocates, or feminist researchers, against family violence researchers; it causes conflict and controversy and detracts from the key goal which is a reduction of domestic and family violence. It is an issue that creates disputes about ideology which detracts from the shift to evidence informed practice. This is an issue that is not seen in other areas of violence research, indeed, as Bates et al. (2017) highlight: "The lack of research-informed practice here is quite unique and does not seem to be as great a factor in less politicized fields" (p. 27). It is hoped that this book could offer an opportunity to bridge the divide between conflicting research groups, and also further bridge the gap between research and practice.

This book is primarily aimed at researchers, practitioners, and educators working in the field of IPV. It will also be of interest and value to policy makers who are reviewing legislation and those involved in commissioning psychological services, perpetrator interventions, and victim services. As a text it challenges current practice with a gender-inclusive, strong, empirical evidence base that could be used as a rationale for making changes in policy and provision. The book is firmly grounded in evidence-based practice, but is also accessible to ensure it can be useful beyond the academic sector.

Outline of chapters

The book is divided into two parts; one covering the most contemporary research in the area, the second covering a commentary on current interventions and practice. The five chapters in Part I of this book offer extensive reviews and empirical research that not only challenge traditional models but provide a compelling evidence-base that supports a more inclusive and evidence-informed approach. Part II, and the latter five chapters, focus on how this evidence-base could, or indeed should, work in practice. It includes a focus on implementing evidence-based practice, but also the obstacles that have been experienced in doing so.

With so much of the historic work on IPV focusing on men's violence towards women, this seems an appropriate place to begin. In her critical exploration of the literature base on men's violence, Elizabeth Bates reviews the existing research on the feminist, or gendered, model of men's IPV and proposes that it would be beneficial to move research and practice beyond this. Using evidence including the sex parity in IPV perpetration (e.g. Archer, 2000), women's use of controlling behaviour (e.g. Bates et al., 2014), the frequency of bidirectional or mutual abuse (e.g. Langhinrichsen-Rohling et al., 2012), and the range of risk factors that predict men's IPV (e.g. Valois, MacDonald, Bretous, Fischer, & Drane, 2002), Bates asserts that it would be more appropriate to consider IPV within the context of both family violence and other general aggression models to allow for more effective interventions to be developed.

The gendered approach to IPV lacks inclusivity; in particular it has focused on working with women as victims, and rarely seeing men's victimisation as anything more than a consequence of women acting in self-defence. The next chapter provides an in-depth exploration of male victims' experiences of female-perpetrated IPV with a specific focus on their contact with the Criminal Justice System. Jessica McCarrick reflects on specific socio-psychological factors that can make men more vulnerable to IPV including childhood socialisation with boys being taught not to hit girls, even in self-defence. She goes on to report on a study working with six British men who reported feeling cast as a perpetrator within their contact with police, and how this perpetuated their trauma responses, leading to psychological difficulties.

The third chapter in this part of the book focuses on attitudes towards IPV victims and perpetrators. Benjamin Hine reports on an empirical study that sought to explore judgements of acceptability, trauma, severity, and blame towards hypothetical IPV scenarios. The findings from the study suggest that perceptions of these issues vary significantly based on the gender of both the perpetrator and victim, with some scenarios judged as being significantly more acceptable and less traumatic than others. Hine goes on to discuss future research implications, with a specific focus on the need to challenge the perceptions of IPV associated with the traditional gender-based models, and how this could impact on other vulnerable victim groups.

The fourth chapter moves the focus towards adolescent dating violence with a strong theme around bidirectional IPV. Katherine Maurer discusses the challenges involved with shifting the focus towards IPV in younger populations as including the distinction of not seeing IPV as a normative teen socialisation process, the limitations that exist when we see IPV as a unilateral issue of one-sided violence (specifically in this model, men's violence towards women), and the need to tailor prevention and intervention strategies to adolescent relationships. Maurer discusses the complexities of adapting intervention strategies that focus on patriarchy and social learning theory as the root cause of couple violence, rather than using psychobiological, developmental, and intergenerational transmission of family violence.

The final chapter in the first part of the book focuses on barriers faced within other neglected victim groups, specifically the LGBTQ+ population. Specifically, Philippa Laskey and Lauren Bolam discuss how IPV within these communities are frequently underreported and unrecognised, and how they are not represented within support services. With a focus on IPV within same-sex relationships in the first part of the chapter, and IPV for transgender individuals in the second part, barriers to support include: homophobia, transphobia, not identifying within the traditional model of IPV, fear of not being believed, and a fear of "outing" themselves.

The second part of the book shifts the focus on to considering IPV within practice settings. It builds on the critical review of literature and empirical studies presented within the first part and explores the practicalities of implementing this in practice-based settings. In the first chapter of this part, John Hamel discusses the evolution of evidence-based treatment approaches in IPV including reflections on his own experience as a practitioner. Developing from some of Hamel's own books, he discusses some of the themes within his experience including how a more informed understanding of IPV characteristics, causes, consequences, and current intervention approaches can increase the impact and effectiveness of future treatment outcomes.

Whilst Hamel discusses a reluctance for some practitioners to move beyond the traditional, Duluth-based models in practice, in the next chapter Amy Ford discusses the development of the UK based "Up2U: Creating Healthy Relationships Programme". This programme utilises the principles of risk, needs, and responsivity (Andrews, Bonta, & Wormith, 2011) offering a gender inclusive, tailored response based on an individual need rather than using an ideological model based on male dominance, power, and control (e.g. Pence & Paymar, 1993). This chapter details the evidence-base and journey of the development and implementation of Up2U, and the University of Portsmouth evaluation and research into its effectiveness. Whilst at the early stages of delivery, initial referrals were overwhelmingly men, there has since been a significant number of referrals of women, and for both partners in an abusive relationship.

The focus on men's violence has had an impact on the field of IPV in many ways. The lack of a strong evidence-base regarding female perpetrators of IPV is the focus of the next chapter; Erica Bowen and Jenny Mackay critically review what is known about IPV perpetration by women in heterosexual relationships. This evidence is then discussed in relation to documented intervention approaches with a view to providing practitioners with a set of guidelines to refer to when seeking to intervene with women who are violent in intimate relationships.

The penultimate chapter involves a reflection on three years of a development project sponsored by the Scottish Government reporting on the progress made and provides an overview of the political and service landscape in Scotland. Nick Smithers' discussion includes an overview of the interplay of legislation, policy, lobbying, activism, and media which perpetuates a public narrative of IPV which has historically excluded male victims and prevented the development of therapeutic interventions for violent and abusive women. Evidence presented includes case studies from the Abused Men in Scotland service delivery mapping exercise and evidence from research carried out with fathers involved in child protection processes, which raises serious questions about domestic abuse policy and practice.

In the final chapter within this practice section of the book Julie Taylor discusses the literature pertaining to children's experiences of living in a domestic violence context. Julie draws upon data from a three-year project working with women who had been sentenced to community payback for largely acquisitive crimes. The women's retrospective phenomenological accounts of growing up in violent homes are explored in relation to their subsequent offending behaviour and current thinking within the field.

The final concluding chapter draws on much of the evidence that has been presented within the book to offer conclusions and recommendations for future research and practice. Scholars and practitioners alike are all working towards the same goal, to reduce violence within the family; it is hoped with more cooperation and cohesion that we could work towards bridging the research practice nexus, and welcome true evidence-based practice.

References

Andrews, D. A., Bonta, J., & Wormith, J. S. (2011). The Risk-Need-Responsivity (RNR) Model: Does adding the Good Lives Model contribute to effective crime prevention?. *Criminal Justice and Behavior*, 38(7), 735–755.

Archer, J. (2000) Sex differences in aggression between heterosexual partners: A meta-analytic review. *Psychological Bulletin*, 126(5), 651–680 doi:10.1037/0033-2909.126.5.651

Babcock, J. C., Green, C. E., & Robie, C. (2004). Does batterer's treatment work? A meta-analytic review of domestic violence treatment. *Clinical Psychology Review*, 23, 1023–1053. doi:10.1016/j.cpr.2002.07.001

Bates, E. A., Graham-Kevan, N., & Archer, J. (2014). Testing predictions from the male control theory of men's partner violence. *Aggressive Behavior*, 40, 42–55. doi:10.1002/ab.21499

Bates, E. A., Graham-Kevan, N., Bolam, L. T., & Thornton, A. J. V. (2017). Review of domestic violence perpetrator programs in the UK. *Partner Abuse*, 8(1), 3–46. doi:10.1891/1946-6560.8.1.37

Birkley, E. L. & Eckhardt, C. I. (2015). Anger, hostility, internalizing negative emotions, and intimate partner violence perpetration: A meta-analytic review. *Clinical Psychology Review*, 37, 40–56. doi:10.1016/j.cpr.2015. 01. 00doi:2

Corvo, K., Dutton, D. G., & Chen, W. Y. (2008). Towards evidence-based practice with domestic violence perpetrators. *Journal of Aggression, Maltreatment and Trauma*, 16(2), 111–130. doi:10.1080/10926770801921246

Dobash, R. E. & Dobash, R. (1979). *Violence against wives*. London: Open Books.

Dobash, R. P. & Dobash, R. E. (2004). Women's violence to men in intimate relationships: Working on a Puzzle. *British Journal of Criminology*, 44, 324–349. doi:10.1093/bjc/azh026

Dutton, D. G. (2006). The gender debate and the feminist paradigm. In Dutton, D. G. (Ed.) *Rethinking domestic violence* (pp. 109–129). Vancouver: UBS Press.

Dutton, D. G. & Corvo, K. (2006). Transforming a flawed policy: A call to revive psychology and science in domestic violence research and practice. *Aggression and Violent Behavior*, 11, 457–483. doi:10.1016/j.avb.2006.01.007

European Institute for Gender Equality (2018). What is gender-based violence? Retrieved from: http://eige.europa.eu/gender-based-violence/what-is-gender-based-violence (Accessed on 15 August, 2018).

Hamel, J. & Nicholls, T. L. (Eds.). (2007). *Family interventions in domestic violence: A handbook of gender-inclusive theory and treatment*. New York: Springer Publishing Company.

Langhinrichsen-Rohling, J., Misra, T. A., Selwyn, C., & Rohling, M. L. (2012). Rates of bidirectional versus unidirectional intimate partner violence across sample, sexual orientations, and race/ethnicities: A comprehensive review. *Partner Abuse*, 3(2), 199–230. doi:10.1891/1946-6560.3.2.199

McHugh, M. C., Livingston, N. A., & Ford, A. (2005). A postmodern approach to women's use of violence: Developing multiple and complex conceptualizations. *Psychology of Women Quarterly*, 29(3), 323–336. doi:10.1111/j.1471–6402.2005.00226.x

Pence, E. (1999). Some thoughts on philosophy. In Shepherd, M. & Pence, E. (Eds.), *Coordinating community responses to domestic violence: Lessons from Duluth and beyond* (pp. 25–40). Thousand Oaks, CA: Sage.

Pence, E. & Paymar, M. (1993). *Education groups for men who batter: The Duluth Model*. New York: Springer Publishing

Valois, R. F., MacDonald, J. M., Bretous, L., Fischer, M. A., & Drane, J. W. (2002). Risk factors and behaviors associated with adolescent violence and aggression. *American Journal of Health Behavior*, 26(6), 454–464. doi:10.5993/AJHB.26.6.6

PART I
Research

2

CHALLENGING THE GENDERED APPROACH TO MEN'S VIOLENCE TOWARDS WOMEN

Elizabeth A. Bates

Up until the 1970s, intimate partner violence (IPV) was routinely ignored in Britain, the United States, and Canada, unless it has escalated to homicide; Dutton (2006a) labelled this the "age of denial" (p. 16); here the sanctity and privacy of the home was valued and to be upheld. However, when Erin Pizzey opened the first women's shelter in 1971 for women who were escaping abusive relationships, a research movement began to explore men's violence against women. What followed was the development of a gendered model of IPV. Proponents of the gendered, or feminist, model (e.g. Dobash & Dobash, 1979, 2004) posit that IPV is an asymmetrical problem of men's violence towards women, with gender ascribed as a causal factor. The violence exhibited is constructed as an extension of the domination and control of wives by their husbands. This male privilege and control narrative has exerted considerable influence since the 1970s and deserves considerable credit for the influence it has had politically and in terms of awareness raising; however, it might now be argued to be in danger of offering a one size fits all response to what is clearly a complex social problem. The fixation on gender as central no longer accounts for a number of contemporary research findings (see Bates, Graham-Kevan, & Archer, 2014) and thus is potentially holding back our understanding of IPV.

Within this feminist literature there are a number of assumptions made about IPV, namely that: the majority of IPV is perpetrated by men as part of a pattern of control towards their female partners (e.g. Dobash & Dobash, 1979, 2004); women's IPV is trivial and is perpetrated in self-defence (e.g. Saunders, 1988); society tolerates men's violence towards women (e.g. Pagelow, 1984); and IPV offenders are different to other types of violent offenders (e.g. Browne, 1987). The aim of this chapter is to challenge and critique the tenets of this theory with evidence from the IPV and general violence literature.

Sex parity in IPV perpetration

There is a wealth of research in the last three decades that details the sexual parity in IPV perpetration. Straus (1979) developed a gender-neutral survey method, the Conflict Tactics Scale (CTS), which has been utilised in many individual studies, and culminated in Archer's (2000) meta-analysis, using 82 studies and a total of over 64,000 participants. Archer found that women reported perpetrating aggressive acts towards their partners more frequently than men. Other more recent studies have also found this difference (e.g. Bates et al., 2014; Bates & Graham-Kevan, 2016)

Since the development of this body of research, more empirical attention has been paid to women's violence. Feminist researchers (e.g. Dobash & Dobash, 1979; Yllo, 1993) have suggested that women's violence only occurs in self-defence or is quite trivial in its outcomes. In contrast, studies examining IPV in community samples often find that it is mutual. For example, Gray and Foshee (1997) found that 66% of their sample reported being in a mutually violent relationship and that this violence was reciprocal, with participants reporting similar amounts of violence as perpetrators and as victims. When examining couples with only one violent partner, they found a higher proportion of men (26%) reported being victims only and a higher proportion of women (29%) reported being perpetrators only. This is further supported by longitudinal research (e.g. O'Leary et al., 1989). Studies that have examined which partner hit out first (e.g. Stets & Straus, 1989) suggest that not only is the violence mutual in severity, but also women more often than men strike the first blow. These studies indicate the presence of mutual violence, but also show that women's perpetration often occurs in the absence of violence from their partner. This does not support the belief that women's violence is mostly motivated by self-defence.

Women's violence is further seen within same-sex relationships; lesbian relationships tend to be significantly more violent than gay male relationships (e.g. Bologna, Waterman, & Dawson, 1987) and more violent than heterosexual relationships (e.g. Lie, Schilit, Bush, Montagne, & Reyes, 1991). Further evidence from Tjaden and Thoennes (2000) suggested that men were no more violent in heterosexual than homosexual relationships, which may indicate that their violence is not a function of dominance, or special attitudes towards women.

Researchers who situate themselves within a feminist, or gendered, model of IPV use crime statistics, such as police data, to support their argument. For example, Melton and Belknap (2003) support this assertion by noting that within police and court data, 86% of the defendants were male and only 14% female. They believe that this adds support to the feminist view that men are much more likely than women to be the perpetrators of IPV. This belief runs counter to a growing body of literature that details the stigma attached to male victimisation; evidence may explain the observed differences in crime reporting by men (e.g. Steinmetz, 1978), and that male victimisation reports are not taken seriously (e.g. Buzawa & Austin, 1993).

Chivalry

Proponents of the gendered model of IPV argue that a patriarchal society allows men to abuse women, and that they are not reprimanded for doing so because they are upholding the patriarchal values and men's absolute power. Felson (2002) is one of several researchers who have argued that the norm of chivalry actually protects women from men in society – he further refers to the inadequacy of the word; it implies that this is just to protect women from men, when it includes the protection of women from other men, other women, children and non-human sources such as natural disasters (e.g. women boarding lifeboats first on the Titanic). Support for this norm comes from studies of helping behaviour; for example, Eagly and Crowley's (1986) meta-analysis revealed women were consistently more likely to receive help from men, with men being more likely to give help compared to women. These sex differences were more pronounced when there were audiences present, suggesting that this chivalrous effect is normative.

Chivalry means that there is a greater moral condemnation of violence when the victim is a woman and also more serious punishments for the offenders. Felson believes that chivalry can reflect an exchange of submission, a sort of benevolent sexism (Glick & Fiske, 2001), which is controversial as it portrays women as weak, and is associated with traditional gender roles. He argued that this is supported by the prevalence of women's violence, but also by research on reactions to violence against women. Many studies have examined evaluations of IPV and whether violence by one sex is condemned more than the other (e.g. Harris & Cook, 1994; Sorenson & Taylor, 2005). Felson and Feld (2009) analysed a large representative sample of 810 American adults and found that participants were more likely to condemn men's assaults on women than any other gender combination, and they were more likely to report this type of assault to the police. Furthermore, participants' condemnation of male violence to women was unaffected by the level of violence committed by women, suggesting that chivalry is not just reserved for those who comply with traditional gender roles.

Control

Coercive control, emotional aggression, psychological aggression, and controlling behaviour are all terms that represent a form of IPV characterised by non-physical aggression and abuse. The use of multiple terms means there have been many definitions of what coercive control is and how it is measured; common themes that are seen amongst the definitions include humiliation, threats, degradation, and isolation (e.g. Follingstad & DeHart, 2000). Within IPV, it entails one partner seeking domination, power, and control over the other using a variety of methods such as stopping contact with friends and family, threatening physical abuse, limiting financial resources, and using children as part of the manipulation. This type of aggression is the most common form of IPV with prevalence averaging around 80%, although there is a wide variation within the literature (Carney & Barner,

2012), attributed to the lack of a clear operationalised definition. Findings from the National Intimate Partner and Sexual Violence Survey found that nearly half of the men and women who took part in the survey reported experiencing some form of coercive control/emotional aggression in their lifetime.

Control and coercion are not present in this way in all relationships; Johnson (1995) sought to create a typology of abuse within relationships that characterised physical aggression both with and without the presence of control. He labelled low control aggression as "situational couple violence", and that characterised by coercion and control as "intimate terrorism". The latter of which Johnson (1995) believed was primarily perpetrated by men against women. Research has since confirmed the credibility of the typology but not the predictions about gender – both men and women are equally as likely to be categorised as aggressive and controlling to their partners (e.g. Bates & Graham-Kevan, 2016; Bates et al., 2014).

In their review, Carney and Barner (2012) found large population surveys revealed that non-physical abuse is more than four times as common as physical aggression by a current partner (Outlaw, 2009). This behaviour is also the most common amongst those also experiencing physical aggression; as well as being common in a mutual or bidirectional sense demonstrating the reciprocal nature of the behaviour (Follingstad & Edmundson, 2010). This is further supported by studies that use both members of the couple as participants; Panuzio and DiLillo (2010) found rates upward of 90% prevalence of emotional and controlling behaviour.

There has been a tendency in the literature to focus on female victimisation (e.g. Kaukinen & Powers, 2015), but Carney and Barner's (2012) review indicated that men and women are equally at risk of being perpetrators and victims with more recent studies supporting this (e.g. Fawson, 2015; Hamberger & Larsen, 2015). For example, Bates et al. (2014) explored IPV, aggression to same-sex non-intimates and controlling behaviour and found women were more physically aggressive, and more controlling, to their partners than men. Control was found to be a significant predictor of both IPV and aggression to same-sex others; men and women in the higher control group perpetrated significantly more aggressive behaviours to partners and same-sex others. Furthermore, it is also something that is found to be reciprocal and mutual; men and women are both perpetrating and experiencing victimisation of this abuse within the same relationships (e.g. Winstok & Smadar-Dror, 2015). Despite this gender parity in experience, Arnocky and Vaillancourt (2014) found participants held more negative attitudes towards male compared to female victims.

Traditional models have historically suggested that patriarchy is the cause of men's use of controlling behaviour towards their female partners. However, these studies demonstrating the gender parity in this behaviour and the overlap with other types of aggression have led researchers to explore other factors. For example, Clift and Dutton (2011) found that participants who recalled parental rejection, borderline personality organisation, trauma, and anger all demonstrated moderately strong relationships with women's self-reported psychological abuse. Females' perpetration of psychological aggression has also been associated with emotional regulation and anger (Shorey, Cornelius, & Idema, 2011).

The literature reviewed here demonstrates that control is not exclusively a characteristic of men's aggression to their partners; this overlap found between IPV, same-sex aggression, and controlling behaviour suggests that IPV can be part of a more generally aggressive interpersonal style (e.g. Langhinrichsen-Rohling, 2010). This is further supported by studies of bullying suggesting that it shares similar risk factors to IPV perpetration. Corvo and deLara (2010) proposed that multiple developmental pathways can lead bullies to adult IPV perpetration, including through adolescent dating aggression. Again, this may indicate a coercive interpersonal style that originates early in development.

Bidirectional and mutual IPV

A key aspect of the debate around the gendered theory of IPV lies in the extent to which violence between partners is unilateral or bidirectional. The development of the CTS (Straus, 1979), and the use of large-scale studies and meta-analyses (e.g. Archer, 2000) have revealed the extent of the symmetry between men's and women's perpetration; a consistent finding that highlights the importance of considering the dynamics that exist within violent relationships. Understanding the behaviour of both members of the couple can further aid our understanding in terms of the context of the violence. Examining the context may provide further insight into motivations and risk factors, as well as hold significant implications for risk assessment.

The Partner Abuse State of Knowledge (PASK) was a comprehensive review of the literature using 48 studies that reported rates of bidirectional versus unidirectional IPV. Langhinrichsen-Rohling, Misra, Selwyn, and Rohling (2012) selected studies for their review based on criteria around the measurement of specifically bidirectional or mutual aggression, and not just the relationship between self-reported perpetration and victimisation. Within their review they explored bidirectional and mutual aggression, and also where there were instances of unilateral aggression within the same samples, and what the sex differences were for these. They calculated a weighted rate of violence across their collated studies of 2,991 sampling units (1,615 women and 1,376 men). The weighted rates showed that prevalence of violence across these samples was 47.0% and of this, 59.6% was bidirectional violence. The remaining 40.4% was unidirectional which was further categorised into 17.5% male to female and 22.9% female to male.

Since the PASK review the examination of bidirectional violence explicitly has waned. However, a number of studies have found significant relationships between IPV perpetration and victimisation (e.g. Bates et al., 2014). Other studies have revealed varying levels of prevalence of bidirectional aggression within a range of samples. For example, Renner, Reese, Peek-Asa, and Ramirez (2015) used a sample of 517 cohabiting rural couples and found 29% occurrence of bidirectional aggression. Whereas, Charles, Whitaker, Swahn, and DiClemente (2011) used a large nationally representative sample of young adults and made comparisons of uni- and bidirectional perpetrators finding that 65.4% were bidirectional.

The implications of the prevalence of bidirectional abuse are important for considering the gendered approach to men's IPV. If bidirectional aggression is the most common found between couples where there is IPV present, then this offers a powerful challenge to a model that suggests the majority of IPV is perpetrated by men against women. Furthermore, when both members of the couple are being aggressive then it suggests causes could be in dyadic areas for example around conflict management (Langhinrichsen-Rohling et al., 2012) or mismatched attachment styles (e.g. Doumas, Pearson, Elgin, & McKinley, 2008). It further highlights the importance of considering women's aggression in uni- or bidirectional relationships. It is even more important to recognise bidirectional violence as a common IPV pattern because research suggests that violent relationships of this type tend to result in worse outcomes and involve more severe violence (e.g. Sullivan, McPartland, Price, Cruza-Guet, & Swan, 2013), a finding that has implications for risk assessment (Bates, 2016).

Are IPV offenders different to other violent offenders?

The gendered model suggests that IPV and other types of violence are etiologically different, that men who commit IPV are different from men who commit other violent crimes. The violence perspective would hold that the motives of IPV are not much different from those of other types of violence (Felson & Lane, 2010). Research by Felson and Messner (1998) found that men and women who murder their partners were equally likely to have violent criminal records as men and women who kill in other circumstances. Additionally, personality factors and IPV perpetration are similar for men and women (e.g. Ehrensaft, Cohen, & Johnson, 2006). Often feminist research that examines these issues has used a prison/treatment sample of male batterers (e.g. Mauricio & Gormley, 2001), or asks women in shelters about their violent partner's behaviour (e.g. Saunders, 1986) which biases the study in favour of the gendered perspective, as it is more likely that Johnson's (1995) "intimate terrorists", or extreme male batterers are being included.

Outside the home, the sex difference in aggression is strongly in favour of men. There are many studies (e.g. Archer, 2004), and crime statistics (e.g. Povey, Coleman, Kaiza, Hoare, & Jansson, 2008), that indicate that men are much more likely to be aggressive outside the home, and outside intimate relationships. This contrasting pattern of sex differences has been explored in the literature through looking at sex-specific, and target-specific effects of aggression. Cross, Tee, and Campbell (2011) presented participants with three conflict scenarios and asked them to rate the likelihood of using physical aggression, verbal aggression, explosive acts, and defusing acts against three opponents: a partner, a same-sex friend, and an opposite-sex friend. This allowed them to separate out the effects of target sex and relationship, or intimacy. They used effect sizes to express the shift in the behaviour from the different opponents. Women were more likely to say that they would use physical and verbal acts of aggression against a partner, and their increase of aggression to a partner appeared to be as a function of intimacy. They found that when examining the difference in aggression for men, the diminution of their aggression from same-sex to partner was as a direct result of the target sex. This finding has been replicated with self-report studies (e.g. Bates et al., 2014), and supports Felson's analysis that norms of chivalry may inhibit men's aggression towards women. Cross et al. (2011) suggest that women's increase in their aggression to partners could be due to the knowledge that their partners would not hit a woman.

Adverse childhood experience and emotion dysregulation

There is a significant body of literature that demonstrates the risk and protective factors associated with men's violence. For example, men's IPV has been found to be predicted by personality disorders (e.g. Ehrensaft et al., 2006), criminality (e.g. Moffitt, 2001), psychopathic traits (Hilton, Harris, Rice, Houghton, & Eke, 2008), alcohol consumption (Caetano, Cunradi, Schafer, & Clark, 2000), as well as by lower levels of empathy (e.g. Jolliffe & Farrington, 2004) and self-control (Bates, Archer, & Graham-Kevan, 2017). Additionally, there is significant overlap found when comparing the risk factors for men's and women's aggression; for example, Medeiros and Straus (2006) found for severe acts of IPV there were nine out of 12 risk factors that were the same for men and women including jealousy, communication problems, and sexual abuse history.

With many of the important risk factors being found to emerge earlier on in development, it is unsurprising the events during formative childhood years become impactful for later behaviour. There is a body literature that has explored the impact of witnessing parental IPV, and the intergenerational transmission of violence through which it is seen in cycles within families (e.g. Straus, 1991). Stith et al. (2000) performed a meta-analysis to examine the relationship between growing up in a violent home and going on to be in a violent relationship: they found a weak to moderate relationship between the two. In support of this, Erin Pizzey's work with men and women involved in domestic violence revealed patterns of destructive behaviour. Pizzey and Shapiro (1982) refer to this pattern as being "prone to violence"; the notion that growing up in a violent family can mean some people have a tendency to be attracted to violent relationships, and are themselves also violent through understanding this as a method of dealing with conflict. What has emerged through the literature that has explored violence within the family is the effects of being exposed to violence as children and the impact this has on the development of future relationships (e.g. Holt, Buckley, & Whelan, 2008).

Witnessing IPV within the family home is an example of a stressful or traumatic experience in childhood. These experiences are often referred to as adverse childhood experiences (ACE), and are thought to have a negative and detrimental impact in adulthood including being associated with health issues, behavioural and social problems (Brown et al., 2009). Indeed, childhood interpersonal trauma has a significant and longstanding impact on adult psycho-relational functioning; different ACE are identified as such based on their actual or potential for harm in the context of a relationship where there is power, trust, and some level of responsibility (Dugal, Bigras, Godbout, & Bélanger, 2016).

Research has demonstrated the impact of ACE individually, but more recently it is thought that there is a cumulative impact of multiple ACE (Dong et al., 2004). For example, Dube, Anda, Felitti, Edwards, and Croft (2002) found each of eight ACE (verbal, physical, and sexual abuse; witnessing parental violence; household substance abuse; mental illness in the household; parent separation/divorce; and incarcerated household members) was associated with an increased risk of alcohol abuse in adulthood. This increased twofold to fourfold when there were experiences of multiple traumatic experiences. This impact of ACE extends to wider negative outcomes including other health behaviours (Dube, Felitti, Dong, Giles, & Anda, 2003), suicide attempts (Dube et al., 2001), and depressive disorders (Chapman et al., 2004). When children experience trauma in their formative years, it impacts on their development, and the way they learn to respond to their experiences. When there is some form of impaired functioning, children find alternative ways to cope with negative or emotional experiences (Dube et al., 2002).

ACE have been found to be associated with perpetration and victimisation of IPV in adulthood (e.g. Whitfield, Anda, Dube, & Felitti, 2003; Ehrensaft et al., 2003), with research demonstrating that men and women who experience childhood victimisation are also at risk for violence victimisation as adults (Desai, Arias, Thompson, & Basile, 2002). ACE and childhood trauma can affect the development of interpersonal skills that are required for adult romantic relationships, for example the ability to trust significant others and the ability to understand and monitor the emotional and mental states of others' behaviour (Godbout, Runtz, MacIntosh, & Briere, 2013). For these adults, their parents were not able to provide a safe and secure base (Dugal et al., 2016), perhaps through their own experiences of ACE, and so as children they may have experienced a "betrayal trauma", when their caregiver or trusted person violates that trust or well-being in some way (Freyd, 1998).

The interdependency that is created within adult relationships renders the possibility of conflict inevitable at some point (Finkel, 2007). People who have experienced ACE and interpersonal trauma generally present a hyperactivation around experiences of abandonment anxiety which may lead to a sensitivity to threats of rejection (perceived or actual), demands for affections, and a desire to have control over a partner's behaviour (Dugal et al., 2016). A situation of conflict and hostility is one where a threat may be perceived to the security of the relationship. This may then be expressed through aggression or attempts to control; indeed, the impact of ACE has been previously linked to higher manifestations of control and domineering behaviour (Messman-Moore & Coates, 2007). This notion links in with what Dutton (1998) described as an "Abusive Personality"; here attachment theory is used as a way of explaining that interpersonal functioning of adults is linked to and related to early childhood experiences with caregivers that impact on the models developed of "self" and "other". Perceived threats to abandonment create intimacy anger which is then directed towards their attachment figure. This anger is then replaced by their fear of abandonment and a cycle is created where anger is followed by violence, and then leads to contrition and dependency. As Dutton (1998) describes it: "These men are literally at their wives' knees or at her throat" (p. 94).

A factor thought to mediate the relationship between ACE and later adult outcomes is that of emotion dysregulation (ED). ED has been defined as a multidimensional construct that involves a lack of awareness and understanding of emotions, a lack of appropriate strategies for coping with intense emotions, and a lack of control around behaviour when emotional distress is high (Gratz & Roemer, 2004). In short, ED reflects maladaptive mechanisms for coping with strong emotions and emotional distress (Gratz, Paulson, Jakupcak, & Tull, 2009). The link between ACE, ED, and IPV victimisation has been found within the literature (e.g. Lilly, London, & Bridgett, 2014).

It is thought ED as a mediator could be more impactful for men due to the way each gender is socialised around experiencing and expressing emotions; it has the potential to intensify the impact of the childhood trauma and increase the likelihood of ED (Gratz et al., 2009). It has been suggested that men utilise and express anger through violence in place of, and as a method of avoidance for, less socially acceptable emotions for men (e.g. fear, upset) and coping strategies that are not consistent with a masculine identity (e.g. crying, talking about emotions; O'Neil & Harway, 1997). Jakupcak, Tull and Roemer (2005) found men's fear of emotions was significantly associated with their overt hostility and anger. The authors concluded these findings were in line with findings that suggest men's aggression is a coping mechanism to deal with distressing feelings, due to them being socialised with fewer alternative emotional expressions.

If the relationship between ACE and IPV is strong as the literature suggests then it not surprising that IPV rates are so high; studies exploring ACE demonstrate how common they are, for example Chapman et al. (2004) report two-thirds of participants had one ACE with a third having at least two. Because ACE are interrelated and not independent (and so co-existing), the authors recommended studying the impact of ACE collectively rather than keeping a narrow focus on one (e.g., witnessing interparental violence). This fits with literature that suggests that witnessing of parental violence is one of many ACE which could co-occur with others; this leads to the notion that a more ecological perspective could be useful in understanding the holistic experiences that are influencing men's violence (Bevan & Higgins, 2002). Rather than social learning theory alone explaining the impact of witnessing violence in the home, the culmination of experiences could lead to the development of a more aggressive interpersonal style that is associated with IPV (Corvo & deLara, 2010; Dugal et al., 2016)

Taken together, this literature suggests childhood experiences appear to be influential over the development of antisocial and aggressive behaviour (both in general and to intimates), and once developed this is often found to remain stable over time. Whilst the gendered model of IPV would proposed men's abusive behaviour is rooted in their patriarchal beliefs about being able to control and dominate women; the evidence presented here indicates that this control is instead rooted in early childhood trauma. Violent experiences in childhood can impact on the development of dysfunctional interaction patterns (Godbout et al., 2013) including abusive and controlling behaviour.

Conclusion

This chapter has presented evidence that challenges the gendered approach to understanding men's violence in relationships. It suggests that the development of abusive behaviour is complex, multi-faceted, and often originates in early childhood relationships and trauma. Interventions aimed at reducing men's violence need to capture this complexity, and be tailored to individual need and risk. Despite this body of evidence, as a theoretical model, the gendered approach is still influential within practice. The Duluth Model was established in the United States in 1981 as an intervention with a curriculum developed by activists within the battered women's movement and five battered women (Pence & Paymar, 1993) who believed IPV was caused by men's patriarchal ideology. Using the "Power and Control Wheel" was central as IPV was understood as being motivated by men's need for power and control over women. Research has been consistent in demonstrating the popularity of this model whilst also indicating a lack of effectiveness of this programme (see Bates et al., 2017 for a full review). Studies that have examined the success rates of the Duluth Model intervention programme have unsurprisingly found it to be unsuccessful (e.g. Babcock, Green, & Robie, 2004). Dutton (2006b) reviewed both its lack of efficacy and the wealth of evidence contradicting its feminist foundations, concluding that its continued use is impeding effective treatment and judicial responses. Despite this, the Duluth model has experienced an "immunity" from having to answer to any external empirical evaluation with political concerns seeming more important than science and a strong evidence base (Corvo, Dutton & Chen, 2008; p. 112). With the increased evidence base detailing both women's perpetration and the prevalence of bidirectional IPV, there is a need to work with perpetrator and victims' groups across the gender and sexuality spectrums to ensure we are developing interventions that are inclusive and effective.

References

Archer, J. (2000). Sex differences in aggression between heterosexual partners: A meta-analytic review. *Psychological Bulletin*, 126, 651–680. doi:10.1037MJ033-2909.I26.5.651

Archer, J. (2004). Sex differences in real world settings: A meta-analytic review. *Review of General Psychology*, 8, 291–322. doi:10.1037/1089-2680.8.4.291.supp

Arnocky, S. & Vaillancourt, T. (2014). Sex differences in response to victimization by an intimate partner: More stigmatization and less help-seeking among males. *Journal of Aggression, Maltreatment & Trauma*, 23(7), 705–724, doi:10.1080/10926771.2014.933465

Babcock, J. C., Green, C. E., & Robie, C. (2004). Does batterers' treatment work? A meta-analytic review of domestic violence treatment. *Clinical Psychology Review*, 23, 1023–1053. doi:10.1016/j.cpr.2002.07.001

Bates, E. A. (2016). Current controversies in intimate partner violence: Overlooking bidirectional violence. *Journal of Family Violence*, 31(8), 937–940. doi:10.1007/s10896-016-9862-1023-1053

Bates, E. A., Archer, J., & Graham-Kevan, N. (2017). Do the same risk and protective factors influence aggression toward partners and same-sex others? *Aggressive Behavior*, 43(2), 163–175. doi:10.1002/ab.21672

Bates, E. A. & Graham-Kevan, N. (2016). Is the presence of control related to help-seeking behavior? A Test of Johnson's Assumptions Regarding Sex-Differences and the Role of Control in Intimate Partner Violence. *Partner Abuse*, 7(1), 3–25. doi:10.1891/1946–6560.7.1.3

Bates, E. A., Graham-Kevan, N., & Archer, J. (2014). Testing predictions from the male control theory of men's partner violence. *Aggressive Behavior*, 40(1), 42–55. doi:10.1002/ab.21499

Bates, E.A., Graham-Kevan, N., Bolam, L. T. & Thornton, A. J. V. (2017). Review of Domestic Violence Perpetrator Programs in the UK. *Partner Abuse*, 8(1), 3–46. doi:10.1891/1946–6560.8.1.37

Bevan, E. & Higgins, D. J. (2002). Is domestic violence learned? The contribution of five forms of child maltreatment to men's violence and adjustment. *Journal of Family Violence*, 17(3), 223–245. doi:10.1023/A:1016053228021

Bologna, M. J., Waterman, C. K., & Dawson, L. J. (1987). Violence in gay male and lesbian relationships: Implications for practitioners and policy makers. *Paper presented at the Third National Conference of Family Violence Researchers, Durham.*

Brown, D. W., Anda, R. F., Tiemeier, H., Felitti, V. J., Edwards, V. J., Croft, J. B., & Giles, W. H. (2009). Adverse childhood experiences and the risk of premature mortality. *American Journal of Preventive Medicine*, 37(5), 389–396. doi:10.1016/j.amepre.2009.06.021

Browne, A. (1987). *When battered women kill.* New York: Free Press.

Buzawa, E. S. & Austin, T. (1993). Determining police response to domestic violence victims: The role of victim preference. *American Behavioral Scientist*, 36, 610–623. doi:10.1177/0002764293036005006

Caetano, R., Cunradi, C. B., Schafer, J., & Clark, C. L. (2000). Intimate partner violence and drinking patterns among white, black, and Hispanic couples in the US. *Journal of Substance Abuse*, 11(2), 123–138. doi:10.1016/S0899–3289(00)00015–00018

Carney, M. M. & Barner, J. R. (2012). Prevalence of partner abuse: Rates of emotional abuse and control. *Partner Abuse*, 3(3), 286–335. doi:10.1891/1946–6560.3.3.286

Chapman, D. P., Whitfield, C. L., Felitti, V. J., Dube, S. R., Edwards, V. J., & Anda, R. F. (2004). Adverse childhood experiences and the risk of depressive disorders in adulthood. *Journal of Affective Disorders*, 82(2), 217–225. doi:10.1016/j.jad.2003.12.013

Charles, D., Whitaker, D. J., Le, B., Swahn, M., & DiClemente, R. J. (2011). Differences between perpetrators of bidirectional and unidirectional physical intimate partner violence. *Partner Abuse*, 2(3), 344–364. doi:10.1891/1946–6560.2.3.344

Clift, R. J. W. & Dutton, D. G. (2011). The abusive personality in women in dating relationships. *Partner Abuse*, 2(2), 166–188. doi:10.1891/1946–6560.2.2.166

Corvo, K. & deLara, E. (2010). Towards an integrated theory of relational violence: Is bullying a risk factor for domestic violence. *Aggression and Violent Behavior*, 15, 181–190. doi:10.1016/j.avb.2009.12.001

Corvo, K., Dutton, D. G., & Chen, W. Y. (2008). Towards evidence-based practice with domestic violence perpetrators. *Journal of Aggression, Maltreatment and Trauma*, 16(2), 111–130. doi:10.1080/10926770801921246

Cross, C. P., Tee, W., & Campbell, A. (2011). Gender symmetry in intimate aggression: An effect of intimacy or target sex? *Aggressive Behavior*, 37(3), 268–277. doi:10.1002/ab.20388

Desai, S., Arias, I., Thompson, M. P., & Basile, K. C. (2002). Childhood victimization and subsequent adult revictimization assessed in a nationally representative sample of women and men. *Violence and Victims*, 17(6), 639.

Dobash, R. E. & Dobash, R. P. (1979). *Violence against wives: A case against the patriarchy.* London: Open Books.

Dobash, R. P. & Dobash, R. E. (2004). Women's violence to men in intimate relationships: Working on a Puzzle. *British Journal of Criminology, 44*, 324–349. doi:10.1093/bjc/azh026

Dong, M., Anda, R. F., Felitti, V. J., Dube, S. R., Williamson, D. F., Thompson, T. J., … & Giles, W. H. (2004). The interrelatedness of multiple forms of childhood abuse, neglect, and household dysfunction. *Child Abuse & Neglect*, 28(7), 771–784. doi:10.1016/j.chiabu.2004.01.008

Doumas, D. M., Pearson, C. L., Elgin, J. E., & McKinley, L. L. (2008). Adult attachment as a risk factor for intimate partner violence: The "mispairing" of partners' attachment styles. *Journal of Interpersonal Violence*, 23, 616–634. doi:10.1177/0886260507313526

Dube, S. R., Anda, R. F., Felitti, V. J., Chapman, D. P., Williamson, D. F., & Giles, W. H. (2001). Childhood abuse, household dysfunction, and the risk of attempted suicide throughout the life span: Findings from the Adverse Childhood Experiences Study. *JAMA*, 286(24), 3089–3096. doi:10.1001/jama.286.24.3089

Dube, S. R., Anda, R. F., Felitti, V. J., Edwards, V. J., & Croft, J. B. (2002). Adverse childhood experiences and personal alcohol abuse as an adult. *Addictive Behaviors*, 27(5), 713–725. doi:10.1016/S0306–4603(01)00204–0

Dube, S. R., Felitti, V. J., Dong, M., Giles, W. H., & Anda, R. F. (2003). The impact of adverse childhood experiences on health problems: Evidence from four birth cohorts dating back to 1900. *Preventive Medicine*, 37(3), 268–277. doi:10.1016/S0091–7435(03)00123–00123

Dugal, C., Bigras, N., Godbout, N., & Bélanger, C. (2016). Childhood interpersonal trauma and its repercussions in adulthood: An analysis of psychological and interpersonal sequelae. In El-Baalbaki, G. (Ed.) *A multidimensional approach to Post-Traumatic Stress Disorder: From theory to Practice.* InTech.

Dutton, D. G. (1998). *The abusive personality: Violence and control in intimate relationships.* New York: Guilford Press.

Dutton, D. G. (2006a). The history of spouse assault. In Dutton, D. G. (Ed.) *Rethinking domestic violence* (pp. 3–17). Vancouver: UBS Press.

Dutton, D. G. (2006b). The gender debate and the feminist paradigm. In Dutton, D. G. (Ed.) *Rethinking domestic violence* (pp. 109–129). Vancouver: UBS Press.

Eagly, A. & Crowley, M. (1986). Gender and helping behavior: A meta-analytic review of the social psychological literature. *Psychological Bulletin*, 100, 283–308. doi:10.1037/0033–2909.100.3.283

Ehrensaft, M. K., Cohen, P., Brown, J., Smailes, E., Chen, H., & Johnson, J. G. (2003). Intergenerational transmission of partner violence: A 20-year prospective study. *Journal of Consulting and Clinical Psychology*, 71(4), 741. doi:10.1037/0022–006X.71.4.741

Ehrensaft, M. K., Cohen, P., & Johnson, J. G. (2006). Development of personality disorder symptoms and the risk for partner violence. *Journal of Abnormal Psychology*, 115, 474–483. doi:10.1037/0021–843X.115.3.474

Fawson, P. R. (2015). Controlling behaviors as a predictor of partner violence among heterosexual female and male adolescents. *Partner Abuse*, 6(2), 217–229. doi:10.1037/t36229–000

Felson, R. B. (2002). *Violence & Gender Re-examined.* Washington D.C.: American Psychological Association.

Felson, R. B. & Feld, S. L. (2009). When a man hits a woman: Moral evaluations and reporting of violence to the police. *Aggressive Behavior*, 35, 477–488. doi:10.1002/ab.20323

Felson, R. B. & Lane, K. J. (2010). Does violence involving women and intimate partners have a special etiology? *Criminology*, 48, 201–218. doi:10.1111/j.1745–9125.2010.00186.x

Felson, R. B. & Messner, S. F. (1998). Disentangling the effects of gender and intimacy on victim-precipitation in homicide. *Criminology*, 36, 405–424. doi:10.1111/j.1745–9125.1998.tb01253.x

Finkel, E. J. (2007). Impelling and inhibiting forces in the perpetration of intimate partner violence. *Review of General Psychology*, 11(2), 193. doi:10.1037/1089–2680.11.2.193

Follingstad, D. R. & DeHart, D. D. (2000). Defining psychological abuse of husbands toward wives: Contexts, behaviors, and typologies. *Journal of Interpersonal Violence*, 15(9), 891–920. doi:10.1177/088626000015009001

Follingstad, D. R. & Edmundson, M. (2010). Is psychological abuse reciprocal in intimate relationships? Data from a national sample of American adults. *Journal of Family Violence*, 25(5), 495–508. doi:10.1007/s10896–10010–9311-y

Freyd, J. J. (1998). *Betrayal trauma: The logic of forgetting childhood abuse.* Cambridge, MA: Harvard University Press.

Glick, P. & Fiske, S. T. (2001) An ambivalent alliance: Hostile and benevolent sexism as complementary justifications for gender inequality. *American Psychologist*, 56, 109–118. doi:10.1037/0003–066X.56.2.109

Godbout, N., Runtz, M., MacIntosh, H., & Briere, J. (2013). Childhood trauma and couple relationships. *Integrating Science & Practice*, 3(2), 14–17.

Gratz, K. L., Paulson, A., Jakupcak, M., & Tull, M. T. (2009). Exploring the relationship between childhood maltreatment and intimate partner abuse: Gender differences in the mediating role of emotion dysregulation. *Violence and Victims*, 24(1), 68–82.

Gratz, K. L. & Roemer, L. (2004). Multidimensional assessment of emotion regulation and dysregulation: Development, factor structure, and initial validation of the difficulties in emotion regulation scale. *Journal of Psychopathology and Behavioral Assessment*, 26(1), 41–54. doi:10.1023/B:JOBA.0000007455.08539.94

Gray, H. M. & Foshee, V. (1997). Adolescent dating violence: Differences between one-sided and mutually violent profiles. *Journal of Interpersonal Violence*, 12, 126–141. doi:10.1177/088626097012001008

Hamberger, L. K. & Larsen, S. E. (2015). Men's and women's experience of intimate partner violence: A review of ten years of comparative studies in clinical samples; Part I. *Journal of Family Violence*, 30(6), 699–717. doi:10.1007/s10896-015-9732-8

Harris, R. J. & Cook, C. A. (1994). Attributions about spouse abuse: It matters who the batterers and victims are. *Sex Roles*, 30, 553–565.doi:10.1007/BF01420802

Hilton, N. Z., Harris, G. T., Rice, M. E., Houghton, R. E., & Eke, A. W. (2008). An indepth actuarial assessment for wife assault recidivism: The Domestic Violence Risk Appraisal Guide. *Law and Human Behavior*, 32(2), 150–163. doi:10.1007/s10979–10007–9088–9086

Holt, S., Buckley, H., & Whelan, S. (2008). The impact of exposure to domestic violence on children and young people: A review of the literature. *Child Abuse & Neglect*, 32(8), 797–810. doi:10.1016/j.chiabu.2008.02.004

Jakupcak, M., Tull, M. T., & Roemer, L. (2005). Masculinity, shame, and fear of emotions as predictors of men's expressions of anger and hostility. *Psychology of Men & Masculinity*, 6(4), 275. doi:10.1037/1524–9220.6.4.275

Johnson, M. P. (1995). Patriarchal terrorism and common couple violence: Two forms of violence against women. *Journal of Marriage and the Family*, 57, 282–294. doi:10.2307/353683

Jolliffe, D. & Farrington, D. P. (2004) Empathy and offending: a systematic review and meta-analysis. *Aggression and Violent Behavior*, 9, 441–476. doi:10.1016/j.avb.2003.03.001

Kaukinen, C. E. & Powers, R. A. (2015). The role of economic factors on women's risk for intimate partner violence: A cross-national comparison of Canada and the United States. *Violence Against Women*, 21(2), 229–248. doi:10.1177/1077801214564686

Langhinrichsen-Rohling, J. (2010). Controversies involving gender and intimate partner violence in the United States. *Sex Roles*, 62, 179–193. doi:10.1007/s11199–11010–9743–0

Langhinrichsen-Rohling, J., Misra, T. A., Selwyn, C., & Rohling, M. L. (2012). Rates of bidirectional versus unidirectional intimate partner violence across sample, sexual orientations, and race/ethnicities: A comprehensive review. *Partner Abuse*, 3(2), 199–230, doi:10.1891/1946-6560.3.2.199

Lie, G., Schilit, R., Bush, J., Montagne, M., & Reyes, L. (1991). Lesbians in currently aggressive relationships: How frequently do they report aggressive past relationships? *Violence and Victims*, 6, 121–135.

Lilly, M. M., London, M. J., & Bridgett, D. J. (2014). Using SEM to examine emotion regulation and revictimization in predicting PTSD symptoms among childhood abuse survivors. *Psychological Trauma: Theory, Research, Practice, and Policy*, 6(6), 644. doi:10.1037/a0036460

Mauricio, A. M. & Gormley, B. (2001). Male perpetration of physical violence against female partners: The interaction of dominance needs and attachment insecurity. *Journal of Interpersonal Violence*, 16(10), 1066–1081. doi:10.1177/088626001016010006

Medeiros, A. & Straus, M. A. (2006). Risk factors for physical violence between dating partners: Implications for gender-inclusive prevention and treatment of family violence. In Hamel, J. & Nicholls, T. (Eds) *Family approaches in domestic violence: A practitioners' guide to gender inclusive research and treatment*. Springer.

Melton, H. C. & Belknap, J. (2003). He hits, she hits: Assessing gender differences and similarities in officially reported intimate partner violence. *Criminal Justice and Behavior*, 30, 328–348. doi:10.1177/0093854803030003004

Messman-Moore, T. L. & Coates, A. A. (2007). The impact of childhood psychological abuse on adult interpersonal conflict: The role of early maladaptive schemas and patterns of interpersonal behavior. *Journal of Emotional Abuse*, 7(2), 75–92. doi:10.1300/J135v07n02_05

Moffitt, T. E. (2001). *Sex differences in antisocial behaviour: Conduct disorder, delinquency, and violence in the Dunedin Longitudinal Study*. Cambridge: Cambridge University Press.

O'Leary, K. D., Barling, J., Arias, I., Rosenbaum, A., Malone, J., & Tyree, A. (1989). Prevalence and stability of physical aggression between spouses: A longitudinal analysis. *Journal of Consulting and Clinical Psychology*, 57, 263–268. doi:10.1037/0022–006X.57.2.263

O'Neil, J. M. & Harway, M. (1997). A multivariate model explaining men's violence toward women: Predisposing and triggering hypotheses. *Violence Against Women*, 3(2), 182–203. doi:10.1177/1077801297003002005

Outlaw, M. (2009). No one type of intimate partner abuse: Exploring physical and non-physical abuse among intimate partners. *Journal of Family Violence*, 24(4), 263–272. doi:10.1007/s10896–10009–9228–9225

Pagelow, M. D. (1984). *Family violence*. New York: Praeger.

Panuzio, J. & DiLillo, D. (2010). Physical, psychological, and sexual intimate partner aggression among newlywed couples: Longitudinal prediction of marital satisfaction. *Journal of Family Violence*, 25(7), 689–699. doi:10.1007/s10896–10010–9328–9322

Pence, E. & Paymar, M. (1993). *Education groups for men who batter: The Duluth model*. New York: Springer Publishing Company.

Pizzey, E. & Shapiro, J. (1982). *Prone to violence*. London: Hamlyn.

Povey, D., Coleman, K., Kaiza, P., Hoare, J., & Jansson, K. (2008). *Homicides, firearm offences and intimate violence 2006/2007*. London, UK: Home Office Statistics Bulletin.

Renner, L. M., Reese, L. M. S., Peek-Asa, C., & Ramirez, M. (2015). Reporting patterns of unidirectional and bidirectional verbal aggression and physical violence among rural couples. *Journal of Family Violence*, 30(8), 1069–1078. doi:10.1007/s10896–10015–9737–9733

Saunders, D. G. (1986). When battered women use violence: Husband abuse or self-defence? *Violence and Victims*, 1, 47–60.

Saunders, D. G. (1988). Wife abuse husband abuse or mutual combat? A feminist perspective on the empirical findings. In Yllo, K. & Bograd, M. (Eds) *Feminist perspectives on wife abuse* (pp. 90–113). Newbury Park, California: Sage Publications.

Shorey, R. C., Cornelius, T. L., & Idema, C. (2011) Trait anger as a mediator of difficulties with emotional regulation and female-perpetrated psychological aggression. *Violence and Victims*, 26(3), 271–282. doi:10.1891/0886–6708.26.3.271

Sorenson, S. B. & Taylor, C. A. (2005). Female aggression toward male intimate partners: An examination of social norms in a community-based sample. *Psychology of Women Quarterly*, 29, 78–96. doi:10.1111/j.1471–6402.2005.00170.x

Steinmetz, S. K. (1978). The battered husband syndrome. *Victimology*, 2, 499–509.

Stets, J. E. & Straus, M. A. (1989). Gender differences in reporting marital violence and its medical and psychological consequences. In Straus, M. A. & Gelles, R. J. (Eds) *Physical violence in American families: Risk factors and adaptations to violence in 8, 145 families* (pp. 227–244). New Brunswick, NJ: Transaction Publishing.

Stith, S. M., Rosen, K. H., Middleton, K. A., Busch, A. L., Lundeberg, K., & Carlton, R. P. (2000). The intergenerational transmission of spouse abuse: A meta-analysis. *Journal of Marriage and Family*, 62(3), 640–654. doi:10.1111/j.1741–3737.2000.00640.x

Straus, M. A. (1979). Measuring intrafamily conflict and violence: The Conflicts Tactics (CT) scales. *Journal of Marriage and the Family*, 41, 75–88

Straus, M. A. (1991). Children as witness to marital violence: A risk factor for life-long problems among a nationally representative sample of American men and women. Paper presented at the Ross Roundtable titled "Children and Violence," Washington, DC.

Sullivan, T. P., McPartland, T., Price, C., Cruza-Guet, M. C., & Swan, S. C. (2013). Relationship self-efficacy protects against mental health problems among women in bidirectionally aggressive intimate relationships with men. *Journal of Counselling Psychology*, 60(4), 641–647. doi:10.1037/a0033406

Tjaden, P. & Thoennes, N. (2000). Prevalence and consequences of male-to-female and female-to-male intimate partner violence as measured by the National Violence Against Women survey. *Violence Against Women*, 6, 142–161. doi:10.1177/10778010022181769

Whitfield, C. L., Anda, R. F., Dube, S. R., & Felitti, V. J. (2003). Violent childhood experiences and the risk of intimate partner violence in adults: Assessment in a large health maintenance organization. *Journal of Interpersonal Violence*, 18(2), 166–185. doi:10.1177/0886260502238733

Winstok, Z. & Smadar-Dror, R. (2015). Sanctions as a tactic used in partner conflicts: Theoretical, operational, and preliminary findings. *Journal of Interpersonal Violence*, 30(12), 1998–2003. doi:10.1177/0886260514552277

Yllo, K. A. (1993). Through a feminist lens: Gender, power and violence. In Gelles, R. J. & Loseke, D. R. (Eds) *Current controversies on family violence*. Newbury Park, CA: Sage.

3

"VICTIM CAST AS PERPETRATOR"

Men's experiences of the Criminal Justice System following female-perpetrated intimate partner violence

Jessica McCarrick

Introduction

At the time of writing this chapter there are waves being made at a government level to redefine and transform how we respond to domestic violence. A government press release (Prime Minister's Office, 2017) highlighted improvements in prosecutions and convictions for domestic violence, but referred to the lack of consistency in the use and effectiveness of different law enforcement measures across the UK. In response to the government plans for a Domestic and Abuse Act, Mark Brookes from Mankind Initiative Charity (Brookes, 2017) emphasised the importance of improving the principles of inclusion, equality, and fairness. He also highlighted the lack of recognition of male survivors within Government policy, which perpetuates the service gap for men across the UK. This lack of recognition is exposed by the terminology used within the 2016–2020 domestic abuse policy "Ending Violence Against Women and Girls Strategy" (Home Office, 2016). This gendered language begins to demonstrate some of the barriers that male victims of domestic violence are faced with.

My interest in this area began during my first year as a Trainee Counselling Psychologist when I completed domestic violence training in a local organisation. Although this organisation was designed to protect women and children, I was still struck by the staunch philosophy that men were the aggressors and women the victims. The philosophy throughout this training was heavily influenced by the feminist paradigm with gendered language being used throughout. As a curious student, I questioned the gendered angle and my critical mind began to wonder about the flipside of the intimate partner violence (IPV) debate. As chance would have it, I later secured a placement in a service which provided psychological therapy and support to men and women who had experienced IPV (sadly this service later closed due to insufficient funding). The experience of working with male survivors further developed my understanding of IPV as an issue to be worked with from the perspective of the individual, rather than their gender. In my clinical practice, I have worked with both men and women who have experienced IPV, which developed my perspective on the experiences of both. However, it was the apparent lack of services available to men, the narratives around not being believed, and being falsely accused of perpetration due to the simple fact they were male that bolstered my passion for researching men's experiences.

The current chapter shall begin with an overview of the history of IPV research and policy development, before moving on to discuss my research which explored men's experiences of the UK Criminal Justice System (CJS) following female-perpetrated IPV (McCarrick, Davis-McCabe, & Hirst-Winthrop, 2015). The chapter will conclude with an overview of the positive developments within IPV campaigning, research, and policy in recent years and recommendations for continued progress.

History of intimate partner violence: research, policy, and practice

In 1976, the Domestic Violence and Matrimonial Proceedings Act (1976) was introduced in Parliament, which gave police powers of arrest in domestic violence situations. The wording of this document appears to be highly influenced by feminism, with the person being arrested being referred to as "he". Seemingly, since this time, public policy response to domestic violence has been defined by activists as the socially sanctioned control of men over women (Dutton & Corvo, 2006). During this time of social change there was a development of "ultra-feminists" who aimed to define women as a victim group who were oppressed by men (Pizzey, Shackleton, & Urwin, 2000). The beliefs held by this group were so extreme that Erin Pizzey was condemned by the ultra-feminist movement following her announcement that 62% of the women who had found refuge in shelters were as violent as their male partners (Pizzey et al., 2000). Indeed, the notion that women could also be perpetrators was so controversial that early researchers discussing this received death threats (Straus, 1999).

Dutton and White (2013) described the IPV perpetrator as a bullying, domineering man who intimidates and assaults a non-violent woman. These ingrained societal beliefs around gender and IPV were revealed by a video filmed by the Mankind Initiative (2014) on the streets of London in 2014[1], which shows public reactions to an IPV incident when the perpetrator was male compared to female. The difference between the two scenarios is palpable, with the female victim eliciting looks of shock and intervention from members of the public trying to protect the woman. The male victim, however, elicited looks of amusement from some onlookers, whilst others turned away to ignore the acts of psychological and physical abuse. Indeed, research has found that gender bias is highly influential in affecting people's perceptions of the severity of IPV. One such study found that acts were more likely to be perceived as psychologically or physically abusive by the public if executed by men (Sorenson & Taylor, 2005). This result remained consistent across all socio-demographic groups. More recent research (Hine & Arrindell, 2015) has demonstrated that IPV vignettes are judged to be more acceptable and more humorous when the victim was male and the perpetrator female. Additionally, this study highlights that people are more likely to assign blame to the victim when the perpetrator is female and the victim is male. It could be argued that as female-perpetrated IPV has not yet been acknowledged to the same extent as male-perpetrated IPV, social norms are less defined as to how to comprehend and respond to such behaviour. Furthermore, professionals are not immune to such bias, with research highlighting that psychologists and family court judges hold gender bias about IPV (e.g. Muller, Desmarais, & Hamel, 2009). Hine and Arrindell (2015) argue that current attitudes about men and masculinity, and the emphasis at a government level on "Violence Against Women and Girls", has contributed to a "cycle of silence" whereby these crimes are concealed from the public psyche.

The gender paradigm within the literature and society overall has evidently had a powerful influence upon public policy and responses to IPV. In addition, masculine roles emphasising self-sufficiency, emotional control, and power are a dominant force within socialisation, and minimises the likelihood of men seeking help (Addis & Mahalik, 2003). Brown (2004) referred to men being caught between the "proverbial rock and a hard place" as men are less likely to receive police protection due to societal beliefs that men can protect themselves, yet if they protect themselves in self-defence they are highly likely to be charged with an offence (Cook, 2009).

There have been several initiatives since the 1990s aimed at improving CJS approaches to IPV. These initiatives include an emphasis upon pro-arrest, and increases in prosecution and conviction. In a study conducted in the North East of England, Hester (2009) reported that the majority of IPV perpetrators recorded by police were male and their victims were predominantly female. Dutton and White (2013) also referred to the issue of under-reporting of IPV by male victims, due to the socialisation of men which reduces the likelihood of men seeking help. George (2007) argued that prejudice against male victims is extreme and has led to under-reporting by police, with more men being put into the CJS if counter charges are made against them. Cook (2009) reported that in some cases, men's calls to police during an episode of IPV were not responded to. In other cases, men were ridiculed by police or wrongly arrested as the primary perpetrator. Statistics reveal that on average, the police receive contact from somebody requiring assistance for IPV once every 30 seconds (HMIC, 2014a; 2014b), which illustrates the importance of research into police response to inform public policy and support positive action. A HMIC report concluded that the overall police response to domestic violence in the UK is "not good enough" (HMIC, 2014a; p. 6). Although this report refers to both male and female victims, it emphasises that women are more likely to be victims than men. This statement is reflected in many IPV policies, studies, and media campaigns, with male victims receiving only a cursory nod. It is likely that this adds to the stigma that men face when reporting IPV and compounds their invisibility across society.

Despite the shortfalls highlighted in the HMIC report, it is important to highlight the complexity of the picture that frontline police officers are faced with when responding to domestic violence calls, particularly when both parties are claiming to be the victim. Decisions made by frontline police are often based on information available to them on the scene to make an accurate assessment, as well as accessing any history of counter-allegations. The use of body-worn cameras is a development which police forces across the UK have begun to implement. The cameras are switched on prior to attending an incident, with the overall aim of improving objectivity in the overall decision made by the Crown Prosecution Service (CPS). However, it could be argued that the ingrained societal belief that men are mostly perpetrators of IPV could continue to influence the interpretation made of video footage by CJS professionals. The aforementioned gender bias which cuts across all layers of society highlights the need for research which promotes the voice of male survivors. Given the need for further research in this area, a study which explored the experiences of men who had contact with the CJS following female-perpetrated IPV was conducted (McCarrick et al., 2015). It was anticipated that the qualitative nature of this study would help promote an understanding of men's experiences and give a voice to men subjected to this hidden crime.

Aim and Methodology

The aim of the study was to analyse the experiences of men who had experienced female-perpetrated IPV, and had subsequent contact with the CJS. A qualitative method was utilised using Interpretative Phenomenological Analysis (IPA) to gain a rich and detailed understanding of participants' experiences.

Participants

Smith, Flowers, and Larkin (2009) suggest between four and ten participants as a reasonable sample size for IPA doctorate studies. In line with this recommendation, six participants were selected for interview. The following inclusion criteria was used: male, over 18 years old, have experienced female-perpetrated IPV (as defined by the Centers for Disease Prevention and Control, 2013), have had contact with the CJS due to their IPV experiences, and are no longer in an abusive relationship, to ensure safety of participants.

Table 3.1 outlines an introduction to the participants.

Findings

Three main themes emerged following analysis of the interviews (see Figure 3.1), which were connected by an umbrella theme of "trauma". Trauma encompassed the overall feel of the six men's experiences, and appeared to stem directly from the original IPV, but was compounded (and in one case helped) through their contact with the CJS. For these participants IPV caused an intense and devastating impact on many dimensions of their lives, including a shattered sense of self due to their masculine identity being challenged; their relationship with friends, families, and

TABLE 3.1 Participants

Pseudonym	Introduction to participant
Lee	Lee is in his early 40s and is eager to change policy for men like him. He experienced eight years of physical and psychological abuse by his ex-wife. His experience of the police was of not being believed and he described subsequently suffering "a nervous breakdown".
Henry	Henry is in his late 40s and experienced four and a half years of physical and psychological abuse by his ex-wife. He was arrested for Actual Bodily Harm after an argument with his wife escalated and he pushed her in self-defence. Henry felt the abuse he sustained had not been taken into consideration.
Martin	Martin is in his late 50s and experienced three years of abuse which began when his ex-partner became unemployed and began misusing alcohol. He described having hot plates of food thrown over him and being threatened with a knife. Following an incident where Martin was physically assaulted, she rang the police and he was subsequently arrested.
Robert	Robert is in his early 60s and described a 20-year period of physical, financial, and psychological abuse by his ex-wife. He described incidents including being stabbed and attacked with a lamp until he was unconscious. Robert described his experience of the CJS as being underlined with the perception that "battered husbands don't exist".
David	David is in his late 40s and experienced four years of control and psychological abuse by his ex-partner. He described several incidents where his ex-partner rang the police following arguments which resulted in David being arrested. He concluded that he felt the psychological factors of the abuse were not considered and felt he was not believed.
Chris	Chris is in his late 50s and described physical violence and psychological control and abuse throughout his 11.5-year relationship. His ex-partner made an allegation of harassment against Chris. He wasn't arrested, but described sensing a "lack of empathy" from the police and felt they didn't listen.

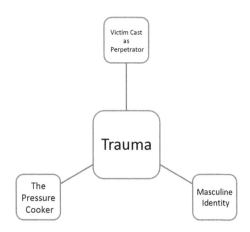

FIGURE 3.1 Main themes from analysis

colleagues being affected due to being "cast as the perpetrator"; a decline in their mental health; and in some cases loss of their careers, ability to trust others, and form new relationships. Throughout the interviews there was a sense of the men needing a space to process their traumatic experiences of their relationships. Where a traumatic event has been brought about by another person there is likely to be heightened feelings of betrayal, abandonment, a perception that others are malicious, and that the world is a dangerous place (Martens, 2005). This appears to fit with the participants, whose experiences were of being abused by their female partner and subsequently being treated like a guilty perpetrator, or not having their experiences believed and validated due to gendered societal beliefs about IPV. Henry and Chris referred directly to the shock they felt because of their experiences with the CJS. These experiences added a layer of further traumatisation, with their "unsafe world" having no protection from outside, and no sense of secure base from which to begin to stabilise and process the trauma.

HENRY: I just felt helpless. I was shocked that he took no interest in it.
CHRIS: I'm going to sound a bit of a drama queen, but I was in a kind of state of shock.

Chris used an interesting choice of words to describe his experiences, which appear to minimise his own emotions and condemn himself for not being "masculine". In line with the lasting psychological effects of living through a traumatic event, Lee described the long-term impact of his experiences. His loss of trust and faith in authority highlighted his feelings of vulnerability and of not being protected by the system.

LEE: I had a nervous breakdown. I now suffer long-term health problems. I'm not able to have faith in any member of authority now.

Victim cast as perpetrator

The first theme of "Victim Cast as Perpetrator" encapsulates how the men were assumed to be, or were treated like, perpetrators (see Figure 3.2). This related to experiences with their partner, the CJS and within wider society, and developed from a narrative in which the men reflected upon their experiences of being treated like a perpetrator, despite being the victim of IPV and feeling dismissed. Subsequently a vicious cycle of abuse was maintained as their abusive partners could successfully use gendered stereotypes to their advantage, placing their male partners in the perpetrator role, and thus further isolating them from sources of support.

By partner

Participants referred to their partners' allegations of IPV despite this being a reversal of the truth.

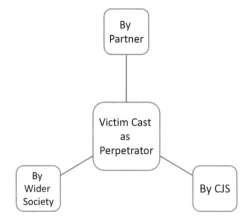

FIGURE 3.2 Sub-themes

CHRIS: The minute I got in contact she was calling the police on me, you know, claiming I was unhinged and that I was harassing her and that she was getting threats.

MARTIN: It's just a big pot of confusion … you know, this woman I thought I was in love with, who I was due to marry, has put me in this situation where I've been manhandled and thrown into a police cell for a false charge.

It appears that the female partners were using gendered stereotypes of IPV to their advantage, to cast their partners as the perpetrator (Dutton & White, 2013). These findings appear to suggest that the pro-arrest policies may also be affected by such stereotypes. Interestingly, participants spoke more about their experiences of being falsely accused of perpetrating violence, rather than coming forward to police as a victim themselves. Given the minimal recognition given to male victims at the time of conducting the study, it is likely they were reluctant to report abuse for fear of not being believed, or the stigma attached to being a male victim. This is supported by statistics which reveal that men are significantly less likely than women to tell anybody about the IPV they experience; indeed, only 10% of men will tell police (compared to 23% of women), 23% will tell somebody in an official position (compared to 43% of women), and 11% will tell a health professional (compared to 23% of women; Mankind Initiative, 2017). These figures highlight the discrepancies in reporting behaviours between men and women whilst emphasising the under-reporting of IPV overall.

By CJS

There was an overriding sense of feeling unfairly treated by the CJS and being cast as a guilty perpetrator despite a lack of evidence. It became apparent that experiences with the CJS could either help or hinder men. This sub-theme highlights the critical role that CJS professionals have, and how psychological outcomes can be impacted positively or negatively by their responses. Martin and Lee highlighted the gender bias experienced by police which influenced experiences and feeling cast as the perpetrator:

MARTIN: I just feel like I'm caught in a web of lies you know, with the law on her side, because they haven't looked into the rest of it, because there's two sides to every story isn't there?

LEE: They prefer to be blinkered, in the fact that, no disrespect to yourself, but whatever a female says is true and whatever a man says is a lie and that is my whole experience in the last 3 years.

Positively, Henry referred to a police officer who was helpful and validated him in an otherwise traumatising situation. Interestingly, this response served as a protective factor as it allowed him to reflect and think whilst in the police cell, where he asked for a pen and paper to write down his experiences. It is noteworthy that without this support, Henry may have reacted in a defensive manner which could have led to more punitive consequences:

HENRY: I remember him saying specifically "learn from this" and he said he had colleagues in the police who'd had the same, much of the same experience, so he was reassuring in a sense.

These findings reflect the conclusions drawn in a literature review of the effectiveness of protection orders issued in incidents of IPV (Russell, 2012), which highlighted that female perpetrators who violated their protection orders were less likely to be convicted and arrested than male perpetrators who did the same. Ultimately, this theme highlights the necessity of maintaining neutrality and abiding by the presumption of innocence until proved guilty. The hidden nature of this crime and the common ambiguity between victim and perpetrator highlight the need to tread carefully and make a thorough assessment which considers all dimensions of IPV, including emotional abuse.

By wider society

Participants described being cast as a perpetrator by society, or their own perception that people would not believe them. This belief appeared to be intrinsically linked to their gender role. The tendency for the general population and various professionals to rely on gendered stereotypes in IPV situations has been found in various studies (Hine & Arrindell, 2015; Sorenson & Taylor, 2005; Follingstad, DeHart, & Green, 2004; Muller et al., 2009). Lee referred to the "whole country" not believing him, perhaps indicative of the powerful gendered messages within society regarding IPV and illustrative of how this message has the potential to perpetuate victimisation:

LEE: Well, to have a whole country not believe what you're saying is a great weight on someone's shoulders, even though you can prove what you're saying, no-one can ever comprehend that unless they've been in that situation.

Henry referred to his experience of being isolated from social support due to abuse sustained by his partner and being cast as the perpetrator:

HENRY: It was a big shock, I felt betrayed. I was shocked that my wife has been trying to turn people against me and I felt as if I'd lost something dear.

Although Henry experienced isolation and adversity from his peers, he also had a more positive experience of a supportive friend who believed him and validated his experiences. This support was invaluable and highlights the importance of raising awareness that IPV is not a gender issue, to develop understanding and increase support within society. Nevertheless, this positive experience was somewhat of an anomaly in the experiences of the men overall, who all described feeling isolated due to being cut off from their social networks. Thus, the subjective experiences of male victims need to be made more visible within society through qualitative research and media campaigning, just as the subjective experiences of female victims have been (Coorey, 1988).

Masculine identity

This theme developed from the role of masculinity in the men's experiences of female-perpetrated IPV (see Figure 3.3). It is indicative of the socialisation of men to "be strong" (Mahalik, Good, & Englar-Carlson, 2003) and "emotionally stoic" (Addis & Mahalik, 2003) which influences the under-reporting of male victims (Steinmetz, 1978). Mahalik et al. (2003) also discussed the link between masculinity and aggression, with societal norms stating that men are usually the violent perpetrators. These norms are present despite statistics suggesting that of those who experienced IPV, a higher proportion of men (37%) endured force than women (29%; Office for National Statistics, 2016). Although these statistics do not clarify whether the perpetrators of this violence were male or female, it is noteworthy that the number of females recorded by the CPS and convicted for domestic violence

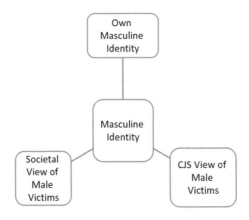

FIGURE 3.3 Sub-themes

crimes has risen from 806 to 5,641 during the period 2004/05 to 2015/16 (Mankind Initiative, 2017). The increase in arrests of women highlights some positive developments, however despite this the CPS continues to frame this crime as "Violence Against Women and Girls".

Own masculine identity

Participants often referred to their physicality and strength when discussing their experiences. Martin highlighted the small physical size of his ex-partner in comparison to his own size and strength, and reflected on the shock he felt when his partner perpetrated violence:

MARTIN: I'm quite a big bloke yeah and she's not big, she's an average sized woman about 5"3 … but, when she goes she just turns into a monster you know? She just comes at you like a bat out of hell sort of thing, it's really, really quite scary.

Chris and David reflected on the loss of their masculine identity, particularly regarding their physical appearance and their perception of being "tough". David reflected upon his declining self-care during the abusive relationship and how this impacted upon his self-worth:

CHRIS: Although I considered myself somewhat of a tough cookie, it didn't prevent me from ending up in therapy.
DAVID: I wasn't looking after myself, I was neglecting myself and I wasn't keeping myself in shape.

The interviews revealed a sense of emasculation and confusion around one's identity as a male victim, which is reflective of the way in which men are socialised to hide their problems, be strong and emotionally stoic (Goldberg, 1979; Addis & Mahalik, 2003). These findings also support the socio-psychological factors which make men vulnerable to female-perpetrated IPV, such as male socialisation which teaches boys not to hit girls, even in self-defence (Brown, 2004; p. 94). Where the abuse had been primarily psychological, such as in David's case, there seemed to be a further layer of confusion as to whether they were the victim or not. This supports previous research which reported that men are more likely to consider themselves a victim if they have been physically abused (Gadd, Farrall, Dallimore, & Lombard, 2003).

Criminal Justice System view of male victims

Participants discussed experiences of not being believed by the police and wider CJS. There appeared to feel a sense of injustice linked to their gender, with the men speaking of disparities in treatment by the CJS. Lee explained his experience of the CPS and his belief that they were only interested in a statistical result at the expense of the "deeper story":

LEE: I felt the CPS and the Police needed to get a statistical result so they could show the world they were dealing with domestic violence against women rather than the deeper story, which was in fact, it was me who was the victim and my daughter and step-son who were being abused by their mother ... and it just wasn't believed.

Chris referred to the "black and white" attitude of the police and other men referred to their beliefs that police were influenced by gender stereotypes present within IPV research, policy, and practice. This supports previous research which highlights the "one size fits all approach" in the CJS based on the assumption of male dominance and female victimisation (Dutton & Corvo, 2006). The ease of relying on such stereotypes is heightened due to the gender paradigm which has emerged within IPV research and the influence of value-laden theories prevailing over scientific accuracy (Dutton & Nicholls, 2005).

Societal view of male victims

Participants discussed inequality between the genders in relation to IPV, with their experiences of being treated unfairly or not being believed. Robert experienced the influence of these beliefs around gender roles within IPV, which seemed to immobilise him from seeking help and led him to retreat into an isolative state:

ROBERT: You couldn't just stand up and say, "I am a battered husband" because battered husbands just didn't exist. Battered women did, but battered men ... nobody believed it.

Robert spoke further about people's perceptions of his "dear, sweet wife", which further added to his experiences of not being believed. Lee explained his wish for change at a government level and referred to his wish for IPV to be considered from a human rights perspective, which echoes the response by McNeely, Cook, and Torres (2001) that domestic violence is a human issue and not a gender issue. He further referred to his feeling of segregation, which supports findings from previous research which highlighted the "non-normative" experience of being a male victim and how this is a barrier to help seeking behaviours (Addis & Mahalik, 2003).

Ultimately, these findings offer an alternative perspective to IPV statistics which report significantly lower numbers of male victims (e.g. Office for National Statistics, 2016). When considering the prevailing stereotypes surrounding IPV which lead to under-reporting by men, as well as men's experiences of being falsely accused, it is possible that the statistics are masking deeper issues which could be understood with a greater emphasis on gathering more qualitative data from all victims of IPV.

The pressure cooker

This theme developed from the experience of psychological distress that the men described (see Figure 3.4). This distress was precipitated by the original abuse perpetrated by their partners and perpetuated by further victimisation within the CJS. The psychological impact contests previous researchers' suggestions that "intimate terrorism" is gendered and relates to the exertion of male dominance over women (Johnson, 1995). The men in the current study experienced physical violence, financial control, threats, isolation, and other means of control, which all fit the definition of "intimate terrorism". The lived experiences of the men in the study highlight that the psychological impact was in line with that of intimate terrorism. The experience of the intense emotional experience was likened by David to a pressure cooker, which illustrates the magnitude of the psychological impact of IPV.

Pressing the trigger

Men spoke about their feelings of anger, both towards their abusive partners and the CJS. Some of the men referred to a trigger point, with some feeling that they could have become the perpetrators themselves due to the intensity of this emotion. Three of the men referred to the high intensity of their anger and how it could have led them to be violent. There was also a sense that the anger the men experienced felt uncontrollable and destructive to their selves:

MARTIN: It made me feel like I wanted to go round and commit the violence that she claimed I had, but, obviously, that's not realistic, but that's what it makes you feel like, that's the kind of emotion is sets up.

DAVID: You can't switch off and you can't be normal and you're always like … anxious and frustrated and angry.

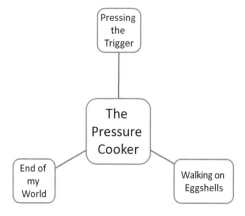

FIGURE 3.4 Sub-themes

CHRIS: You're sitting in a room somewhere, probably at home, hating this person and ... the only person you're hurting is yourself.

Previous research has reported that depression manifests itself differently in men, such as through anger or aggression, attributed to masculinity norms that view sadness as a weakness, which is socially unacceptable for men (Martin, Neighbors, & Griffith, 2013). When the societal expectations and gender norms for men are considered, it appears that the anger experienced by the men in the study is a manifestation of their emotional pain, due to their lived experiences. These experiences appeared to be directly related to decreased psychological health, with reference made to anxiety, and not being able to switch off from anger, with Chris adding that the emotion was so intense that he eventually "sought help" for it.

The feelings of anger appear to be a response to the abuse they had lived through by their ex-partners and perpetuated by their experiences with the CJS. Interestingly, the analysis of Henry's interview did not reveal similar themes of anger, which may be due to individual differences. However, it is also worth noting that this could be reflective of the positive experiences of being listened to and validated by his friend and the police officer, which allowed him a better space for reflection and decreased his need to act out defensively.

Walking on eggshells

The DSM-5 (American Psychiatric Association, 2013) attributes several symptoms to a diagnosis of Post-Traumatic Stress Disorder (PTSD). In the current study, the men spoke of several dimensions to their experience which are attributable to PTSD symptoms. Henry's experience reflects the symptom of recurrent, distressing dreams which relates to a traumatic event:

HENRY: I had a nightmare that the police were actually after me and tried to pin a very serious crime on me. I think it was murder and they found something, they dug something up.

Robert and Henry also described their difficulties with sleep, which is in line with the PTSD symptom of sleep disturbance. In Henry's case this sleep disturbance had begun due to a direct aspect of the abuse by his partner who would actively prevent him from sleeping.

ROBERT: I used to be unable to sleep and trying to carry on holding down a responsible job and yet not being able to sleep ... it's very difficult.
HENRY: A nurse diagnosed me with something called acute sleep deprivation and I told my wife that and she would still prevent me from sleeping.

The men in the study reflected on their experiences of depression, having constant "dark thoughts" and contemplating suicide. The men also highlighted a diminished interest in significant activities, with one explaining that he begun to avoid leaving his house. Henry described his fears of the police coming after him whereas Martin and David discussed this in relation to the control they were under by their abusive partners. This highlights the "parallel process" which occurred, whereby the men felt threatened both at home by their partners and outside their homes by the police.

End of my world

Participants reflected upon the losses they had experienced because of the violence. The enormity of this loss was captured by David, who referred to it feeling as though it was "the end of my world". These losses were varied, with some representing the impact of the controlling nature of their abusive relationships.

A dominant aspect was that of isolation, with the abuse leading some of the men to avoid future relationships due to their fear of abuse recurring and their sense of trust being shattered. Whilst David spoke about losing friendships, Robert referred to the loss of the relationships with his children. Both losses were a direct consequence of the controlling behaviours of their abusive partners:

DAVID: I lost my friends, seeing them regularly, being able to chill with them, relax with them, talk to them. I lost me, keeping fit, which made me feel good.
ROBERT: You end up retreating into your own world.

Other men in the study discussed loss in other regards, including the loss of careers, the loss of their sense of self and identity, and the loss of their relationships with their abusive ex-partners:

MARTIN: It's just a big pot of confusion … you know, this woman that I thought I was in love with, who I was due to get married to, has put me in a situation where I've been manhandled and thrown into a police cell for a false charge.
CHRIS: I'm still single. I'm having … well I don't even try anymore. The relationships I've tried to have in the intervening period, I've just found I have too much baggage with me really … and too much fear.

Migliaccio (2002) highlighted the impact that IPV has on men's self-esteem, which hinders their ability to leave the abusive relationship and perpetuates their isolation. These findings were supported by the experiences of the men in the current study, highlighting the intense psychological impact of IPV, due to the control and abuse which is further exacerbated by gendered societal beliefs.

A period of social change?

In the time since this study, there have been signs of social change, for example, best practice guidance has been published by Stafford Borough Council and Stoke on Trent City Council on how to work with male victims of IPV. These guidelines highlight the importance of believing the person disclosing the abuse and adopting a non-judgemental attitude. Guidance for supporting male victims at this local level highlights a step forward in responding to IPV in a less gendered manner. However, the guidance also highlights the lack of male refuges in that local area, with male victims having to declare themselves as homeless to escape an abusive relationship. Indeed, across the UK there are only 19 organisations which offer refuge or safe house provision for men, having a total of 78 spaces and only 20 which are dedicated to male victims. Areas including London, Lancashire, South East England, East Anglia, North Eastern England, and Northern Ireland have a distinct lack of safe house provision for men. This emphasises the need for the current government plans to increase spending in domestic violence and open more safe refuges for men across the UK.

Even more recently, Northumbria Police and Crime Commissioner Vera Baird has provided funding for organisations to increase therapeutic support for male victims of domestic violence (Northumbria Press Release, 2015). The research described here revealed the importance of funding services which are accessible to male victims, so they can receive specialist support tailored to their emotional and psychological needs. These services may also benefit from group interventions overseen by a skilled clinician, where men can share experiences and thus lower their sense of isolation and stigmatisation.

The study also identified the prevalence of CJS re-traumatisation and how this can be experienced as invalidation; a finding that indicates a need for police training to be reviewed enabling a less gendered response to IPV. Just as an increase in research around violence against women developed our awareness of the magnitude of this epidemic (Watts & Zimmerman, 2002), the same must now be done for men. The discourse around IPV needs to move away from gendered language and begin discussing this crime in terms of the psychological, developmental, and societal drivers which perpetuate the problem. Ultimately, an inclusive discourse will enable victims' voices to be heard regardless of their gender. Small pockets of good practice have developed across different sectors in the UK, however what is crucial is top-down support from a government level in terms of policy change and funding. Only then can the grass-roots organisations and community police responses be fully facilitated to provide a timely, effective, and supportive response to men affected by IPV.

Note

1 See video at: www.youtube.com/watch?v=u3PgH86OyEM

References

Addis, M. E. & Mahalik, J. R. (2003). Men, masculinity, and the contexts of help seeking. *American Psychologist*, 58(1), 5–14. doi:10.1037/0003–066X.58.1.5

American Psychiatric Association. (2013). *Diagnostic and statistical manual of mental disorders* (5th ed.). Arlington: American Psychiatric Publishing.

Brookes, M. (2017, February 18). New Domestic Violence and Abuse Act must lead to full and equal recognition for male victims. *Mankind Initiative Press Release*. Retrieved from:

http://new.mankind.org.uk/wp-content/uploads/2015/05/2-New-Domestic-Violence-and-Abuse-Act-Statement.pdf

Brown, G. A. (2004). Gender as a factor in the response of the law-enforcement system to violence against partners. *Sexuality and Culture*, 8(3–4), 3–139. doi:10.1007/s12119–12004–1000–1007

Centers for Disease Prevention and Control. (2013). Intimate Partner Violence: Definitions. Retrieved from: www.cdc.gov/violenceprevention/intimatepartnerviolence/definitions.html (Accessed on 10 June, 2017).

Cook, P. W. (2009). *Abused men: The hidden side of domestic violence*. Westport, CT: Praeger Publishers.

Coorey, L. (1988). Domestic violence and the police: Who is being protected? Unpublished Masters dissertation. University of Sydney, Australia.

Domestic Violence and Matrimonial Proceedings Act. (1976). Retrieved from: www.legislation.gov.uk/ukpga/1976/50/pdfs/ukpga_19760050_en.pdf (Accessed 10 June, 2017).

Dutton, D. G. & Corvo, K. (2006). Transforming a flawed policy: A call to revive psychology and science in domestic violence research and practice. *Aggression and Violent Behaviour*, 11 (5), 457–483. doi:10.1016/j.avb.2006.01.007

Dutton, D. G. & Nicholls, T. L. (2005). The gender paradigm in domestic violence research and theory: Part 1 – The conflict of theory and data. *Aggression and Violent Behaviour*, 10 (6), 680–714. doi:10.1016/j.avb.2005.02.001

Dutton, D. G. & White, K. R. (2013). Male victims of domestic violence. *New Male Studies: An International Journal*, 2(1), 5–17.

Follingstad, D. R., DeHart, D. D., & Green, E. P. (2004). Psychologists' judgments of psychologically aggressive actions when perpetrated by a husband versus a wife. *Violence and Victims*, 19(4), 435–452.

Gadd, D., Farrall, S., Dallimore, D., & Lombard, N. (2003). Male victims of domestic violence. *Criminal Justice Matters*, 53(1), 16–17. doi:10.1080/09627250308553565

George, M. J. (2007). The "great taboo" and the role of patriarchy in husband and wife abuse. *International Journal of Men's Health*, 6(1), 7–21.

Goldberg, H. (1979). *The new male: From macho to sensitive but still all male*. New York: New American Library.

Hester, M. (2009). Who does what to whom? Gender and domestic violence perpetrators. Violence Against Women Research Group/University of Bristol with Northern Rock Foundation. Retrieved from: www.nrfoundation.org.uk/downloads/Who%20Does%20What%20to%20Whom.pdf

Hine, B. & Arrindell, O. (2015). 'Yeah but, it's funny if she does it to him': comparing ratings of acceptability, humour, and perpetrator and victim blame in female-to-male versus male-to-female domestic violence scenarios. Male Psychology Conference 2015, London, UK. (Unpublished). Retrieved from http://repository.uwl.ac.uk/id/eprint/2094/

HMIC. (2014a). Everyone's business: Improving the police response to domestic abuse. Retrieved from: www.justiceinspectorates.gov.uk/hmic/wp-content/uploads/2014/04/improving-the-police-response-to-domestic-abuse.pdf

HMIC. (2014b). Policing in austerity: Meeting the challenge. Retrieved from: www.justiceinspectorates.gov.uk/hmic/wp-content/uploads/policing-in-austerity-meeting-the-challenge.pdf

Home Office. (2016, March 8). Ending Violence against Women and Girls. Strategy 2016–2020. HM Government. Retrieved from: www.gov.uk/government/uploads/system/uploads/attachment_data/file/522166/VAWG_Strategy_FINAL_PUBLICATION_MASTER_vRB.PDF

Johnson, M. (1995). Domestic violence: An overview. In *Family violence and the caring professions* (pp. 101–126). Macmillan Education UK.

Mahalik, J. R., Good, G. E., & Englar-Carlson, M. (2003). Masculinity scripts, presenting concerns and help seeking: Implications for practice and training. *Professional Psychology: Research and Practice*, 34(2), 123. doi:10.1037/0735–7028.34.3.239

Mankind Initiative. (2014, May 16). Violence is violence: Domestic abuse advert. Retrieved from: http://new.mankind.org.uk/media-and-policy/media

Mankind Initiative. (2017). Male victims of domestic and partner abuse 30 key facts. Retrieved from: http://new.mankind.org.uk/wp-content/uploads/2015/05/30-Key-Facts-Male-Victims-February-2017-1.pdf

Martens, W. H. J. (2005). Multidimensional model of trauma and correlated antisocial personality disorder. *Journal of Loss and Trauma*, 10, 115–129. doi:10.1080/15325020590908821

Martin, L. A., Neighbors, H. W., & Griffith, D. M. (2013). The experience of symptoms of depression in men vs women: Analysis of the national comorbidity survey replication. *JAMA Psychiatry*, 70(10), 1100–1106. doi:10.1001/jamapsychiatry.2013.1985

McCarrick, J. A., Davis-McCabe, C., & Hirst-Winthrop, S. (2015). Men's experiences of the UK Criminal Justice System following female-perpetrated intimate partner violence. *Journal of Family Violence*, 31(1), 1–11. doi:10.1007/s10896–10015–9749-z

McNeely, R. L., Cook, P. W., & Torres, J. B. (2001). Is domestic violence a gender issue, or a human issue? *Journal of Human Behavior in the Social Environment*, 4(4), 227–251. doi:10.1300/J137v04n04_02

Migliaccio, T. A. (2002). Abused husbands: A narrative analysis. *Journal of Family Issues*, 23(1), 26–52. doi:10.1177/0192513X02023001002

Muller, H., Desmarais, S., & Hamel, J. (2009). Do judicial responses to restraining order requests discriminate against male victims of domestic violence? *Journal of Family Violence*, 24(8), 625–637. doi:10.1007/s10896–10009–9261–9264

Northumbria Press Release. (2015). Male victims of domestic violence supported by commissioner funding. Retrieved from: http://verabaird.info/articles/male-victims-of-domestic-violence-supported-by-commissioner-funding/

Office for National Statistics (British Crime Survey). (2016, February 9). Focus on violent crime and sexual offences, England and Wales: Year ending Mar 2016. Retrieved from: www.ons.gov.uk/peoplepopulationandcommunity/crimeandjustice/compendium/focusonviolentcrimeandsexualoffences/yearendingmarch2016

Pizzey, E., Shackleton, J. R., & Urwin, P. (Eds) (2000). *Women or men – who are the victims?* London: Institute for the Study of Civil Society.

Prime Minister's Office. (2017, February 17). Press release: Prime Minister's plans to transform the way we tackle domestic violence and abuse. Retrieved from: www.gov.uk/government/news/prime-ministers-plans-to-transform-the-way-we-tackle-domestic-violence-and-abuse

Russell, B. (2012). Effectiveness, victim safety, characteristics, and enforcement of protective orders. *Partner Abuse*, 3(4), 531–552. doi:10.1891/1946–6560.3.4.531

Smith, J. A., Flowers, P., & Larkin, M. (2009). *Interpretative phenomenological analysis: Theory, method and research*. Los Angeles: SAGE.

Sorenson, S. B. & Taylor, C. A. (2005). Female aggression toward male intimate partners: an examination of social norms in a community-based sample. *Psychology of Women Quarterly*, 29(1), 79–96. doi:10.1111/j.1471–6402.2005.00170.x

Steinmetz, S. (1978). The battered husband syndrome. *Victimology*, 2, 499–509.

Straus, M. A. (1999). The controversy over domestic violence by women: A methodological, theoretical and sociology of science analysis. In Arriaga, X. B. & Oskamp, S. (Eds) *Violence in intimate relationships* (pp. 17–44). Thousand Oaks, CA: Sage.

Watts, C. & Zimmerman, C. (2002). Violence against women: global scope and magnitude. *The Lancet*, 359(9313), 1232–1237. doi:10.1016/S0140–6736(02)08221–08221

4

"IT CAN'T BE THAT BAD, I MEAN, HE'S A GUY"

Exploring judgements towards domestic violence scenarios varying on perpetrator and victim gender, and abuse type

Benjamin A. Hine

Introduction

I was sat in the backseat of a car a few months ago with a couple who live on my road, Sarah and David. David was driving and Sarah was in the passenger seat. For some reason, we all began discussing what celebrities we found attractive (and no, I will not divulge my choices!). Sarah said that she thought the actor Jamie Dornan "was really fit … like *really* fit". David acted affronted, joking "Are you just going to say that in front of me? Like I'm not even here?!". She replied that she did not care, and laughed. David then mentioned that he found a particular female celebrity very attractive (unfortunately, the name escapes me). With this comment, Sarah turned in the passenger seat, and slapped David on the arm as hard as she could. I could practically feel the stinging sensation it must have produced. "What was that for?!", David exclaimed. Sarah explained that he should not be saying such things in front of her, and should know better. I laughed awkwardly. I then paused and thought, just imagine if the scenario had been reversed. How might I, or anyone as it happens, have reacted differently if David had been the one to slap Sarah? I would have been outraged, shocked, appalled, and would have intervened immediately, questioning his actions and making sure Sarah was "OK". I probably would have wondered whether there was something more sinister going on. Was David abusing Sarah in private? How would I speak to her about it? As it happens, however, no such thoughts occurred. We all brushed past it, and drove on.

This scenario is one that typifies the importance of our perceptions, interpretations, prejudices, and stereotypes in how we react to a whole variety of events, including cases of violence between two people. And, whilst I can reassure readers that this incident (as far as I know) is not indicative of a more sinister pattern of behaviour, serious issues and questions are still present. Why are acts of aggression such as these tolerated or even found humorous when performed by women? Are the aggressive acts of women ever seen as abuse? If not, why not? Conversely, why are we unable to see men as victims of domestic violence, particularly at the hands of women? And how do we evaluate violence within same-sex relationships? In an attempt to answer some of these questions, this chapter first outlines the possible role of social cognition in informing judgements towards incidences of intimate partner violence, before reviewing existing research examining perceptions and judgements of such abuse. Original research in this area exploring judgements towards hypothetical incidents of domestic violence occurring in opposite-sex and same-sex couples, and of differing abuse types, is then outlined. Finally, outcomes of this research are discussed, as is the need for broader and more inclusive discourse in this area.

The "domestic violence stereotype"

It has been argued that an extremely narrow conceptualisation of domestic violence exists in society, including in academic circles (Dutton & White, 2013). Operating as a "gender paradigm" within the literature, the idea that domestic violence is predominantly perpetrated by violent men towards helpless women has proven a guiding principle for academic research, as well as policy development and implementation, for nearly 50 years. However, as is increasingly highlighted by a small group of scholars, this representation of domestic violence is dramatically limited, and does not correspond to the statistics available that demonstrate substantial victimisation amongst men (Drijber, Reijnders, & Ceelen, 2013; Dutton & Nicholls, 2005; Dutton & White, 2013), parity of perpetration in men and women (Archer, 2000), and similar prevalence levels within same-sex relationships (Bacchus et al., 2017). Such representations also present domestic violence as largely physical and unidirectional in nature, when in reality violence within relationships encompasses a wide variety of behaviours, such as psychological abuse (Capezza & Arriaga, 2008), and is frequently bidirectional (Langhinrichsen-Rohling, Misra, Selwyn, & Rohling, 2012). Why, therefore, when evidence exists to the contrary, and in a time when legislative definitions of domestic violence are increasingly broad, inclusive, and purposely highlight that no limit of gender or sexuality exists on the performance or receipt of such behaviours, do such narrow depictions of domestic violence endure?

The role of social cognition

The way the brain decodes and responds to social situations and interactions may be in part responsible for the formulation and subsequent propagation of the "domestic violence stereotype". Social cognition describes how people process, store, and apply information about other people and social situations, focusing particularly on the cognitive processes engaged by the brain when making sense of our social world (Hogg & Vaughan, 2014). An important part of this process is the development of schemas, described as patterns of thought or behaviour that organise and build relationships between information, producing a mental structure of preconceived ideas or "frameworks" about how the world operates (Fiske & Taylor, 1991). We build up numerous schemas, including person schemas (e.g. "best friend"), role schemas (e.g. a police officer), scripts (e.g. what happens during certain particular "events"), and self-schemas (e.g. knowledge about yourself; Hogg & Vaughan, 2014), and use these as sources of information in both familiar and novel situations. Importantly, schema tend to remain unchanged even in the face of contradictory information, and people are more likely to notice things that fit into their schemas and ignore things that do not (otherwise known as "confirmation bias"; Plous, 1993).

As part of this process, we will likely build up a representation or "script" for domestic violence, either through direct experience (e.g. growing up witnessing abuse), indirect representations (e.g. in the media), or both. For many this will likely result in a schema representing a "traditional" image of domestic violence, due to the prevalence of this stereotype within society. This stereotype will then become reinforced as information that matches this schema is absorbed and logged, and incongruent information ignored. This will, in turn, perpetuate the stereotype further, and so on. Relationships *between* schemas also exist, providing even greater amounts of information to inform decision making. For example, some of the most well-developed schemas are those about gender. Representations of men, and by association masculinity, as being aggressive, independent, strong, stoic, unemotional, and sexually dominant, and of women (and femininity) as non-aggressive, inter-dependent, weak, passive, emotional, nurturing, and sexually submissive (Bem, 1981; Gerber, 1991; Lueptow, Garovich-Szabo, & Lueptow, 2001) are learnt from a very young age, and from a wide variety of sources (Blakemore, Berenbaum, & Liben, 2009; Ruble, Martin, & Berenbaum, 2006). Children, and the adults they become, also learn associations between these gender characteristics and the corresponding activities, preferences, and roles appropriate for each sex. This is particularly important in the case of domestic violence, as it is easy to see how the attributes associated with men and masculinity are more synonymous with perpetration of abuse (particularly physical aggression), and feminine attributes with victimisation.

Other cognitive processes, such as heuristics, then help to shape our reactions to domestic violence by providing mental shortcuts to the wealth of information stored, including our stereotypes (Hogg & Vaughan, 2014). Thus, when con-fronted with an incident that we think might be domestic violence, heuristics help guide us in our decision making, (e.g. when determining perpetration, or in deciding whether something is even domestic violence at all). In most instances, such mental processes are useful, as they allow us to engage in rapid decision making, particularly in unfamiliar or ambiguous situations. However, they can produce "cognitive biases" that result in judgemental errors, often by not encouraging or allowing for all of the information to be assessed. In the context of domestic violence, this process can therefore have severe consequences. Specifically, incidences of intimate partner violence which do not "fit" with our pre-existing conceptualisations are likely to be subjected to sub-standard evalua-tive processes which result in appraisals that seek to preserve our existing schema, for example minimisation or even outright dismissal.

The influence of victim and perpetrator gender

An increasing number of studies have highlighted the possible influence of such processes by examining perceptions of, and judgements towards, incidences of domestic violence. For example, recent studies utilising layperson and undergraduate populations show (amongst a whole raft of findings) that incidents are viewed as more serious and are rated as more likely to result in injury when the victim is female, regardless of perpetrator gender (Ahmed, Aldén, & Hammarstedt, 2013; Poorman, Seelau, & Seelau, 2003; Seelau, Seelau, & Poorman, 2003; Seelau & Seelau, 2005). In addition, incidents involving male perpetrators are rated as more serious, more likely to cause injury, and are more likely to receive a recommendation of citation/arrest by police. Interestingly, when interactions between victim and perpetrator gender do occur, it is the most stereotypical version of abuse (male perpetrator, female victim) that receives the highest seriousness ratings, is most likely to have police intervention recommended, and is the most likely to receive a recommendation that the victim call the police (Ahmed et al., 2013; Poorman et al., 2003; Seelau et al., 2003; Seelau & Seelau, 2005). This is supported by earlier studies showing that incidences in which men abuse women are invariably perceived more negatively than those in which women abuse men, as male-on-female violence is rated more severe than female-on-male violence and harsher penalties are awarded to male as compared to female perpetrators (Arias & Johnson, 1989; Feather, 1996; Gerber, 1991; Harris & Cook, 1994; Home, 1994; O'Toole & Webster, 1988; Sorenson & Taylor, 2005; Willis, Hallinan, & Melby, 1996). Other studies suggest that male victims of female perpetrators are also considered least worthy of assistance, with incidences of male-on-female, gay, and lesbian domestic violence more likely to be deemed illegal, and to receive a recommendation of police intervention and action, than female-on-male violence (Sorenson & Thomas, 2009). Such results therefore suggest that violence by men towards women is regarded as particularly serious, with the opposite true for violence by women towards men.

These studies are further supported by qualitative research, which suggests that both non-abused young adults and male victim-survivors have strongly held stereotypes about gender, domestic violence, and about male victim-survivors in particular (Shum-Pearce, 2015). For example, non-abused adults believe that "men are powerful", and therefore have control over any given situation, could leave easily, and that they do not need help. This is complemented by the belief that "women are incapable of harm", reflecting the commonly held stereotype of women as weak and physically unintimidating. Male victim-survivors reported that they felt "invisible" and that they "shouldn't need help" when victimised (Shum-Pearce, 2015), and other studies support the idea that these men feel bound by prevalent stereotypes about gender and violence, characterised by a lack of recognition (Wallace, 2018). It is therefore no surprise that male victim-survivors struggle to find support among their social networks upon disclosure (Tsui, 2014; Tsui, Cheung, & Leung, 2010), and that they often shy away from reporting their abuse for fear of embarrassment, ridicule, and the lack of available support services (Barber, 2008).

These "internal" barriers to reporting are likely fuelled through perceptions and stereotypes of abuse held by service providers, and those within the criminal justice system. When interviewing male victim-survivors, McCarrick, Davis-McCabe and Hirst-Winthrop (2016) found that their experiences with police officers were overwhelmingly negative, mirroring earlier work (Buzawa & Austin, 1993). Other studies show that male victim-survivors are more likely to be blamed for their victimisation (Stewart & Maddren, 1997), that prejudice towards male victim-survivors is extreme (George, 1994), and that they are often completely ignored by police and other services (Cook, 2009; George & Yarwood, 2004). When comparing male versus female perpetrator cases, the same actions are judged as actionable when performed by men compared to women (Sorenson & Taylor, 2005), and when cases are progressed, female perpetrators are likely to receive lower sentences or have their cases dismissed (Henning & Feder, 2005). Officers are also less likely to reinforce protection orders in female-perpetrated cases (Connolly, Huzurbazar, & Routh-McGee, 2000; Renzetti, 1989). It is no wonder then that male victim-survivors report believing that officers will not be able to help them to a greater extent than women do (Drijber et al., 2013).

Victim-survivors in same-sex relationships also expect negative experiences with law enforcement (Finneran & Stephenson, 2013), and have difficulty accessing services (Stiles-Shields & Carroll, 2015). Indeed, as outlined in Chapter 6, major barriers are identified in the help-seeking abilities of LGBTQIA+ victim-survivors, including lack of understanding and stigma (Calton, Cattaneo, & Gebhard, 2016). Even counsellors and therapists have been shown to place greater seriousness on violence in opposite-sex compared to same-sex relationships (Wise & Bowman, 1997). This is likely due, in part, to cultural heterosexism, a system of attitudes, biases, and discrimination in favour of opposite-sex sexuality and relationships (Herek, 1995). Moreover, such cultural attitudes will also influence the development of multiple different schemas, including those about relationships, gender, sexuality, and domestic violence. Importantly, the studies outlined earlier demonstrate that the narrow representation of domestic violence as perpetrated exclusively by men towards women serves to minimise the importance and limit the recognition of male victim-survivors of female abuse, as well as same-sex abuse and those involved. Crucially, such beliefs and attitudes are only further fuelled by the academic, political, and social dialogue purporting domestic abuse as "gendered", as discussed in other chapters of this book.

Abuse type

The stereotype of domestic violence outlined earlier also suggests that such violence is predominantly physical. However, statistics routinely indicate widespread prevalence of other forms of abuse (such as psychological or emotional aggression; see Black et al., 2011). And yet, even fewer studies have examined the impact of abuse type on perceptions and judgements towards other incidences of abuse. One such study by Langhinrichsen-Rohling and colleagues showed participants one of two videos depicting either a psychologically aggressive conflict or a conflict that involved both psychological and physical aggression. Results indicated that physical aggression added to perceptions of seriousness, above and beyond the effect of psychological aggression (Langhinrichsen-Rohling, Shlien-Dellinger, Huss, & Kramer, 2004). Capezza and Arriaga (2008) compared physical and psychological aggression more extensively, presenting participants with either a low, medium, or high physical abuse scenario, or a low versus high psychological abuse scenario. They then asked about the negativity of the behaviour, the acceptability of the behaviour, and the severity of conflict. They found that participants' judgements became significantly more negative with increasing physical abuse, but no corresponding change was found with increased psychological abuse. Physical abuse is also much more likely to be rated as illegal compared to other forms of violence (Sorenson & Thomas, 2009). These limited results suggest that physical abuse within relationships is considered more serious than psychological forms of aggression. This is alarming considering that psychological aggression has been found to be a larger predictor of victim-survivors' fears of future abuse (Sackett & Saunders, 1999), and that experiencing this type of abuse is more strongly associated with negative health outcomes, such as depression or substance misuse (Coker et al., 2002).

The present study

A prevalent stereotype undoubtedly exists regarding intimate partner violence (Dutton & White, 2013), which is related to, and constructed around, deeply ingrained beliefs about gender (Gerber, 1991). As such, a widespread disbelief and minimisation towards male victim-survivors, as well as victim-survivors within same-sex relationships, exists (Calton et al., 2016; McNeely, Cook, & Torres, 2001), both within the general population, and in specialist populations such as those providing services and support, and those within the criminal justice system. Crucially, negative beliefs also appear to be internalised by victim-survivors and may be partially responsible for chronically low reporting rates in these groups. However, more research is needed to explore judgements made towards scenarios involving male versus female perpetrators and victims, to understand how these incidences are evaluated against such a stereotype. In addition, research exploring the impact of abuse type on perceptions and judgements (for example, lesser known types of aggression and coercive control), or how gender and abuse type interact (e.g. male-perpetrated physical abuse versus female-perpetrated emotional abuse) is needed, as some forms of aggression may be linked to gender stereotypes (e.g. verbal/psychological aggression being thought of as more typical in women). The present study therefore explored undergraduates' judgements towards hypothetical intimate partner violence scenarios varying by victim-perpetrator gender and abuse type.

Method

Design

This study adopted a between-subjects design with two factors: abuse type (with three levels: physical, psychological/emotional, and financial) and perpetrator-victim gender (with four levels: male-male, male-female, female-female, and female-male). These factors constituted the independent variables in this study. Thirty questions measuring perceptions of the scenario itself, reaction and intervention preferences, perceptions of the victim and perpetrator, perceptions of the relationship, the outcome of the incident, and the frequency of occurrence acted as separate dependent variables in this study.

Participants

Participants were 243 undergraduate students (M = 22.83 years, SD = 5.39, min = 18.00, max = 54.00, 138 women) at a university in West London, UK. Most were third year undergraduate students (102), coming from a variety of ethnic backgrounds (63% were white, 19% were black, 10% were Asian, with the remainder identifying as belonging to another ethnic group). Furthermore, 87.7% of participants (213) identified as heterosexual, with 4.9% and 3.7% identifying as bisexual and gay respectively (3.7% were asexual or "other"). Finally, and importantly for this study, 21.8% of participants (53) reported some history of domestic violence.

Materials and procedure

A vignette depicting an incident of domestic violence was adapted from Seelau and Seelau (2005). This previous study utilised two vignettes for each scenario, giving accounts from the perspective of both the victim and the perpetrator. However, the volume of information provided in these vignettes may have placed too much strain on participants, as well as skew or prime participants' perspectives through their identification with either the victim or perpetrator based on gender. The vignettes utilised in this study therefore describe the event from a neutral perspective, and are shorter, to provide more control over effects observed. Within these vignettes, variation of victim and perpetrator gender (using different names and associated pronouns), as well as the type of violence, created 12 vignettes in total. All other factors remained constant. Participants read only one of the 12 scenarios, and presentation of these vignettes was randomised. An example vignette (male perpetrator, male victim, financial abuse) is given in the following:

> Please read the following account of a dispute involving a romantically involved couple, Matt and Tom, both 26-year-old males. They have been

together for approximately two years. They both weigh roughly 11 stone, are both around 5 foot 10 inches tall, and both have full-time jobs.

One night Tom returns home late after stopping off at a local bar after work and drinking with friends. Matt is suspicious of Tom, and begins yelling at him and accusing him of being unfaithful. Tom says that Matt is being stupid, that he hasn't been unfaithful, and that he is tired and wants to go to bed. Matt insists that they continue to talk, again accusing Tom of being more interested in his friends than in him. As the argument escalates, Tom decides he has had enough and goes to leave the room. Matt shouts at Tom to try and stop him leaving. Tom pauses, and then continues towards the bedroom. Matt shouts at Tom again and demands that Tom show him the receipts for the night. When Tom refuses, Matt says that he clearly can't be trusted and until he can trust him he shouldn't have access to their money. He insists Tom hands over his wallet so that he can take away his card to the joint account they both pay their wages into. Tom, now visibly upset, hands over his wallet and goes into the bedroom. Tom shuts the door, and Matt stays in the main room.

Participants then answered 30 questions adapted from previous research in this area (Poorman et al., 2003; Seelau, et al., 2003; Seelau & Seelau, 2005). Most involved answering on a Likert scale from 1 (Not at all) to 7 (Extremely). Some questions (e.g. should the victim in this scenario call the police?) invited categorical responses (e.g. yes or no). An electronic version of the questionnaire battery was presented using the survey software Qualtrics. If participants consented to participation following the briefing, they were asked demographic questions, before being presented with one of the 12 different domestic violence scenarios. They were asked to read this carefully, and to answer the questions presented honestly. Once participants were finished, they were presented with debriefing information, including contact information for local support services if required.

Results

Several 3 (abuse type) x 4 (perpetrator-victim gender) between-subject ANOVAs were computed for the 24 questions requiring Likert scale responses. MANOVAs were not appropriate, as few correlations between questions were found. For the four questions requiring categorical responses, separate chi-square analyses were conducted to assess the influence of abuse type and perpetrator-victim gender on participants' choices. One-way within-subject ANOVAs were computed for the four questions measuring appropriateness of intervention, and judgements of frequency for each perpetrator-victim combination.

Perpetrator-victim gender

Some main effects were found for perpetrator-victim gender. Importantly, significant differences were found for judgements of seriousness, $F(3,231) = 2.58$, $p < .05$, with scenarios involving female victims (male perpetrator, M = 5.09, SD = 1.55; female perpetrator, M = 4.93, SD = 1.49) rated as more serious than those involving male victims (male perpetrator, M = 4.56, SD = 1.29; female perpetrator, M = 4.47, SD = 1.45). This suggests that, regardless of perpetrator gender, incidents of abuse towards male victims are not awarded the same gravity as those towards women. It was also much more likely that participants would say that victims should call the police in M-F scenarios than in any other, χ^2 (3) = 8.63, p < .05. This again points to the seriousness that participants may place on scenarios involving female victims, particularly when at the hands of male abusers. M-F couples were also rated as lowest on closeness (M = 3.29, SD = 1.26), compared to F-F couples (M = 3.99, SD = 1.47), with M-M and F-M couples falling in-between, $F(3,231)$ = 2.58, p < .05. Finally, significant differences were found for ratings of perpetrator masculinity/femininity, $F(3,197)$ = 3.59, p < .05. Tukey HSD post hoc tests revealed that participants gave the highest masculinity rating to perpetrators in the M-F scenario (M = 37.74, SD = 29.42) compared to F-F (M = 50.97, SD = 22.37) and F-M scenarios (M = 51.71, SD = 22.33), with M-M scenarios falling in-between (M = 46.13, SD = 24.87). This could suggest that being abusive towards a female victim is also synonymous with increased masculinity.

Participants also differed significantly in their judgements of appropriateness of intervention by law enforcement, $F(3,717)$ = 4.61, p < .01. Predictably, participants believed intervention to be most appropriate in M-F scenarios (M = 6.15, SD = 1.15) compared to M-M (M = 6.04, SD = 1.24), F-M (M = 6.03, SD = 1.25), and F-F scenarios (M = 6.01, SD = 1.27). This further supports the idea that participants regard M-F incidents as more serious, and therefore worthy of investigation by police officers. This could partly be due to the fact that participants also rated M-F incidents to be more frequently occurring in society (M = 5.55, SD = 1.41) than M-M (M = 4.72, SD = 1.51), F-F (M = 4.42, SD = 1.52), and F-M scenarios (M = 4.6, SD = 1.60), F (3,687) = 64.22, p < .01. However, combined with the results for seriousness outlined earlier, these results most likely suggest a bias in participants towards M-F scenarios.

Abuse type

Several main effects were also found for abuse type. Participants were: more likely to try and intervene, $F(2,231)$ = 3.50, p < .05, less likely to do nothing and more likely to call the police, χ^2 (6) = 15.26, p < .05, more likely to recommend that the victim call the police, χ^2 (2) = 25.16, p < .001, less likely to recommend the police should talk to the couple and more likely to recommend an arrest, χ^2 (2) = 27.09, p < .001, more likely to believe the police can help, $F(2,231)$ = 8.08, p < .001, believed the perpetrator more capable of harm, $F(2, 230)$ = 8.16, p < .001, and serious injury, F (2,230) = 9.47, p < .001, and more likely to award more severe punishments, F (2,230) = 4.47, p < .05, in physical compared to psychological/emotional and financial scenarios. These results all suggest that participants view physical incidents as more serious, and therefore worthier of police investigation and punishment within the criminal justice system. This is particularly interesting considering that all the types of abuse utilised in this study are covered by the current definition of domestic violence provided by the UK government. An interesting additional finding is that participants rated victims of financial abuse as more feminine than victims of other abuse types, $F(2,230) = 4.47$, $p < .05$. This suggests that participants may view those who suffer from certain types of abuse as more likely to be one gender or the other. No interactions between factors were found.

Discussion

This study examined the influence of perpetrator and victim gender, as well as abuse type, on judgements towards hypothetical domestic violence scenarios. This is the first study to examine these factors in combination, and to do so using such a wide range of measures. A number of differences were found for both factors, with scenarios involving male violence towards women, and physical violence, receiving the most severe ratings. These results support the notion that stereotypes about domestic violence exist, and that these conceptualisations may influence judgements upon occurrence. The importance of such results cannot be understated, as both internal and external reactions to abuse are critical in the decision by victim-survivors to report, as well as the quality of care received once they have done so.

The male-female effect

Participants rated scenarios involving female victims as more serious than those involving male victims. This supports findings from previous studies suggesting that participants may view women as more vulnerable, and men less so, in abuse scenarios (Ahmed et al., 2013; Seelau et al., 2003; Seelau & Seelau, 2005; Shum-Pearce, 2015). Differences in evaluations of seriousness are extremely important, as such judgements serve to reinforce negative attitudes towards male victim-survivors, particularly a prevalence of disbelief towards male victimisation (McNeely et al., 2001). Judgements in this study also appeared to reflect a bias towards "traditional" abuse scenarios (e.g. those involving a male perpetrator and a female victim), with a higher probability of a recommendation for the victim to call the police, and a higher level of appropriateness for police intervention, awarded in these situations. This supports previous work (Poorman et al., 2003), and suggests that participants therefore view these scenarios as particularly serious (thus deserving of police involvement). Considering the academic, political, and social narrative surrounding domestic violence which places an emphasis on the abuse of women by men, as well as established gender beliefs regarding the qualities of men and women synonymous with perpetration and victimhood respectively, it is unsurprising that participants view violence towards women as more serious, particularly when at the hands of men. However, this presents serious issues for both male victim-survivors of female abuse, and victim-survivors within same-sex relationships. Lesser seriousness placed on abuse in these contexts is likely to be internalised by victim-survivors themselves, resulting in a decreased impetus to report victimisation, and to gain adequate support and assistance (Barber, 2008; Dutton & White, 2013). Furthermore, unfortunately, decisions by victim-survivors in such scenarios not to report may then result in an associated reinforcement of the idea that abuse in this context is less common, and therefore, less important, thus perpetuating the cycle.

Physical aggression equals abuse

Mirroring results from previous research (Capezza & Arriaga, 2008; Langhinrichsen-Rohling et al., 2004; Sorenson & Thomas, 2009), physical abuse received higher ratings than psychological/emotional or financial abuse on several measures related to seriousness and intervention. These results therefore suggest that participants' judgements may be informed by a typically narrow representation of intimate partner violence as almost exclusively involving physical acts of aggression (Capezza & Arriaga, 2008). This again presents serious consequences for victim-survivors of non-physical abuse, as they may not receive support from social networks or services following victimisation, or even believe that they have been victimised in the first instance. This is particularly alarming as the severe impact of psychological abuse on physical and mental health outcomes is outlined in previous research (Coker et al., 2002; Sackett & Saunders, 1999). It is also surprising considering that definitions of domestic violence provided by the UK government, like many Western countries, are increasingly inclusive of various coercive and controlling behaviours, including psychological abuse.

Limitations

A number of sample-related issues present. First, this study was conducted using under-graduate students, many of whom were studying a psychology degree programme at the time. In addition, many of these students were in the second or third year of their degree and would have completed modules exploring gender psychology in an applied context, and forensic psychology. As such, these students would have been more informed than typical populations on the issues outlined in this chapter, and may have therefore responded in a manner representative of that increased awareness. Furthermore, approximately 20% of participants reported that they had suffered from domestic abuse at some point in their lives. These participants may have therefore provided judgements that are informed by their own personal experiences, which may have been more sympathetic to victim-survivors, regardless of gender. Future research should therefore seek to obtain more representative samples (e.g. using members of the general public) as well as those within law enforcement and service agencies, in order to capture judgements made by those whose opinions prove pivotal for victim-survivors.

Methodological limitations also exist. First, the scenarios presented in this study depicted a one-time, unidirectional incident of violence. In reality, domestic violence is often much more complicated, involving a pattern of behaviour over time, with dual perpetration and victimisation. Again, this presented a narrow sample of domestic violence, as dual-perpetration or "intimate partner terrorism" is also common (Langhinrichsen-Rohling et al., 2012). Future research should seek to examine how factors such as length of abuse and share of perpetration influence judgements of domestic violence, by male and female perpetrators, and across abuse types.

Implications and conclusion

Research in this area is still in its infancy, and many more studies, specifically those addressing some of the limitations outlined earlier, are needed. However, the results from research to date provides clear evidence that substantial variation exists in evaluations of domestic abuse scenarios across a variety of measures. Notably, participants appear to be guided by a stereotype of abuse that is narrow, misrepresentative, and not supported by the information available regarding the context, nature, and frequency of domestic violence in Western countries. As already outlined, this has serious implications for victim-survivors who do not meet the "cognitive criteria" created by our schemas and stereotypic beliefs, including critical physical and mental health outcomes associated with internalisation of false-victimhood beliefs, and continued abuse. As such, several important steps are recommended to improve the experiences of all those suffering from intimate partner violence:

1. Greater efforts are needed to challenge the current political and societal narrative that portrays women as the exclusive victim-survivors of domestic violence. For example, the creation of a corresponding, male-oriented version of the "Violence Against Women and Girls" strategy, or making such strategies fundamentally gender inclusive, would help acknowledge the experiences, needs, and existence of male victim-survivors, and, importantly, may help rectify inequalities in funding and support (e.g. the absence of male-only refuges in London). In addition, greater explicit recognition of the needs and vulnerabilities of the LGBTQIA+ community in the context of domestic violence is also needed at this level.
2. Services (e.g. police forces, prosecution services, and other professional bodies) need to respond, immediately, to the specific needs of male victim-survivors, and those in same-sex relationships, in their provision of training and support. Importantly, whilst many services argue that their training is "gender neutral", this often means that the very specific and nuanced experiences of female, male, and LGBTQIA+ victim-survivors are not fully considered. Put simply, a dedicated effort to provide "gender-inclusive" as opposed to "gender neutral" training is urgently required.
3. The academic community must continue investigating which factors influence judgements and attitudes towards domestic violence, in order to inform policy and discourse. Moreover, greater efforts must also be made to use more diverse methodology to examine abuse in ways that are more representative of its occurrence (e.g. occurring over longer periods of time, and with dual-perpetration). Furthermore, non-politicised models of domestic violence require urgent development. In other words, models are required that *account* for gender, but are not determined or driven by specific, political, and gendered narratives (i.e. feminism and the Duluth Model)

4. Finally, the media needs to increasingly provide varied and more nuanced representations of domestic violence to audiences, to broaden stereotypical understandings of abuse. This is particularly important considering a) the broad reach of the media (including social media and the internet) in today's world and b) the powerful indirect effects that this type of material can have on stereotype formation. On a broader, societal level, we must increasingly open our minds to the complexities of domestic violence and abuse as a crime, and guard against utilising stereotypes when confronted with a victim-survivor in need of our help.

Only by taking such substantive and immediate actions will we, as a society, begin to break down the powerful and pervasive stereotypes surrounding domestic violence, and thus acknowledge the wide range of perpetrators and victim-survivors, as well as behaviours and circumstances, involved in intimate partner violence. By doing so, we may finally begin to provide all victim-survivors of domestic violence with the acknowledgement, support, and assistance they deserve.

References

Ahmed, A. M., Aldén, L., & Hammarstedt, M. (2013). Perceptions of gay, lesbian, and heterosexual domestic violence among undergraduates in Sweden. *International Journal of Conflict and Violence*, 7, 249–260. doi:0070-ijcv-2013216

Archer, J. (2000). Sex differences in aggression between heterosexual partners: A meta-analytic review. *Psychological Bulletin*, 126, 651–680. doi:10.1037/0033-2909.126.5.651

Arias, I. & Johnson, P. (1989). Evaluations of physical aggression among intimate dyads. *Journal of Interpersonal Violence*, 4, 298–307. doi:10.1177/088626089004003004

Bacchus, L. J., Buller, A. M., Ferrari, G., Peters, T. J., Devries, K., Sethi, G., … Feder, G. S. (2017). Occurrence and impact of domestic violence and abuse in gay and bisexual men: A cross sectional survey. *International Journal of STD & AIDS*, 28, 16–27. doi:10.1177/0956462415622886

Barber, C. F. (2008). Domestic violence against men. *Nursing Standard*, 22, 35–39. doi:10.7748/ns2008.08.22.51.35.c6644

Bem, S. (1981). Gender schema theory: A cognitive account of sex typing. *Psychological Review*, 88, 354–364.

Black, M. C., Basile, K. C., Breiding, M. J., Smith, S. G., Walters, M. L., Merrick, M. T., & Stevens, M. R. (2011). The national intimate partner and sexual violence survey (NISVS): 2010 summary report. Atlanta, GA: National Center for Injury Prevention and Control, Centers for Disease Control and Prevention.

Blakemore, J. E. O., Berenbaum, S. A., & Liben, L. S. (2009). *Gender development*. New York: Psychology Press.

Buzawa, E. S. & Austin, T. (1993). Determining police response to domestic violence victims. *American Behavioral Scientist*, 36, 610–623.

Calton, J. M., Cattaneo, L. B., & Gebhard, K. T. (2016). Barriers to help seeking for lesbian, gay, bisexual, transgender, and queer survivors of intimate partner violence. *Trauma, Violence, & Abuse*, 17, 585–600. doi:10.1177/1524838015585318

Capezza, N. M. & Arriaga, X. B. (2008). You can degrade but you can't hit: Differences in perceptions of psychological versus physical aggression. *Journal of Social and Personal Relationships*, 2, 225–245. doi:10.1177/0265407507087957

Coker, A. L., Davis, K. E., Arias, I., Desai, S., Sanderson, M., Brandt, H. M., & Smith, P. H. (2002). Physical and mental health effects of intimate partner violence for men and women. *American Journal of Preventive Medicine*, 23, 260–268. doi:10.1016/S0749-3797(02)00514-7

Connolly, C., Huzurbazar, S., & Routh-McGee, T. (2000). Multiple parties in domestic violence situations and arrest. *Journal of Criminal Justice*, 28, 181–188. doi:10.1016/S0047-2352(00)00034-9

Cook, P. W. (2009). *Abused men: The hidden side of domestic violence*. Westport, CT: Praeger Publishers.

Drijber, B. C., Reijnders, U. J. L., & Ceelen, M. (2013). Male victims of domestic violence. *Journal of Family Violence*, 28, 173–178. doi:10.1007/s10896-012-9482-9

Dutton, D. G. & Nicholls, T. L. (2005). The gender paradigm in domestic violence research and theory: Part 1 – The conflict of theory and data. *Aggression and Violent Behavior*, 10, 680–714. doi:10.1016/j.avb.2005.02.001

Dutton, D. G. & White, K. R. (2013). Male victims of domestic violence. *New Male Studies: An International Journal*, 2, 5–17.

Feather, N. T. (1996). Domestic violence, gender, and perceptions of justice. *Sex Roles*, 35, 507–519. doi:10.1007/BF01544134

Finneran, C. & Stephenson, R. (2013). Gay and bisexual men's perceptions of police helpfulness in response to male=male intimate partner violence. *Western Journal of Emergency Medicine*, 14, 354–362. doi:10.5811/westjem.2013.3.15639

Fiske, S. T. & Taylor, S. E. (1991). *Social cognition* (2nd ed.). New York, NY: McGraw-Hill.

George, M. J. (1994). Riding the donkey backwards: Men as the unacceptable victims of marital violence. *The Journal of Men's Studies*, 3, 137–159.

George, M. J. & Yarwood, D. J. (2004). Male domestic violence victims survey 2001: Main findings. Retrieved from: www.dewar4research.org/DOCS/mdv.pdf

Gerber, G. L. (1991). Gender stereotypes and power: Perceptions of the roles in violent marriages. *Sex Roles*, 24, 439–458. doi:10.1007/BF00289333

Harris, R. J. & Cook, C. A. (1994). Attributions about spouse abuse: It matters who the batterers and victims are. *Sex Roles*, 30, 553–565. doi:10.1007/BF01420802

Henning, K. & Feder, L. (2005). Criminal prosecution of domestic violence offenses. *Criminal Justice and Behavior*, 32, 612–642. doi:10.1177/0093854805279945

Herek, G. (1995). Psychological heterosexism in the United States. In D'Augelli, A. R. & Patterson, C. J. (Eds) *Lesbian, gay, and bisexual identities over the lifespan: Psychological perspectives* (pp. 321–346). Oxford: Oxford University Press.

Hogg, M. A. & Vaughan, G. M. (2014). *Social psychology* (7th ed.). London, UK: Pearson.

Home, A. M. (1994). Attributing responsibility and assessing gravity in wife abuse situations: A comparative study of police and social workers . *Journal of Social Service Research*, 19, 67–84. doi:10.1300/J079v19n01_04

Langhinrichsen-Rohling, J., Misra, T. A., Selwyn, C., & Rohling, M. L. (2012). Rates of bidirectional versus unidirectional intimate partner violence across sample, sexual orientations, and race/ethnicities: A comprehensive review. *Partner Abuse*, 3, 199–230. doi:10.1891/1946-6560.3.2.199

Langhinrichsen-Rohling, J., Shlien-Dellinger, R. K., Huss, M. T., & Kramer, V. L. (2004). Attributions about perpetrators and victims of interpersonal abuse. *Journal of Interpersonal Violence*, 19, 484–498. doi:10.1177/0886260503262084

Lueptow, L. B., Garovich-Szabo, L., & Lueptow, M. B. (2001). Social change and the persistence of sex typing: 1974–1997. *Social Forces*, 80, 1–36.

McCarrick, J., Davis-McCabe, C., & Hirst-Winthrop, S. (2016). Men's experiences of the criminal justice system following female perpetrated intimate partner violence. *Journal of Family Violence*, 31, 203–213. doi:10.1007/s10896-015-9749-z

McNeely, R. L., Cook, P. W., & Torres, J. B. (2001). Is domestic violence a gender issue, or a human issue? *Journal of Human Behavior in the Social Environment*, 4, 227–251. doi:10.1300/J137v04n04_02

O'Toole, R. & Webster, S. (1988). Differentiation of family mistreatment: Similarities and differences by status of victim. *Deviant Behavior*, 9, 347–368. doi:10.1080/01639625.1988.9967791

Plous, S. (1993). *The psychology of judgment and decision making*. New York, NY: Mcgraw-Hill

Poorman, P. B., Seelau, E. P., & Seelau, S. M. (2003). Perceptions of domestic abuse in same-sex relationships and implications for criminal justice and mental health responses. *Violence and Victims*, 18, 659–670. doi:10.1891/vivi.2003.18.6.659

Renzetti, C. M. (1989). Building a second closet: Third party responses to victims of lesbian partner abuse. *Family Relations*, 38, 157–163. doi:10.2307/583669

Ruble, D. N., Martin, C. L., & Berenbaum, S. (2006). Gender development. In Eisenberg, N. (Ed.) *Handbook of child psychology: Vol. 3. Social, emotional, and personality development* (6th ed., pp. 858–932). New York: Wiley.

Sackett, L. A. & Saunders, D. G. (1999). The impact of different forms of psychological abuse on battered women. *Violence and Victims*, 14, 105–117.

Seelau, E. P., Seelau, S. M., & Poorman, P. B. (2003). Gender and role-based perceptions of domestic abuse: Does sexual orientation matter? *Behavioral Sciences and the Law*, 21, 199–214. doi:10.1002/bsl.524

Seelau, S. M. & Seelau, E. P. (2005). Gender-role stereotypes and perceptions of heterosexual, gay and lesbian domestic violence. *Journal of Family Violence*, 20, 363–371. doi:10.1007/s10896-005-7798-4

Shum-Pearce, A. (2015). Young men talk about abuse. Paper presented at the Male Psychology Conference, University College London, London, UK.

Sorenson, S. B. & Taylor, C. A. (2005). Female aggression toward male intimate partners: An examination of social norms in a community-based sample. *Psychology of Women Quarterly*, 29, 79–96. doi:10.1111/j.1471-6402.2005.00170.x

Sorenson, S. B. & Thomas, K. A. (2009). Views of intimate partner violence in same-sex and opposite-sex relationships. *Journal of Marriage and the Family*, 71, 337–352. doi:10.1111/j.1741-3737.2009.00602.x

Stewart, A. & Maddren, K. (1997). Police officers' judgements of blame in family violence: The impact of gender and alcohol. *Sex Roles*, 37, 921–933. doi:10.1007/BF02936347

Stiles-Shields, C. & Carroll, R. A. (2015). Same-sex domestic violence: Prevalence, unique aspects, and clinical implications. *Journal of Sex & Marital Therapy*, 41, 636–648. doi:10.1080/0092623X.2014.958792

Tsui, V. (2014). Male victims of intimate partner abuse: Use and helpfulness of services. *Social Work*, 59, 121–130. doi:10.1093/sw/swu007

Tsui, V., Cheung, M., & Leung, P. (2010). Help-seeking among male victims of partner abuse: Men's hard times. *Journal of Community Psychology*, 38, 769–780. doi:10.1002/jcop.20394

Wallace, S. (2018). *An investigation into the needs of men experiencing domestic abuse and current service provision (Wales)* (PhD thesis). University of South Wales/Prifysgol De Cymru, Pontypridd, Wales.

Willis, C. E., Hallinan, M. N., & Melby, J. (1996). Effects of sex role stereotyping among European American students on domestic violence culpability attributions. *Sex Roles*, 34, 475–491. doi:10.1007/BF01545027

Wise, A. J. & Bowman, S. L. (1997). Comparison of beginners counselors' responses to lesbian vs. heterosexual partner abuse. *Violence and Victims*, 12, 127–135.

5

DISTINCTIONS IN ADOLESCENT DATING VIOLENCE

An exploration of etiology, scope, and prevention strategies of intimate partner violence in adolescence

Katherine Maurer

Introduction

Early family violence research (see Straus, Gelles, & Steinmetz, 1980) over-looked the mediating role of "courtship violence" between exposure to child-hood family violence and marital violence (Makepeace, 1981). It is now an entire field of study and has generated a diversity of terminology including: adolescent relationship abuse, teen/adolescent dating violence, dating aggression (e.g. Jennings, Okeem, Piquero, Sellers, & Theobald, 2017; Wincentak, Con-nolly, & Card, 2017). To be inclusive, the term adolescent intimate partner violence (AIPV) is used in this discussion to refer to a continuum of behaviours perceived as injurious in the context of an intimate relationship between two adolescents.

Considerable research (e.g. Cui, Gordon, Ueno, & Fincham, 2013; Johnson, Giordano, Manning, & Longmore, 2015; Whitaker, Le, & Niolon, 2010) supports Makepeace's (1981) hypothesis that a substantial proportion of adult intimate partner violence (IPV) is a continuation of behaviour initiated in ado-lescence. Though desistence is the norm, research suggests that about 30–50% of adult IPV includes individuals who were involved in some form of AIPV prior to the age of 18 (Johnson, Giordano et al., 2015; Whitaker et al., 2010). Even for those who do not go on to become perpetrators and/or victims, the negative effects may persist into adulthood (Johnson, Giordano et al., 2015) manifesting in: enduring psychopathology (Ackard, Eisenberg, & Neumark-Sztainer, 2007), poor physical health (Copp, Giordano, Longmore, & Manning, 2016), decreased social functioning (Exner-Cortens, Eckenrode, & Rothman, 2013), associated involvement in other forms of violence within (Hamby, Finkelhor, & Turner, 2012) and outside of the family (Chang, Foshee, McNaughton Reyes, Ennett, & Halpern, 2015; Vivolo-Kantor, Olsen, & Bacon, 2016).

The conceptual frameworks of adult (see Winstok, 2007) and adolescent (see Capaldi & Langhinrichsen-Rohling, 2012; Pepler, 2012) IPV have changed substantially in the past decade, shifting away from the initial socio-cognitive etiological theory of IPV (i.e. patriarchy) for one model of married couple violence (cis-male perpetrator/cis-female victim this should be victim not perpetrator; e.g. Pence & Paymar, 1993). To address the many definitional, theoretical, methodological, and ideological issues of AIPV, researchers and theorists have developed a multidisciplinary integrative approach that focuses less on violent behaviour and more on the interactions in which violence occurs. AIPV is conceptualised as fundamentally dyadic and interactive within a social ecology of systems that shift over time relative to the multiple stages of adolescent development. This life course perspective on the dynamic socio-biological stages of adolescence is the foundation of a novel developmental-ecological-systems (DES) model of AIPV (Capaldi & Langhinrichsen-Rohling, 2012; Pepler, 2012).

Revisions in the who, what, and why of AIPV have generated three central challenges: 1) accounting for substantive between and within group heterogeneity; 2) advancing causal, risk, and persistence/desistence theories of AIPV that are developmentally and ecologically informed; 3) tailoring prevention and intervention strategies to the heterogeneity of adolescent relationships, multiple developmental stages, and diverse social environments (e.g. De Koker, Mathews, Zuch, Bastien, & Mason-Jones, 2014). Throughout this discussion, in addition to describing and advancing the DES perspective, an anti-oppressive practice lens will be applied to a critical analysis of discourses informing AIPV approaches and cultural and identity factors that influence AIPV trajectories (e.g. Yerke & DeFeo, 2016; Barrenger, Stanhope, & Atterbury, 2017).

AIPV identities (the who and the what)

AIPV epidemiological research can span nearly two decades from age 11–29 (e.g. Johnson, Giordano et al., 2015), reflecting the expansion of the bounds of adolescence. Between and within individual countries (e.g. provincial differences across Canada), ages of consent for legal autonomy, sexual activity, and marriage vary greatly and influence the boundaries between adolescence and adulthood. Many European and North American researchers make developmental distinctions of early adolescence (ages 11–13), mid-adolescence (14–16), late adolescence (17–19), with early or emergent adulthood starting around 21 years old (Arnett, 2000). These developmental distinctions influence variation in engagement, type, quantity, and persistence in estimates of AIPV.

For both adults and adolescents, the types of relationships and the forms of abuse that constitute IPV have evolved greatly from the initial focus on gendered unidirectional physical and sexual abuse within cisgender heterosexual marriage (Bates, 2016; Espinoza & Warner, 2016; Straus, 2010), largely informed by the experiences of white middle-class North Americans and Western Europeans (e.g. Pence & Paymar, 1993). Who constitutes a couple of interest in IPV research now includes same-sex, cohabiting, transgender, gender non-binary, bi/pansexual, and dating couples, not solely married cisgender heterosexuals. Despite the known diversity of identities now included in AIPV definitions, the majority of IPV and AIPV research remains focused on heterosexual cisgender intimate partners (Murray & Mobley, 2009; Yerke & DeFeo, 2016).

Forms of IPV range from psychological, emotional, and economic to physical and sexual assault, among others (Hamby & Turner, 2013; Pepler, 2012; Ybarra, Espelage, Langhinrichsen-Rohling, Korchmaros, & Boyd, 2016). Some mechanisms of AIPV no longer require physical proximity, such as electronic communication (e.g. texting, social media; Draucker & Martsolf, 2010). Forms of psychological violence, such as controlling behaviours, may manifest substantively differently in the context of non-cohabiting adolescent couples (e.g. texting) as compared to cohabitating adult couples (e.g. Cutbush & Williams, 2016). The binary of male perpetrator and female victim was the de facto definition of domestic violence or spousal abuse, precursors to the more general term of IPV (Mills, 2008; Straus, 2010). However, these categories of IPV are only part of the mosaic of perpetration and victimisation (e.g. Saint-Eloi Cadely et al., 2017; Johnson, 2008). Substantial evidence shows that the majority of adult couples reporting IPV in fact report co-occurring or bidirectional perpetration and victimisation (see Bates 2016; Espinoza & Warner, 2016), meaning that either both partners report perpetrating IPV or one partner reports both perpetration and victimisation within the same relationship of 50% or more (Capaldi, Kim, & Shortt, 2007; Whitaker, Haileyesus, Swahn, & Saltzman, 2007). AIPV is also predominantly bidirectional (e.g. Taylor & Mumford, 2016; Ybarra et al., 2016); rates of bidirectional IPV are consistently highest in late adolescence and early adulthood. The crucial exception to this pattern is sexual abuse and rape, which, for heterosexual cisgender adults and adolescents, is characterised predominantly by unidirectional male perpetration and female victimisation (e.g. Hamby & Turner, 2013; Ybarra et al., 2016). The limited research on the continuum of sexual identity and gender suggests much greater variation (Yerke & DeFeo, 2016).

The conceptualisation, terminology, and measurement of the overlap of perpetration and victimisation, and gender differentials is one of the most highly contested topics in IPV research (see Baker & Stein, 2016; Bates, 2016; Hamby & Turner, 2013; Straus, 2010; Winstok, 2007); bidirectional data have greatly influenced the shift to a dyadic perspective in IPV and AIPV research. Patterns indicate that the rate of female perpetration is commensurate with that of males (e.g. Bates, 2016; Straus, 2010), with the exception of sexual assault (Jennings et al., 2017; Wincentak et al., 2017). Yet there are many challenges to the validity of these data. Gender is an important lens for AIPV theory, research, and practice. However, this analysis focuses primarily on aggregate data along a continuum of gender identities.

Further complicating the AIPV terrain is the overlap when family violence is intergenerational. Retrospective reports of childhood family violence exposure are associated with almost four times the risk of adult IPV (Whitfield, Anda, Dube, & Felitti, 2003). Longitudinally, 20–30% of participants reporting adolescence-only family violence victimisation reported AIPV involvement (e.g. Smith, Ireland,

Park, Elwyn, & Thornberry, 2011). In addition, up to 60% of families report co-occurring parental IPV (victimisation/perpetration) and child maltreatment (Heyman & Slep, 2002), even in adolescence (e.g. Smith et al., 2011). Victim and perpetrator co-exist in the same person more often than not.

AIPV involvement overlaps frequently with non-family-based violence, such as bullying, neighbourhood violence, racial/ethnic/gender discrimination, and socio-economic segregation as well (see Hamby & Grych, 2012; Jain, Buka, Subramanian, & Molnar, 2010; Yerke & DeFeo, 2016). Research suggests that individual and structural categories of violence may have more, rather than less, in common, and interact heterogeneously (e.g. Jain et al., 2010). Hamby and Grych (2012) propose the concept of a "web of violence" as a heuristic to encompass the multiple and interactive forms of violence exposure teens (and adults) experience. Interactive measuring of exposure to multiple forms of violence is relatively new in IPV and AIPV research. The considerable heterogeneity of AIPV that has emerged is complex and challenges many assumptions of the IPV scope, etiology, and intervention literature.

The nature and scope of IPV

Assessing the scope of AIPV is severely challenged (as is IPV; Winstok, 2007) by a lack of common definitions and measurement, significant differences in quantity and severity across different sample sites and characteristics. What may be more useful for understanding the DES approach is an assessment of the nature of AIPV through patterns replicated consistently across sampling and measurement variance. Three key patterns emerge in AIPV data: the age-curve, heterogeneity of perpetration and victimisation by type and frequency, and relationship instability.

The age-curve is a phenomenon in interpersonal violence research that demonstrates peak rates of engagement in late adolescence/young adulthood with a precipitous decline moving into adulthood (Johnson, Giordano et al., 2015; Laub & Sampson, 2003). In AIPV, progressive increases in dating involvement drive the curve. Longmore, Manning, and Giordano (2001) reported that dating nearly tripled in early adolescence (7% age 11 to 30% by age 13), nearly doubled again (48% to 83%) in mid-adolescence (14–16), and by age 17, 94% of adolescents had dated. In longitudinal data over ten years, AIPV perpetration rose from 13% ($M = 15$ years old) to 22% ($M = 22$ years old) to 14% ($M = 25$ years old; Kaufman-Parks, DeMaris, Giordano, Manning, & Longmore, 2018). Given the variance of participation in dating activities across different stages of adolescence, AIPV prevalence rates may be skewed to the experiences of late adolescence/early adulthood (e.g. Ybarra et al., 2016).

Across many studies reporting data by type, rates of reported psychological violence are often highest, with sexual abuse the least frequently reported (e.g. Ybarra et al. 2016) and rates of physical abuse falling in between. Taylor and Mumford (2016) reported incident rates by type, abuse role, and age in an analysis of the U.S. National Survey on Teen Relationships and Intimate Violence ($n = 1,804$) of youth age 12–18. The age-curve (Johnson, Giordano et al., 2015) is reflected in progressive increases in both physical and sexual abuse perpetration and victimisation. Reported rates of psychological AIPV were five times greater than sexual abuse victimisation and perpetration, rates of which also reflected a substantial gender differential. In all categories except sexual AIPV, bidirectional perpetration and victimisation were more common than unidirectional categories.

The binary measurement of AIPV/no AIPV obscures the heterogeneity of the frequency and severity of the quantity of acts of perpetration and victimisation upon which dose response theories depend to predict differential exposure outcomes (e.g. Whitfield et al., 2003). Count measures (e.g. the Conflict Tactics Scale [CTS], Straus, Hamby, Boney-McCoy, & Sugarman, 1996) assess aggression on three intersecting axes of frequency (number of acts), severity (minor/severe), and directionality (perpetrator/victim). Although count data are much contested (e.g. Hamby & Turner, 2013), the method allows for a more fine-grained analysis when unpacking the heterogeneity of AIPV. The CTS and similar measures have been highly criticised for ignoring context or effect of IPV (see Hamby & Turner, 2013; Winstok, 2007).

In research that presents incidence data by count, several clear patterns emerge: with the exception of clinical samples, the majority of individuals report no AIPV. When count data are analysed by frequency, most report three or fewer acts of AIPV. Only a very small percentage will report more than five acts (Straus et al., 1996). Ybarra et al. (2016) tested heterogeneity using prevalence data from a US sample of 1,058 14–21-year-olds to examine overlap of type and role of AIPV. Although 59% reported no acts of psychological victimisation, 41% reported one to two acts, and 2% reported four acts. Perpetration of psychological AIPV rates were equivalent. Physical AIPV was less common: 82% reported no victimisation and 81% no perpetration, with 13% and 14% respectively reporting one to two acts of physical AIPV. Only 3% reported more than five acts of either physical AIPV victimisation or perpetration. These distinctions do not minimise the effect of experiencing even one act of AIPV. Yet, these data demonstrate the extensive within-group variance that is obscured by statistical analyses relying on dichotomisation. Similar differentials are found when assessing severity. Count data are useful to formulate a more nuanced picture of AIPV heterogeneity (e.g. Ybarra et al., 2016).

A critical consideration of any data is the sampling site bias. For example, data from a school sample (e.g. Johnson, Giordano et al., 2015) may not include many of the most at-risk youth. AIPV-engaged youth may already be involved with the criminal justice or child welfare systems and be underrepresented in school samples that exclude subpopulations of expelled students, homeless – particularly LGBTQ+ and indigenous – youth, youth in care, and youth who may not attend mainstream school or school at all (Petering, Wenzel, & Winetrobe, 2014). Private schools are often not included in studies, presenting a potential socio-economic bias and excluding low-risk adolescents. Community sampling, even when accounting for ethnic and economic diversity (e.g. Jain et al., 2010; Ybarra et al., 2016), may still exclude adolescents not living with their families. In clinical samples, given the consistent overrepresentation of low-income and racialised children in juvenile justice and child welfare systems, these data may be inherently skewed by structural sampling biases. Criminal justice-involved and LGBTQ+ youth populations often report higher cumulative incident rates of AIPV that may be linked with higher overall exposure to violence, a risk factor for AIPV itself (Jennings et al., 2017; Petering et al., 2014).

A final consideration that is fundamental to AIPV and distinct from its adult counterpart is relationship stability. Adult IPV is perceived as consistent over time, within the couple and with future partners (Fritz & Slep, 2009). Adolescence, however, is marked by multiple short-term relationships or churning (multiple breakups and reunions; Jennings et al., 2017). Johnson, Manning, Giordano, and Longmore (2015) assessed for relationship continuity prospectively longitudinally across adolescence with the TAR Study sample and report a nearly three-fold increase in partnership stability from age 13 to 24. By age 29, 39% report no lifetime AIPV while only 8% of participants report AIPV in each past relationship over the length of the study; 53% report some discontinuity. Fritz and Slep's (2009) analysis shows considerable variability of relationship stability by physical and psychological AIPV over 12 months; 45% of 10th and 11th graders report having the same partner across the study.

The trajectory of adolescence is considerably more variable in terms of shifting social relationships than even early adulthood. Changes of engagement in intimate partnerships and frequency and severity of AIPV over time are driven by developmental and social processes. These findings merit further unpacking to account for the processes or mechanisms that influence persistence and desistence. The stress response system (SRS) plays a central role in our understanding of violent behaviour during adolescent development and is useful for contextualising the patterns of change across adolescence.

AIPV etiology: biological sensitivity to context

The shift in AIPV theory and research to a DES model that considers dyadic and systems/environment interactions across multiple developmental stages necessitates complex modelling of dyadic interactions and looping effects. At the biological level, SRS is the central processing mechanism of the interaction between the individual and their social environment (Ellis, Del Giudice, & Shirtcliff, 2017). Thus, it has been a logical shift in AIPV research to begin to incorporate the substantial knowledgebase of psychobiology research on the process of self-regulation in the context of interpersonal violence (see Cicchetti & Rogosch, 2002; Pepler, 2012).

Self-regulation is an interactive process between external (social) stimuli, internal cognitive and emotional reactions to the external stimuli, and the ability to moderate the reactivity (affect) to stimuli for an optimal behavioural outcome (Davidson, Putnam, & Larson, 2000; Ellis et al., 2017). This feedback loop is the essence of dyadic interaction. The capacity to self-regulate during interactions is a cornerstone of psychological well-being and the central developmental task of adolescence

(Nader, 2011). However, adolescence is also a window of heightened vulnerability of the SRS, alterations to which may lead to psychopathology that endures into adulthood (see Ellis et al., 2017 for a detailed description of the psychobiology of SRS).

Self-regulation is a core concept in AIPV theory grounded in the DES framework. AIPV etiology theories had been dominated by socio-cognitive processes of social learning of cultural (i.e. patriarchy), and family norms accepting of IPV and violence in general. With the shift to DES, AIPV researchers have begun to focus on self-regulation as a central mechanism to understanding the trajectory of AIPV across adolescence and towards adulthood as a mechanism by which a variety of stressful experiences in childhood, including structural marginalisation and oppression, might affect adolescent and subsequent adult behaviours (Ehrensaft & Cohen, 2012; Pepler, 2012).

Until recently, most AIPV etiological research was conducted using diathesis-stress or cumulative risk models (e.g. Fraser, Richman, Galinsky, & Day, 2009; Sameroff, 2009). These models share the standpoint that greater vulnerability – genetic, physiological, or temperamental – to an environmental stressor increases risk for adverse proximal and distal outcomes (Sameroff, 2009). Dose-response theory suggests that the more stress (risk factors) the greater likelihood of negative outcomes (e.g. Whitfield et al., 2003). Specific interactions with chronic or severe stress, through repeated activation, may lead to enduring psychopathology (see Ellis et al., 2017). This is how past experiences get encoded in the body and become predictors of future behaviour (Ellis et al., 2017). Nonetheless, the majority of individuals exposed to environmental stressors exhibit resiliency and do not develop a stress regulation disorder (Ellis et al., 2017; Nader, 2011), just as the majority of family violence-exposed children exhibit resiliency and do not become AIPV involved (Smith et al., 2011).

Biological sensitivity to context and adaptive calibration

In seeking to understand the differential effects of socio-biological risk factors such as these, researchers developed a theory of biological sensitivity to context (BSC) which has been substantially empirically validated (see Ellis et al., 2017). The BSC theory posits that there is considerable individual variance in stress reactivity, the purpose of which is to mediate vulnerability or sensitivity to external stimuli, which may range from injurious to protective (Del Giudice, Ellis, & Shirtcliff, 2011). This sensitivity is distributed on a U-shape curve such that on either side of the U are highly sensitive individuals. In supportive environments, these individuals are flexible to change and thrive in it; conversely, in hostile, unsupportive environments, high stress facilitates attunement to threat and danger. The lower portion of the curve represents the experience of most children who are in neither very dangerous nor absolutely reliable environments; they develop a buffered, less environmentally responsive SRS compared to the heightened reactivity of the upper zone of the U-shape (Del Giudice et al., 2011).

The current iteration of BSC theory is the Adaptive Calibration Model (ACM; see Del Giudice et al., 2011 for a discussion of the model) which posits that changes in the SRS in relation to environment are adaptive and meant to optimise experience and functioning. In positive environments, the sensitive individuals will be very engaged with their environment and alterations in their SRS will serve to maximise the opportunities they encounter. Although sensitive individuals in unstable dangerous environments will also be very engaged, the alterations in their SRS will serve to protect and defend them. As this second group matures and gets involved in relationships outside of their original environment, the adaptations that have optimised their engagement may be maladaptive to the new environment. For example, considerable research has shown that adolescents and adults who grew up in unpredictable environments have a very heightened perception of threat. This kept them safe as a child. As an adolescent or young adult, they may react to a perceived threat from their partner well out of proportion to the actual level of threat (Del Giudice et al., 2011) and respond maladaptively and violently. Pluess and Belsky (2013) have further postulated that within the high sensitivity group, there are individuals who are particularly sensitive to positive experiences (vantage sensitivity), to which others will have a buffered response. They are currently developing an evidence base for the construct.

AIPV heterogeneity and BSC/ACM

As noted, the considerable heterogeneity across multiple axes fits poorly with dominant AIPV etiology models. Not only is there substantial role overlap in AIPV, there is substantial overlap of multiple forms of AIPV (Ybarra et al., 2016) as well as other forms of interpersonal, family, and community violence (Chang et al., 2015; Vivolo-Kantor et al., 2016). Many of the roles and types of violence share common risk factors even though they are conceptualised as discreet. Thus, it is conceptually difficult to reconcile why risk factors for perpetration and victimisation might be the same from a standpoint of patriarchy as the primary cause of couple violence. Similarly, there are few differences in risk profiles between heterosexual and same-sex couples, yet a patriarchy-based AIPV theory suggests they cannot have the same etiological trajectory.

From the stress physiology standpoint of BSC and ACM, this is congruent because the focus is on stress responsivity to a challenging environment, rather than specific and disparate social context of the stressor (type of aggression/violence). Thus, a person who is relatively sensitive to the environment may be more likely to engage in aggression or violence, experience more fear as a victim, and, if these responses loopback dyadically, may be both perpetrator and victim of AIPV. The heterogeneity of patterns of engagement and desistence in AIPV, particularly the individual level data that show these patterns shifting from partner to partner (Johnson, Manning et al., 2015), may be manifestations of a differential stress response based on a change in environmental stimuli between different partners. Thus, Ellis et al. (2017) argue that rather than stigmatise and pathologise (even criminalise) AIPV involvement, through the BSC/ACM lens, we can understand aggressive reactivity as AIPV behaviour that was adaptive in another context yet is maladaptive in a new environment. Using the ACM frame, there are a plethora of biopsychosocial intervention options available as compared to the narrow socio-cognitive approach that is common (Ellis et al., 2017).

AIPV interventions

In North America, two comprehensive AIPV interventions were developed based on a DES model: *Dating Matters*^{TM} (CDC, n.d.) in the US (which includes a *Safe Dates* component; Foshee et al., 2004) and the *Fourth R* (Wolfe, n.d.) in Canada. Both interventions take a public health approach to promoting the development of skills and behaviours associated with healthy relationships in general and include AIPV as a specific intervention target. Rather than focus solely on AIPV, these programmes acknowledge the interconnectedness of exposure to violence across multiple systems – family, school, community, society – and abuse roles (CDC, n.d.; Wolfe, n.d.), the "web of violence" (Hamby & Grych, 2012), as well as engagement in other risk behaviours, including substance abuse. Each programme takes a developmental perspective of prevention, targeting youth before or as they enter into intimate relationships. Furthermore, the interventions include an ecological perspective by including components that target the individual, relationships (family, peers, intimate partners), community (neighbourhoods, schools, workplace), and society (cultural norms, socio-economic policies, historical oppression). The manualised interventions include training of facilitators and access to extensive support materials (CDC, n.d.; Wolfe, n.d.).

Recent reviews (e.g. De Koker et al., 2014; Petering et al., 2014) of AIPV interventions note that although many of the interventions showed pre-post-test changes in attitudes about AIPV, very few (e.g. *Safe Dates*, Foshee et al., 2004) showed any lasting changes in AIPV behaviours. In contrast, Wolfe et al. (2009) reported that at 2.5 years follow up, the *Fourth R* intervention group reported less physical AIPV in 11th grade compare to the control group (9.8% versus 7.4%, respectively; adjusted OR, 2.42; 95% CI, 1.00–6.02; $p = .05$).

To date, no results have been published on the implementation of *Dating Matters*^{TM}. However, Niolon, Taylor, Latzman, Vivolo-Kantor, and Valle (2016) have reported on the demographics of the pilot study sample from four urban cities in the US for students grades 7–9. The sample is racially and economically diverse and self-reports high levels of pre-intervention AIPV perpetration and other forms of violence involvement. Patterns of self-reported AIPV perpetration were similar to those in other studies, with girls reporting higher perpetration than boys in all categories, except sexual abuse and stalking; the highest rate of perpetration was verbal/emotional abuse 82% versus 72% ($p < .001$), followed by physical abuse 43% versus 20% ($p < .001$), measured with the Conflict in Adolescent Dating Relationships Inventory (Wolfe et al., 2001). Crooks, Scott, Ellis and Wolfe (2011) noted that levels of violence engagement (defined as at least two of seven acts of delinquent behaviour) varied across schools from 5–35%, suggesting that heterogeneity at the community level as well as the individual level is an important factor to consider in implementation of interventions.

Parents are an integral component in the DES model (Olsen, Parra, & Bennett, 2010). Niolon et al. (2016) discussed barriers faced when implementing *Dating Matters*^{TM} (CDC, n.d.) to engage parents, even in survey participation. Given the high co-occurrence of family violence and AIPV (Heyman & Slep, 2002), engagement with parents is a priority for reducing environmental stress or to bolster family support (Olsen et al., 2010). Considerable resources might be needed to engage parents; an alternative source of behavioural change support – peer mentorship – could also serve as a booster for interventions.

Intervention boosting has improved longitudinal outcomes in adolescent intervention research (see Foshee et al., 2004; Guilamo-Ramos et al., 2011). Peer mentors could be recruited from past intervention participants, an accessible resource, particularly if there is low parental engagement. Peer mentoring shifts power from a professional expert (e.g. teacher, therapist) to acknowledge the expertise of lived experience shared between mentor and mentee. This type of mentoring is an integral component in mental health recovery used to support and reinforce behavioural changes (Solomon, 2004). Barrenger et al. (2017) suggest that peer mentoring is also a means to challenge dominant stigmatising discourses such as those AIPV-involved adolescents face, particularly within educational settings where behaviours may significantly impact school participation in the advent of criminal justice involvement (see Petering et al., 2014).

Peer attitudes, particularly associations with friend groups in which AIPV is normative, are strong risk factors for AIPV involvement (Olsen et al., 2010). Conversely, peer mentorship may be an alternative to help adolescents apply skills they have learned through the intervention in their ongoing relationships supported by a network of individuals who have completed the intervention and successfully desisted from AIPV perpetration and victimisation. Peer mentors may offer needed support if there is low parental engagement or if there is ongoing family violence. The *Fourth R* (Wolfe, n.d.) includes peer-mentoring specific to Indigenous students, though no data are available on the effects. Mentorship may also provide essential counterbalance to the heteronormative discourse of AIPV for LGBTQ+ adolescents and provide community-specific support (Yerke & DeFeo, 2016). Introducing a peer mentorship component to DES-modeled interventions is one approach to structurally supporting individual and group level change post-intervention.

In addition to challenges of sustaining positive changes following AIPV interventions, a crucial and little discussed issue is responding to AIPV persistence, post-intervention. The results of multiple reviews (e.g. De Koker et al., 2014; Petering et al., 2014) confirm that post-intervention, there often will be future AIPV. As noted earlier, most AIPV is characterised by low frequency and low severity of acts (e.g. Ybarra et al., 2016) that may not warrant criminal justice involvement yet may involve school-level discipline, even perhaps expulsion. However, learning is predicated on making mistakes. Can we approach AIPV desistance as a process that might involve future acts of AIPV and provide ongoing support for learning desistance? From the SRS perspective, rate of change is too variable at the individual level to predict expectable times to desistance (Ellis et al., 2017) and no data yet exist at the group level. Thus, how can institutions invested in DES model interventions best address infractions that may be part of a behavioural change process?

One possibility is to include an adaptation of a restorative justice model for IPV perpetrators (e.g. Grauwiler & Mills, 2004). The approach includes mediation, family group conferencing, healing circles, and community engagement. Being solution-focused may help engage populations with negative histories with mainstream criminal justice, including women (Randall, 2013), immigrants, LGBTQ+, racialised and Indigenous communities. The approach is a good fit to DES intervention models in its focus on behavioural change and relationship building. Additionally, it is adaptable to bidirectional perpetration, whereas criminal justice interventions are dependent on delineating victim-perpetrator roles.

Given the instability of adolescent relationships, this approach may be more useful as it promotes healing and change that may benefit future intimate partnerships rather than being linked to a specific couple. Further, because schools and other institutions in which DES-based AIPV interventions may be staged are often closed or small communities, taking a more process and solution-based approach to healing relationships that are likely to continue after dissolution of the couple seems a very promising approach.

Conclusion

The shift in AIPV research to a DES model, with its dyadic interactive focus, affords consideration of new etiological frameworks, such as BSC and ACM (Ellis et al., 2017) to explain the patterns of heterogeneous AIPV across adolescence. In turn, interventions that incorporate expanded opportunities to improve self-regulation over time, with ongoing supports such as peer mentoring and restorative justice to address AIPV persistence, may increase the effectiveness of existing intervention models (CDC, n.d.; Wolfe, n.d.). It is important that any interventions be informed by an anti-oppressive practice perspective and take into account the multiple systemic stressors that increase risk of AIPV specific to histories of marginalisation, oppression, and exclusion for racialised, immigrant, low-income, non-cis gender/sex, female, neurodiverse individuals. The secondary and primary benefits of teaching relationship skills, self-regulation, community-based change models in secondary schools and social service agencies may have many benefits beyond the urgent goal of preventing the initiation and persistence of AIPV. Advancing the DES model of AIPV in theory, research, and policy holds promise to improve outcomes for all adolescents (Capaldi & Langhinrichsen-Rohling, 2012).

References

Ackard, D., Eisenberg, M. E., & Neumark-Sztainer, D. (2007). Long-term impact of adolescent dating violence on the behavioral and psychological health of male and female youth. *Journal of Pediatrics*, 151(5), 476–481. doi:10.1016/j.jpeds.2007.04.034

Arnett, J. J. (2000). Emerging adulthood: A theory of development from the late teens through the twenties. *American Psychologist*, 55, 469–480.

Barrenger, S. L., Stanhope, V., & Atterbury, K. (2017). Challenging dominant discourses: Peer work as social justice work. *Journal of Progressive Human Services*, 1–21. doi:10.1080/10428232.2017.1399036

Baker, C. & Stein, N. (2016). Obscuring gender-based violence: Marriage promotion and teen dating violence research. *Journal of Women, Politics and Policy*, 37(1), 87–109.

Bates, E. (2016). Current controversies within intimate partner violence: Overlooking bidirectional violence. *Journal of Family Violence*, 31(8), 937–940. doi:10.1007/s10896-016-9862-7

Capaldi, D. M., Kim, H. K., & Shortt, J. W. (2007). Observed initiation and reciprocity of physical aggression in young, at-risk couples. *Journal of Family Violence*, 22(2), 101–111.

Capaldi, D. M. & Langhinrichsen-Rohling, J. (2012). Informing intimate partner violence prevention efforts: Dyadic, developmental, and contextual considerations. *Prevention Science*, 13(4), 323–328.

CDC (Centers for Disease Control) (n.d.). Dating MattersTM : Strategies to promote healthy teens relationships. Retrieved from: https://vetoviolence.cdc.gov/dating-matters

Chang, L., Foshee, V. A., McNaughton Reyes, H. L., Ennett, S. T., & Halpern, C. T. (2015). Direct and indirect effects of neighbourhood characteristics on the perpetration of dating violence across adolescents. *Journal of Youth and Adolescence*, 44(3), 727–744. doi:10.1007/s10964-014-0190-z

Cicchetti, D. & Rogosch, F. A. (2002). A developmental psychopathology perspective on adolescence. *Journal of Consulting and Clinical Psychology*, 70, 6–20.

Copp, J. E., Giordano, P. C., Longmore, M. A., & Manning, W. D. (2016). The development of attitudes toward intimate partner violence: An examination of key correlates among a sample of young adults. *Journal of Interpersonal Violence*, 1–31. doi:10.1177/0886260516651311

Cui, M., Gordon, M., Ueno, K., & Fincham, F. D. (2013). The continuation of intimate partner violence from adolescence to young adulthood. *Journal of Marriage and Family*, 75(2), 300–313.

Cutbush, S. & Williams, J. (2016). Teen dating violence, sexual harassment, and bullying among middle school youth: Examining measurement invariance by gender. *Journal of Research on Adolescence*, 26(4), 918–926. doi:10.1111/jora.12244

Davidson, R. J., Putnam, K. M., & Larson, C. L. (2000). Dysfunction in the neural circuitry of emotion regulation: A possible prelude to violence. *Science*, 289(5479), 591–594.

De Koker, P., Mathews, C., Zuch, M., Bastien, S., & Mason-Jones, A. J. (2014). A systematic review of interventions for preventing adolescent intimate partner violence. *Journal of Adolescent Health*, 54(1), 3–13.

Del Giudice, M., Ellis, B. J., & Shirtcliff, E. A. (2011). The adaptive calibration model of stress responsivity. *Neuroscience and Biobehavioral Reviews*, 35, 1562–1592.

Draucker, C. B. & Martsolf, D. S. (2010). The role of electronic communication technology in adolescent dating violence. *Journal of Child and Adolescent Psychiatric Nursing*, 23(3), 133–142. doi:10.1111/j.1744-6171.2010.00235.x

Ehrensaft, M. K. & Cohen, P. (2012). Contribution of family violence to the intergenerational transmission of externalizing behavior. *Prevention Science*, 13(4), 370–383.

Ellis, B. J., Del Giudice, M., & Shirtcliff, E. A. (2017). The adaptive calibration model of stress responsivity: Concepts, findings, and implications for developmental psychopathology (pp. 237–276). In Beauchaine, T. P. & Hinshaw, S. P. (Eds) *Child and adolescent psychopathology* (3rd ed.). New York, NY: Wiley & Sons.

Espinoza, R. C. & Warner, D. (2016). Where do we go from here? Examining intimate partner violence by bringing male victims, female perpetrators, and psychological sciences into the fold. *Journal of Family Violence*, 31(8), 959–966.

Exner-Cortens, D., Eckenrode, J., & Rothman, E. (2013). Longitudinal associations between teen dating violence victimization and adverse health outcomes. *Pediatrics*, 131(1), 71–78. doi:10.1542/peds.2012-1029

Foshee, V. A., Bauman, K. E., Ennett, S. T., Linder, G. F., Benefield, T., & Suchindran, C. (2004). Assessing the long-term effects of the Safe Dates program and a booster in preventing and reducing adolescent dating violence victimization and perpetration. *American Journal of Public Health*, 94(4), 619–624.

Fraser, M. W., Richman, J. M., Galinsky, M. J., & Day, S. H. (2009). *Intervention research: Developing social programs*. New York, NY: Oxford University Press.

Fritz, P. A. T. & Slep, A. M. S. (2009). Stability of physical and psychological adolescent dating aggression across time and partners. *Journal of Clinical Child & Adolescent Psychology*, 38(3), 303–314. doi:10.1080/15374410902851671

Grauwiler, P. & Mills, L. G. (2004). Moving beyond the criminal justice paradigm: A radical restorative justice approach to intimate abuse. *Journal of Sociology & Social Welfare*, 31(1), 49–69.

Guilamo-Ramos, V., Bouris, A., Jaccard, J., Gonzalez, B., McCoy, W., & Aranda, D. (2011). A parent-based intervention to reduce sexual risk behavior in early adolescence: Building alliances between physicians, social workers, and parents. *The Journal of Adolescent Health: Official Publication of the Society for Adolescent Medicine*, 48(2), 159–163. doi:10.1016/j.jadohealth.2010.06.007

Hamby, S., Finkelhor, D., & Turner, H. (2012). Teen dating violence: Co-occurrence with other victimizations in the national survey of children's exposure to violence (NatSCEV). *Psychology of Violence*, 2(2), 111–124. doi:10.1037/a0027191

Hamby, S. & Grych, J. (2012). *The web of violence: Exploring connections among different forms of interpersonal violence and abuse*. Dordrecht: Springer.

Hamby, S. & Turner, H. (2013). Measuring teen dating violence in males and females: Insights from the National Survey of Children's Exposure to Violence. *Psychology of Violence*, 3(4), 323–339. doi:10.1037/a0029706

Heyman, R. E. & Slep, A. M. S. (2002). Do child abuse and interparental violence lead to adulthood family violence? *Journal of Marriage and Family*, 64(4), 864–870. doi:10.1111/j.1741-3737.2002.00864

Jain, S., Buka, S. L., Subramanian, S. V., & Molnar, B. E. (2010). Neighborhood predictors of dating violence victimization and perpetration in young adulthood: A multilevel study. *American Journal of Public Health*, 100(9), 1737–1744. doi:10.2105/AJPH.2009.169730

Jennings, W. G., Okeem, C., Piquero, A. R., Sellers, C. S., & Theobald, D. (2017). Dating and intimate partner violence among young persons ages 15–30: Evidence from a systematic review. *Aggression and Violent Behavior*, 33, 107–125. doi:10.1016/j.avb.2017.01.007

Johnson, M. P. (2008). *A typology of domestic violence: Intimate terrorism, violent resistance, and situational couple violence*. Boston, MA: Northeastern University Press.

Johnson, W. L., Giordano, P. C., Manning, W. D., & Longmore, M. A. (2015). The age-IPV curve: Changes in the perpetration of intimate partner violence during adolescence and young adulthood. *Journal of Youth and Adolescence*, 44(3), 708–726.

Johnson, W.L., Manning, W. D., Giordano, P. C., & Longmore, M. A. (2015). Relationship context and intimate partner violence from adolescence to young adulthood. *Journal of Adolescent Health*, 57(6), 631–636.

Kaufman-Parks, A., DeMaris, A., Giordano, P., Manning, W., & Longmore, M. (2018). Intimate partner violence perpetration from adolescence to young adulthood: Trajectories and the role of familial factors. *Journal of Family Violence*, 33(1), 27–41. doi:10.1007/s10896-017-9924-5

Laub, J. H. & Sampson, R. J. (2003). *Shared beginnings, divergent lives: Delinquent boys to age 70*. Cambridge, MA: Harvard University Press.

Longmore, M. A., Manning, W. D., & Giordano, P. C. (2001). Preadolescent parenting strategies and teens' dating and sexual initiation: A longitudinal analysis. *Journal of Marriage and Family*, 63(2), 322–335. doi:10.1111/j.1741-3737.2001.00322.x

Makepeace, J. M. (1981). Courtship violence among college students. *Family Relations*, 30(1), 97–102. doi:10.2307/584242

Mills, L. G. (2008). *Violent partners: A breakthrough plan for ending the cycle of abuse*. New York, NY: Basic Books.

Murray, C. E. & Mobley, A. K. (2009). Empirical research about same-sex intimate partner violence: A methodological review. *Journal of Homosexuality*, 56(3), 361–386. doi:10.1080/00918360902728848

Nader, K. (2011). Trauma in children and adolescents: Issues related to age and complex traumatic reactions. *Journal of Child and Adolescent Trauma*, 4(3), 161–180.

Niolon, P. H., Taylor, B. G., Latzman, N. E., Vivolo-Kantor, A. M., & Valle, L. A. (2016). Lessons learned in evaluating a multisite, comprehensive teen dating violence prevention strategy: Design and challenges of the evaluation of dating matters: Strategies to promote healthy teen relationships. *Psychology of Violence*, 6(3), 452–458. doi:10.1037/vio0000043

Olsen, J. P., Parra, G. R., & Bennett, S. A. (2010). Predicting violence in romantic relationships during adolescence and emerging adulthood: A critical review of the mechanisms by which familial and peer influences operate. *Clinical Psychology Review*, 30(4), 411–422.

Pence, E. & Paymar, M. (1993). *Education groups for men who batter: The Duluth model*. New York, NY: Springer.

Petering, R., Wenzel, S., & Winetrobe, H. (2014). Systematic review of current intimate partner violence prevention programs and applicability to homeless youth. *Journal of the Society for Social Work & Research*, 5(1), 107–135. doi:10.1086/675851

Pepler, D. (2012). The development of dating violence: What doesn't develop, what does develop, how does it develop, and what can we do about it? *Prevention Science*, 13(4), 402–409. doi:10.1007/s11121-012-0308-z

Pluess, M. & Belsky, J. (2013). Vantage sensitivity: Individual differences in response to positive experiences. *Psychological Bulletin*, 139(4), 901–916. doi:10.1037/a0030196

Randall, M. (2013). Restorative justice and gendered violence; From vaguely hostile sceptic to cautious convert: Why feminists should critically engage with restorative approaches to law. *Dalhousie Law Journal*, 36, 461.

Saint-Eloi Cadely, H., Pittman, J. F., Pettit, G. S., Lansford, J. E., Bates, J. E., Dodge, K. A., & Holtzworth-Munroe, A. (2017). Classes of intimate partner violence from late adolescence to young adulthood. *Journal of Interpersonal Violence*, doi:10.1177/0886260517715601

Sameroff, A. J. (2009). Conceptual issues in studying the development of self-regulation. In Olson, S. L. & Sameroff, A. J. (Eds) *Regulatory processes in the development of behavior problems: Biological, behavioral, and social-ecological perspectives* (pp.1–18). Cambridge, UK: Cambridge University Press.

Smith, C. A., Ireland, T. O., Park, A., Elwyn, L., & Thornberry, T. P. (2011). Intergenerational continuities and discontinuities in intimate partner violence. *Journal of Interpersonal Violence*, 26(18), 3720–3752. doi:10.1177/0886260511403751

Solomon, P. (2004). Peer support/peer provided services underlying processes, benefits, and critical ingredients. *Psychiatric Rehabilitation Journal*, 27(4), 392–401. doi:10.2975/27.2004.392.401

Straus, M. A. (2010). Thirty years of denying the evidence on gender symmetry in partner violence: Implications for prevention and treatment. *Partner Abuse*, 1(3), 332–362. doi:10.1891/1946-6560.1.3.332

Straus, M., Gelles, R., & Steinmetz, S. K. (1980). *Behind closed doors: A survey of family violence in America*. New York, NY: Anchor Press/Doubleday

Straus, M. A., Hamby, S. L., Boney-McCoy, S., & Sugarman, D. B. (1996). The revised conflict tactics scales (CTS2): Development and preliminary psychometric data. *Journal of Family Issues*, 17, 283–316.

Taylor, B. G. & Mumford, E. A. (2016). A national descriptive portrait of adolescent relationship abuse: Results from the national survey on teen relationships and intimate violence. *Journal of Interpersonal Violence*, 31(6), 963–988.

Vivolo-Kantor, A., Olsen, E. O., & Bacon, S. (2016). Associations of teen dating violence victimization with school violence and bullying among US high school students. *Journal of School Health*, 86(8), 620–627. doi:10.1111/josh.12412

Whitaker, D.J., Le, B., & Niolon, P. H. (2010). Persistence and desistance of the perpetration of physical aggression across relationships: Findings from a national study of adolescents. *Journal of Interpersonal Violence*, 25(4), 591–609.

Whitaker, D. J., Haileyesus, T., Swahn, M., & Saltzman, L. S. (2007). Differences in frequency of violence and reported injury between reciprocal and nonreciprocal intimate partner violence. *American Journal of Public Health*, 97(5), 941–947. doi:10.2105/AJPH.2005.079020

Whitfield, C. L., Anda, R. F., Dube, S. R., & Felitti, V. J. (2003). Violent childhood experiences and the risk of intimate partner violence in adults: Assessment in a large health maintenance organization. *Journal of Interpersonal Violence*, 18, 166–185.

Wincentak, K., Connolly, J., & Card, N. (2017). Teen dating violence: A meta-analytic review of prevalence rates. *Psychology of Violence*, 7(2), 224–241. doi:10.1037/a0040194

Winstok, Z. (2007). Toward an interactional perspective on intimate partner violence. *Aggression and Violent Behavior*, 12(3), 348–363. doi:10.1016/j.avb.2006.12.001

Wolfe, D. A. (n.d.). The Fourth R; Strategies for healthy youth relationships. Retrieved from: https://youthrelationships.org/

Wolfe, D. A., Crooks, C., Jaffe, P., Chiodo, D., Hughes, R., Ellis, W. … Donner, A. (2009). A school based program to prevent adolescent dating violence: A cluster randomized trial. *Archives of Pediatric Adolescent Medicine*, 163(8), 692–699. doi:10.1001/archpediatrics.2009.69

Wolfe, D. A., Scott, K., Reitzel-Jaffe, D., Wekerle, C., Grasley, C., & Straatman, A. (2001). Development and validation of the conflict in adolescent dating relationships inventory. *Psychological Assessment*, 13(2), 277–293. doi:10.1037/1040-3590.13.2.277

Ybarra, M. L., Espelage, D. L., Langhinrichsen-Rohling, J., Korchmaros, J. D., & Boyd, D. (2016). Lifetime prevalence rates and overlap of physical, psychological, and sexual dating abuse perpetration and victimization in a national sample of youth. *Archives of Sexual Behavior*, 45(5), 1083–1099.

Yerke, A. & DeFeo, J. (2016). Redefining intimate partner violence beyond the binary to include transgender people. *Journal of Family Violence*, 31(8), 975–979. doi:10.1007/s10896-016-9887-y

6

BARRIERS TO SUPPORT IN LGBTQ+ POPULATIONS

Philippa Laskey & Lauren T. Bolam

The experiences of heterosexual female victims of intimate partner violence (IPV) are well documented in research and policy (Langenderfer-Magruder, Whitfield, Walls, Kattari & Ramos, 2016). In addition, heterosexual men are starting to receive more research attention in terms of their victimisation experiences (e.g. Hines & Douglas, 2011; Próspero & Kim, 2009). In terms of gender and sexuality, the LGBTQ+ community is severely underrepresented in IPV research, policy, and victim support provision (Morin, 2014). It is this victim support provision that is most crucial to this community; there is little point in raising awareness of IPV victimisation in the LGBTQ+ community through research and policy change, if the support for victims is inadequate or unavailable.

IPV is a significant and damaging experience for all victims, regardless of gender or sexuality. Victims can experience a wide range of different types of abuse from their partners including physical, psychological, emotional, sexual, and financial abuse (Centers for Disease Control and Prevention, 2017). Abusive behaviours can range from the overt punching, kicking, or pushing (Jaffe & Schub, 2011) to the more covert behaviours such as isolation, threats, or stalking (Grose & Cabrera, 2011). Traditionally, IPV has often been framed within a gendered or feminist model, with men being perpetrators and women being victims (Graham-Kevan, 2007). However, as research and practice in the field of IPV moves forward, it is becoming clearer that violence within an intimate relationship is far more complex than was once thought. Importantly, IPV is found outside of the traditional male perpetrator–female victim conceptualisation. This implies that it is unlikely that gender and sexuality are the causes of IPV, rather their prominence may be attributable to the nature of the relationships within which it occurs, an intimate relationship. With this in mind it is important that research and practice are focussed on all victims of IPV, rather than the majority group of women in heterosexual relationships.

This chapter aims to highlight the issues surrounding IPV in the LGBTQ+ community and the barriers this community face when accessing support. In light of the unique issues that are associated with different members of the LGBTQ+ community, this chapter will discuss LGB victims and transgender victims separately. This is to make the distinction clear between sexuality and gender, as often the two are conflated within the literature. While transgender people can be LGB, and people who are LGB can be transgender, we assert that it is important to discuss sexuality and gender separately so that each population receives adequate attention.

History of LGB relationships

Over the past few decades a strong gay and lesbian movement has been forged and more recently this has expanded to include bisexual and transgender communities. This movement has been significant within Western society. These communities helped many who identified as LGBTQ+ find acceptance, whereas in the past members of this community frequently reported extreme isolation and no sense of belonging, as well as an absence of social support (e.g. family, friends, peers) as a result of their sexual orientation or gender identity (Harper & Schneider, 2003). This movement has paved the way for a significant shift in the level and availability of support for the LGBTQ+ community. Support services emerged, including local and national agencies which worked hard to support the LGBTQ+ community and helped to increase understanding and acceptance (e.g. Stonewall, Albert Kennedy Trust, GLAAD). These organisations helped improve social, legal, and political relationships; which in turn resulted in a shift in recognition of the human rights issues previously faced by members of this community.

Agencies created support and awareness of the innumerable forms of LGBTQ+ related oppression and discrimination that members of this community faced on a regular basis (Dworkin, 2003). Organisations were finally able to help this minority community who were previously "hidden" and whose "voices" were silenced. The LGBTQ+ community had experienced oppression and misconceptions causing high levels of stigmatisation. Events such as the Stonewall riot in 1969 have been recognised as pivotal in starting the process of social and political change (Poindexter, 1997). Harper and Schneider (2003) reported that the threat of violence during this period was a part of the everyday lives of members of the LGBTQ+ population, especially for those in younger groups. Research, such as that conducted by Edwards and Sylaska (2013), found significant reports of bullying, harassment, and physical violence within multiple settings (e.g. home, school, friendships, and romantic relationships).

Members of the LGBTQ+ community have historically experienced harassment and violence within many aspects of their lives. A situation that was compounded further by active discrimination and stigmatisation in areas such as employment, housing, education, and human services. During the time when this LGBTQ+ movement was emerging and gathering momentum, these negative behaviours were frequently left unchallenged in law, with little legislation available to acknowledge and contest the discrimination and stigmatisation faced by individuals within this population (Harper & Schneider, 2003).

Taking this context into account, violence between partners within the LGBTQ+ community may involve similar experiences of abuse, but could also include different power dynamics; this was a particularly common finding of research conducted in the 1980s and 1990s. Some LGBTQ+ individuals who had "come out" were ostracised from their family, lost their employment, and also found friendships were terminated. Some were thrown out of their homes and would move in with their partners; in a violent relationship, this was reported to exacerbate any imbalances of power and create opportunities to exert control. With the fear of homelessness, many victims of IPV would not leave their partner despite this abuse. This may also be true for individuals losing their employment, where the unemployed partner may lose financial independence and so become vulnerable to abuse involving financial control (Renzetti, 1992).

For LGBTQ+ intimate relationships, harassment and violence in their lives may cause additional strain on their relationships. These extant strains were found to be greater where drug and alcohol use were prominent (Renzetti, 1992); indeed, substance abuse has been found to be associated with increased risk of IPV (Halpern, Young, Waller, Martin, & Kupper, 2004), therefore agencies offering support to members of the LGBTQ+ population may need to recognise and address such issues, constructing these factors as potentially precipitating violence.

Prevalence of intimate partner violence in same-sex relationships

Halpern et al. (2004) reported prevalence rates for IPV in LGB relationships in the United States at around 25%, with one in ten reporting acts of physical violence. IPV data collected by SafeLives (an IPV charity based in the UK) found that within their LGB sample, 69% of participants had experienced some form of IPV. More recent research such as Carvalho, Lewis, Derlega, Winstead and Viggiano (2011) found prevalence rates ranging from 25% and 50% in gay and lesbian relationships. Bartholomew, Regan, Oram, and White (2008a) found 41% of GB males reported being a victim of at least one incidence of physical abuse; 35% reported to reacting violently to these behaviours; 12% of participants reported that they were both the perpetrator and victim of abuse; this indicates that bidirectional violence was clearly present within some of the relationships reported by this study. This finding supports work investigating bidirectional violence within opposite-sex relationships (Bates, 2016), suggesting similar patterns of behaviour within intimate relationships regardless of the gender and sexuality of those involved. These prevalence rates suggest that IPV is indeed a serious societal problem for LGBTQ+ communities.

Considering behaviours beyond physical abuse, a relatively large-scale study by Turell (2000) found that the rates for a myriad of abusive acts were high. Monetary abuse was found to be reported by 40% of the sample of 492 individuals; coercive abuse was found to be high with 51% reporting this behaviour. Victims also reported the perpetration of shaming abuse in 70% of the sample and threatening behaviour at 52%. Physical abuse was reported at a level of 50%. Telesco's (2001) research on psychological abuse found high prevalence rates including: 71%

reported angry stares, and name calling was reported at 55%. Jealous behaviour was found to be prevalent within 41% of relationships. Furthermore, Frankland and Brown's (2014) study, which featured coercive control within same-sex IPV, found that forms of dominance and emotional control were most commonly reported using the Controlling Behaviour Scale (CBS-R; Graham-Kevan & Archer, 2005).

Similarly, Halpern et al. (2004) found that a progressively common form of coercive control within a same-sex relationship was "outing". "Outing" refers to someone intimidating their partner by threatening to reveal their sexual orientation and relationship status to family, friends, peers, and employers who are unaware of their sexuality. Halpern et al.'s (2004) research reported that bisexual men were five times more likely than lesbian women and gay men to be victims of the controlling behaviour in the form of "outing", and bisexual women were found to be four times more likely to be threatened with "outing". Maladaptive behaviours in relationships are becoming what IPV researchers argue as a "norm" within abusive relationships regardless of gender and sexuality (Bartholomew, Regan, White, & Oram, 2008b; McHugh, 2005).

These statistics reveal how prevalent the issue of IPV is within this minority population and that it is just as common, if not more so, within LGB relationships; however, it is underreported and sometimes ignored due to the dynamics of the relationships. For example, police classing acts of physical violence within a same-sex relationship as cases of non-intimate aggression due to the nature of the relationship (Pattavina, Hirschel, Buzawa, Faggiani, & Bentley, 2007). There is also a reported common misconception that violence within same-sex relationships is always bidirectional (West, 1998).

Exposure to IPV has been reported to increase a number of adverse outcomes related to health (Ard & Makadon, 2011). One such health risk that can affect both IPV and mental health outcomes is internalised homophobia and internalised transphobia, which can arise from attitudes towards the LGBTQ+ population; these views can be shaped by family, friends, other peers, and outlets such as the media. This can be attributed to the misconception that being heterosexual or being cisgendered is "normal", and that being a part of the LGBTQ+ community is somehow "different" or "not normal". This attitudinal bias may be responsible for young people and adults experiencing high rates of bullying, and can result in the individual developing their own form of internalised homophobia/transphobia and self-dislike (Carvalho et al., 2011). This negative view that having a LGBTQ+ identity is somehow "not normal" can increase issues such as depression and self-injury (Frost & Meyer, 2009; Igartua, Gill, & Montoro, 2009).

Barriers to support for LGB victims

Calton, Cattaneo, and Gebhard (2016) argue that there are three main barriers to victims seeking help for IPV in LGBTQ+ relationships. The first being that there is a limited understanding of IPV within these groups which creates significant issues in developing tailored support services. Consequently, appropriate training could be costly which has led to calls on pragmatic grounds for LGBTQ+ individuals to use services already available to support non-LGBTQ+ victims. In addition to potential costs incurred for additional training there will be methodological considerations needed to ensure that future research to underpin these services is both robust and relevant to the LGBTQ+ populations. In particular, measures should be tailored to ensure nuances of abuse within LGBTQ+ relationships are captured.

The second barrier identified was the stigma associated with being part of the LGBTQ+ community as well as being a victim of IPV. This was found to be a particular issue for gay men who reported that they were reluctant to seek support because they felt embarrassed or ashamed of the abuse (Simmons, Farrar, Frazer & Thompson, 2011). Turell and Cornell-Swanson (2005) found LGBTQ+ IPV survivors reported being very dissatisfied with formal support services. These services included domestic violence agencies, shelters, crisis lines, and the Criminal Justice System (Turell & Cornell-Swanson, 2005; Merrill & Wolfe, 2000). The National Transgender Discrimination Survey reported 19% of respondents were refused care by professionals because of their gender identity. Whilst difficult to defend this may be a consequence of confusion over where these victims should go to receive support.

Calton et al. (2016) stated that the third barrier was systemic inequities. They argued that if LGBTQ+ IPV survivors do not feel comfortable seeking support from an agency, they will not reach out for help in fear of discrimination. Whilst some services include help providers such as victim advocates, the victims may not seek help from the organisation due to links with official agencies (e.g. government agencies), and an associated fear or lack of faith in how the Criminal Justice System has contributed to oppression within these groups.

Charities such as SafeLives report that LGB individuals are underrepresented within partner violence services for a range of reasons: they do not identify with the stereotype of IPV, they do not believe the services are aimed at them, a lack of trust in mainstream agencies such as the Criminal Justice System, and a fear of "outing" themselves in order to make use of such services. Examining the situation in Wales, Harvey, Mitchell, Keeble, McNaughton Nicholls, and Rahim (2014) found that LGBT people who experience domestic and sexual violence may face specific barriers to accessing support services. These included "individual barriers" related to their knowledge and perceptions, "interpersonal barriers" related to control and abuse from/by other people on the basis of their sexual orientation and gender identity, and "structural and cultural barriers" that related to the way existing services have been designed with the needs of heterosexual women in mind. Relating to the latter, Houston and McKirnan (2007) found that gay men have a reluctance to seek help from agencies because they are typically used by heterosexual female victims. Within this study, gay men reported feeling that they are not a priority within these services and some gay men seek help for their abuse via mental health services instead, due to their abuse compromising and significantly impacting on this aspect of their health and well-being. Mental health practitioners have reported in some instances that whilst they are experienced in supporting victims of IPV, they may be inexperienced responding to LGB victims.; this is also reported by community therapists. This knowledge can ultimately discourage LGB victims from seeking help.

The barriers affecting victims from seeking help and accessing care and support can cause many issues with the victims of abuse who feel they do not have anywhere to turn to. These feelings can be exacerbated by the stigma of LGB relationships, discrimination, lack of understanding in services such as the Criminal Justice System (Letellier, 1994) and what can be argued as a general cultural insensitivity towards LGB people who are abused within their relationships (Houston & McKirnan, 2007). Lie and Gentlewarrier (1991) surveyed over 1,000 lesbians asking whether they would be likely to use a service for IPV (this was whether they identified as a perpetrator or victim), and if they perceived they were both accessible and available. Over two-thirds of the sample reported that they would not use a service or support agency. Similarly, Renzetti (1989) also found low rates of help seeking from services. This trend is not found just within the lesbian population. Island and Letellier (1991) found gay men were reluctant to seek help from legal and social agencies in relation to partner violence.

Pagelow (1981) argued that feelings of shame and a fear of retaliation may prevent all victims from seeking help. For LGB groups, there were reported concerns over revealing their sexual or gender orientation to service providers, as well as family, friends, and peers due to fear of personal repercussions (Calton et al., 2016). Homophobia and discriminatory practices were argued to still be apparent in services for the wider community and therefore the LGBTQ+ community reported a need for specific services. Renzetti (1989) found many lesbians reported that agencies refused to help victims; whilst laws have been implemented to stop this type of discrimination, there have also been reports of support services denying the seriousness of violence within a same-sex relationship. Gay men have also reported these issues when seeking help from professionals.

West (1998) stated that services for same-sex IPV are needed to create an appropriate assessment tool for measuring abuse within a same-sex relationship. For example, within the LGBTQ+ community there are some unique forms of violence that can be used within this type of relationship dynamic, such as the prevalence of homophobic control which includes "outing" which can have severe consequences for individuals. Furthermore, the presence of a HIV-positive status can be used as a form of control or emotional abuse within the relationship. Assessments would also be advised to measure the influences of homophobia within relationships, both societal and internalised. Current assessment tools are not designed to measure the prevalence and effects of these behaviours within same-sex relationships. Without appropriate assessment tools for this community, specific support services cannot be created, impacting on the health of individuals within the LGBTQ+ community when exposed to IPV.

Transgender people and intimate partner violence

The needs of transgender people tend to be little understood by both healthcare providers and the general public (Winter et al., 2016). Transgender is an umbrella term which refers to anyone whose gender identity or gender expression is different from the gender associated with the sex that they were assigned at birth (Hughto, Reisner, & Pachankis, 2015). For clarity, gender identity is an individual's sense of their own gender, and gender expression is how someone chooses to express their gender identity through behaviour and appearance. Some examples of the gender identities and gender expressions that are included under the transgender umbrella are as follows: Male-to-female (MTF) transgender, female-to-male (FTM) transgender, drag king and drag queen, genderqueer, non-binary, androgyne, and bigender (Beemyn & Rankin, 2011). There are many more identities and expressions than this but they all share the central characteristic of being different to the binary (male and female) sex that was assigned at birth.

Often, transgender people face oppression and marginalisation in their everyday lives, and historically transgender people have not always been accepted in society (Lombardi, Wilchins, Priesing, & Malouf, 2001). Transgender people can face a wide variety of hostility throughout their lives, from their family not accepting their gender identity or gender expression, to being a victim of hate crime from strangers (Stotzer, 2009). Notably, they can even experience marginalisation from sexual minority cultures, who would be expected to be supportive (Levitt & Ippolito, 2014). This is concerning as it is thought that the presence of multiple oppressed identities (e.g. transgender and sexual minority) can lead to mental health issues as a result of cumulative burden (Bariola et al., 2015). Further to this, there is evidence that these minority groups of transgender people face a greater risk of being discriminated against (Shires & Jaffee, 2015). Further discrimination is seen through opposition of the transgender population from feminist practitioners who believe that transgender people (especially MTF transgender people) are a threat to their "women only" spaces (Elliot, 2016). Janice Raymond (1994) has been particularly vocal about the fact that transgender people are not "real" men and women. She has also stated that she believes that a man who wishes to be the opposite sex is the ultimate manifestation of a man possessing a woman within a patriarchal society. Such opposition from these supposedly supportive groups can only add to the pervasive discrimination transgender people experience on a regular basis. When this everyday discrimination is then paired with an abusive relationship, the difficulties of a transgender person are further exacerbated.

There is a limited amount of research concerning transgender people and IPV victimisation (Whitton, Newcomb, Messinger, Byck, & Mustanski, 2016); however, what research there is suggests that transgender people can experience more IPV than their cisgender (meaning those whose gender identity corresponds with the sex they were assigned at birth; Chakraborti & Garland, 2015) counterparts (Langenderfer-Magruder et al., 2016). One particular report, which examines transgender peoples' experience of IPV in Scotland, provides useful prevalence rates which have relevance more widely here in the UK (The Scottish Trans Alliance, 2010). The report used a relatively small sample ($n = 60$ for some of the analysis, $n = 45$ for the remaining analysis), but it is one of the only pieces of research that has examined transgender peoples' experiences of IPV victimisation specifically. Eighty percent of the respondents stated that they had experienced emotional, physical, or sexual abuse by a partner. However, only 60% of these people actually recognised the behaviour as IPV. When looking at specific types of abuse the report states that the most common type of abuse was transphobic emotional abuse (73% of participants reported this). In terms of the impact that this abuse had on the participants, the majority of respondents to this part of the survey (98%) reported experiencing at least one negative effect on their well-being; the most common negative effect experienced was psychological or emotional problems (76%). These results demonstrate the significant impact IPV has on these transgender victims, but also highlights the fact that not all of them recognise their partner's behaviour as abuse. For this to change, greater emphasis needs to be placed on investigating IPV in transgender populations, as often the unique experiences of this victim group are amalgamated into studies on LGBTQ+ IPV victimisation in general.

As stated earlier in the chapter, transgender people experience unique issues when facing IPV. When transgender people are on the receiving end of IPV they experience types of abuse that other victim groups experience, but some abuse can be targeted specifically at vulnerabilities that are associated with the person's gender identity (Brown, 2011). Some of these abusive tactics can include using inappropriate pronouns, telling the victim that they are not a "real" man/woman, ridiculing the victim's gender identity, denying access to medical treatment such as hormones, hiding tools that enable the person to express their gender identity, and threatening to "out" the victim to their family and friends (FORGE, 2011). There are also examples of an abuser taking advantage of the everyday difficulties a transgender person can experience; for example, transgender people can face employment discrimination and can therefore be financially dependent on their partner which can lead to the abuser demanding "compensation" in the form of forced participation in activities such as prostitution or the drug trade (Goldberg, 2003). It is clear that, while transgender victims of IPV experience abuse that other victim groups experience, some abuse tactics exploit the vulnerabilities that this population already struggle with daily. This reinforces the need for specialised support for this victim group, which is equipped to deal with the distinctive issues they face.

Barriers to support for transgender victims

Regardless of whether a transgender person is the victim of IPV, access to support systems generally for the transgender population is challenging. There can often be a stigma associated with being transgender, and this can result in transgender people being reluctant to disclose their gender identity. They can even be reluctant in disclosing their gender identity to healthcare professionals because of a fear that they will be the victim of discrimination (Roberts & Fantz, 2014). Even though the transgender community is growing globally, there can still be a distinct lack of knowledge or awareness in healthcare professionals. In fact, there is evidence that there can be resistance from clinicians in treating transgender people, and some can be abusive and discriminatory (Shuster, Reisner, & Onorato, 2016). This kind of discrimination is not only perpetrated by staff in healthcare settings; Criminal Justice professionals can also be responsible. When transgender people report crime victimisation, they are often concerned about being treated with respect, or about whether their case will be handled appropriately; there can also be cases of revictimisation at the hands of Criminal Justice professionals as a result of discrimination (Stotzer, 2014). This is important when considering the barriers to support for IPV victimisation because if a transgender person has experienced discrimination from help providers in the past, then they are unlikely to seek help for abuse in their relationship because of mistrust and fear (Bradford, Reisner, Honnold, & Xavier, 2013).

As with LGB victims, transgender victims of IPV also experience significant barriers when attempting to access support for victimisation. Similar to the abuse they experience, the problems they face when accessing support for their victimisation are more often than not as a result of their gender identity or gender expression. The main issue with the currently available support for transgender victims of IPV is that it is simply not adequate or appropriate for the distinctive issues this population experience. In the UK, most of the current support provision for transgender victims of IPV is limited to organisations that are aimed at female victims in heterosexual relationships, organisations that are specific to the LGBTQ+ community but are not victims' services, and services which offer helplines that have time constraints (Walker, 2015). In fact, the large majority of victim support provision in the UK is aimed at heterosexual women. While female victims of male violence may be seen to represent the majority of IPV victims, this does not justify the lack of services for other victim groups. Further to this, transgender victims could be less likely to report their abuse because they do not see themselves represented in IPV policies, campaigns, and support services (Bornstein, Fawcett, Sullivan, Senturia, & Shiu-Thornton, 2006), therefore the true prevalence rates of abuse suffered by transgender people may not be known. All of this points to a lack of services that are equipped to specifically help the transgender population with the complex issue of IPV victimisation.

Even with the paucity of IPV victim services available to them, transgender people still encounter barriers when they are able to engage with support. These barriers can be different depending on the transgender person's gender identity or gender expression, but they have the common characteristics of being directly linked to their gender identity not matching the sex they were assigned at birth. One major barrier facing MTF transgender victims of IPV when accessing support is how much they "pass" as their gender identity when attempting to access women's organisations (Goldberg & White, 2011). However, even this does not account for the rest of the transgender community (e.g. FTM transgender people, or people who do not identify with a gender binary) trying to access support for IPV victimisation. Support for male victims of IPV is not widely available and most of the available support is based on a victim being either male or female. Sometimes FTM transgender victims of IPV have the choice of risking further harm within the male shelter system, or having to hide their gender identity to be able to use the female shelters (Brown, 2011). This relates back to a previous point of, if transgender people do not feel as though the support available is meant for them, they are probably less likely to seek any support (Walker, 2015). Other barriers to transgender victims seeking help include not wanting to seek help out of a fear of creating negative views towards the transgender community (Walker, 2015), the disclosure of a person's birth name during criminal proceedings (Brown, 2011), and the fact that they may have to undergo a medical examination with a medical professional who has little knowledge of transgender people (Goldberg, 2003). All of these barriers are likely to be addressed with increased knowledge on the part of medical and Criminal Justice personnel and on the part of society in general.

If help for IPV victimisation continues to be framed using the gender binary, then many victims are still without the support they need. It has been suggested by some that a sense of community within the transgender population (Nuttbrock et al., 2015) or seeking help from friends (Guadalupe-Diaz & Jasinski, 2017) can counteract the mental health issues associated with being a victim of abuse; however, this may not be an option for many transgender victims if their abuser has isolated them from both the transgender community and their friends (Bornstein et al., 2006).This also does not replace effective transgender-specific support which addresses victims' individual needs. Currently, transgender people can often face the difficult decision of choosing to stay in a violent relationship or accessing support systems which have a high possibility of being discriminatory (Yerke & DeFeo, 2016). For this reason, it could be argued that it is crucial for appropriate support services for transgender victims to be put in place to help this often-forgotten population. This can only be done by raising awareness of the unique issues that transgender victims of IPV experience. In fact, Merrill (1996, p. 20) challenged researchers to develop "theories which explain phenomena for every group that experiences it, not only the majority group". This can also be extended to the provision of support services to IPV victims.

Conclusion

It is clear that the needs of the LGBTQ+ community are complex and varied, both in everyday life and as IPV victims. Indeed, LGBTQ+ people can face harassment and discrimination on a daily basis. When combined with an abusive relationship, their issues can only increase. From the evidence presented in this chapter, it can be seen that the prevalence rates of IPV in LGBTQ+ relationships are equal, if not significantly higher, than their heterosexual, cisgender counterparts. This is in obvious opposition to the traditional view of IPV presented by the feminist perspective, and certainly warrants further investigation. However, further investigation may prove to be problematic, as IPV in LGBTQ+ relationships is not fully understood, and currently there is no specific assessment tool that incorporates the unique abuse tactics (e.g. "outing") that people from this population can face. What is needed is research that investigates both prevalence rates of IPV in LGBTQ+ relationships on a large-scale, and also further examines the abusive behaviours that are unique to this population. This in turn can only strengthen any attempt at creating and sustaining IPV victim support services that are tailored to the LGBTQ+ community.

In addition to highlighting the experiences of LGBTQ+ IPV victims, this chapter has also discussed some of the issues this population can experience when seeking support for abuse in their relationship. Before victims from the LGBTQ+ community even access support they face barriers, most notably the fear of discrimination. It has been found that this fear of discrimination may not be unfounded, as health professionals, Criminal Justice personnel, and support services may not have the appropriate knowledge of this population in order to provide satisfactory, non-discriminatory support. LGBTQ+ victims of IPV can often not recognise their experiences as abuse, which is further compounded by the fact that they do not feel as though support services are aimed at them. Unfortunately, this can result in LGBTQ+ IPV victims choosing between an abusive relationship and discriminatory support services that are often not equipped to help them. Moving forward from here it is important to acknowledge that understanding the experiences of all victims of IPV, regardless of gender or sexuality, are paramount when developing support services. Only then can support for IPV victims be truly inclusive.

References

Ard, K. L. & Makadon, H. J. (2011). Addressing intimate partner violence in lesbian, gay, bisexual, and transgender patients. *Journal of General Internal Medicine*, 26(8), 930–933.

Bates, E. A. (2016). Current controversies within intimate partner violence: overlooking bidirectional violence. *Journal of Family Violence*, 31(8), 937–940. doi:10.1007/s10896-016-9862-7

Bariola, E., Lyons, A., Leonard, W., Pitts, M., Badcock, P., & Couch, M. (2015). Demographic and psychosocial factors associated with psychological distress and resilience among transgender individuals. *American Journal of Public Health*, 105(10), 2108–2116.

Bartholomew, K., Regan, K. V., Oram, D., & White, M. A. (2008a). Correlates of partner abuse in male same-sex relationships. *Violence and Victims*, 23(3), 344–360. doi:10.1891/0886–6708.23.3.344

Bartholomew, K., Regan, K. V., White, M. A., & Oram, D. (2008b). Patterns of abuse in male same-sex relationships. *Violence and Victims*, 23(5), 617–636. doi:10.1891/0886–6708.23.5.617

Beemyn, G. & Rankin, S. (2011). *The lives of transgender people*. New York: Columbia University Press.

Bornstein, D., Fawcett, J., Sullivan, M., Senturia, K., & Shiu-Thornton, S. (2006). Understanding the experiences of lesbian, bisexual and trans survivors of domestic violence. *Journal of Homosexuality*, 51(1), 159–181. doi:10.1300/J082v51n01_08

Bradford, J., Reisner, S., Honnold, J., & Xavier, J. (2013). Experiences of transgender-related discrimination and implications for health: Results from the Virginia transgender health initiative study. *American Journal of Public Health*, 103(10), 1820–1829.

Brown, N. (2011). Holding tensions of victimisation and perpetration: Partner abuse in trans communities. In Ristock, J. (Ed.), *Intimate partner violence in LGBTQ lives* (pp. 153–168). Oxon, UK: Routledge.

Calton, J. M., Cattaneo, L. B., & Gebhard, K. T. (2016). Barriers to help seeking for lesbian, gay, bisexual, transgender, and queer survivors of intimate partner violence. *Trauma, Violence, & Abuse*, 17(5), 585–600.

Carvalho, A. F., Lewis, R. J., Derlega, V. J., Winstead, B. A., & Viggiano, C. (2011). Internalized sexual minority stressors and same-sex intimate partner violence. *Journal of Family Violence*, 26(7), 501–509. doi:10.1007/s10896-011-9384-2

Centers for Disease Control and Prevention. (2017). Intimate partner violence. Retrieved from: www.cdc.gov/violenceprevention/intimatepartnerviolence/index.html (Accessed 7 June, 2017).

Chakraborti, N. & Garland, J. (2015). *Hate crime: Impact, causes & responses* (2nd ed.). London, UK: SAGE Publications Ltd.

Dworkin, S. H. & Yi, H. (2003). LGBT identity, violence, and social justice: The psychological is political. *International Journal for the Advancement of Counselling*, 25(4), 269–279.

Edwards, K. M. & Sylaska, K. M. (2013). The perpetration of intimate partner violence among LGBTQ college youth: The role of minority stress. *Journal of Youth and Adolescence*, 42(11), 1721–1731. doi:10.1007/s10964-012-9880-6

Elliot, P. (2016). *Debates in transgender, queer, and feminist theory: Contested sites*. Surrey, UK: Ashgate Publishing Limited.

FORGE. (2011). Transgender & SOFFA domestic violence/sexual assault resource sheet. Retrieved from: www.forge-forward.org/publications-resources/anti-violence-publications/page/7/ (Accessed on 6 June, 2017).

Frankland, A. & Brown, J. (2014). Coercive control in same-sex intimate partner violence. *Journal of Family Violence*, 29(1), 15–22. doi:10.1007/s10896–10013–9558–9551

Frost, D. M. & Meyer, I. H. (2009). Internalized homophobia and relationship quality among lesbians, gay men, and bisexuals. *Journal of Counseling Psychology*, 56(1), 97.

Goldberg, J. M. (2003). Trans people in the criminal justice system: A guide for criminal justice personnel. Retrieved from: www.jibc.ca/search/gss/trans%20people%20criminal%20justce (Accessed on 7 June, 2017).

Goldberg, J. M. & White, C. (2011). Reflections on approaches to trans anti-violence education. In Ristock, J. (Ed.) *Intimate partner violence in LGBTQ lives* (pp. 153–168). Oxon, UK: Routledge.

Graham-Kevan, N. (2007). Domestic violence: research and implications for batterer programmes in Europe. *European Journal on Criminal Policy & Research*, 13, 213–225.

Graham-Kevan, N. & Archer, J. (2005). Investigating three explanations of women's relationship aggression. *Psychology*, 29, 270–277. doi:10.1177/0886260503256656

Grose, S. & Cabrera, G. (2011). Intimate partner violence: Psychological aspects. *Cinahl information systems*.

Guadalupe-Diaz, X. & Jasinski, J. (2017). "I wasn't a priority, I wasn't a victim": Challenges in help seeking for transgender survivors of intimate partner violence. *Violence against Women*, 23(6), 772–792. doi:10.1177/1077801216650288

Halpern, C. T., Young, M. L., Waller, M. W., Martin, S. L., & Kupper, L. L. (2004). Prevalence of partner violence in same-sex romantic and sexual relationships in a national sample of adolescents. *Journal of Adolescent Health*, 35(2), 124–131.

Harper, G. W. & Schneider, M. (2003). Oppression and discrimination among lesbian, gay, bisexual, and transgendered people and communities: A challenge for community psychology. *American Journal of Community Psychology*, 31(3–4), 243–252.

Harvey, S., Mitchell, M., Keeble, J., McNaughton Nicholls, C., & Rahim, N. (2014). *Barriers faced by lesbian, gay, bisexual and transgender people in accessing domestic abuse, stalking and harassment, and sexual violence services* (p. 80). Cardiff: Welsh Government Social Research.

Hines, D. A. & Douglas, E. M. (2011) Symptoms of posttraumatic stress disorder in men who sustain intimate partner violence: A study of help-seeking and community samples. *Psychology of Men and Masculinity*, 12, 112–127. doi:10.1037/a0022983.

Houston, E. & McKirnan, D. J. (2007). Intimate partner abuse among gay and bisexual men: Risk correlates and health outcomes. *Journal of Urban Health*, 84(5), 681–690. doi:10.1007/s11524–11007–9188–0

Hughto, J., Reisner, S., & Pachankis, J. (2015). Transgender stigma and health: A critical Review of stigma determinants, mechanisms, and interventions. *Social Science & Medicine*, 147, 222–231. doi:10.1016/j.socscimed.2015.11.010

Igartua, K. J., Gill, K., & Montoro, R. (2009). Internalized homophobia: A factor in depression, anxiety, and suicide in the gay and lesbian population. *Canadian Journal of Community Mental Health*, 22(2), 15–30.

Island, D. & Letellier, P. (1991). *Men who beat the men who love them: Battered gay men and domestic violence*. Psychology Press.

Jaffe, S. & Schub, T. (2011). Intimate partner violence: Physical abuse. *Cinahl information systems*.

Langenderfer-Magruder, L., Whitfield, D., Walls, N., Kattari, S., & Ramos, D. (2016). Experiences of intimate partner violence and subsequent police reporting among lesbian, gay, bisexual, transgender, and queer adults in Colorado: Comparing rates of cisgender and transgender victimisation. *Journal of Interpersonal Violence*, 31(5), 855–871. doi:10.1177/0886260514556767

Letellier, P. (1994). Gay and bisexual male domestic violence victimization: Challenges to feminist theory and responses to violence. *Violence and Victims*, 9(2), 95–106.

Levitt, H. & Ippolito, M. (2014). Being transgender: Navigating minority stressors and developing authentic self-presentation. *Psychology of Women Quarterly*, 38(1), 46–64doi:10.1177/0361684313501644

Lie, G. Y. & Gentlewarrier, S. (1991). Intimate violence in lesbian relationships: Discussion of survey findings and practice implications. *Journal of Social Service Research*, 15(1–2), 41–59.

Lombardi, E., Wilchins, R., Priesing, D., & Malouf, D. (2001). Gender violence: Transgender experiences with violence and discrimination. *Journal of Homosexuality*, 42(1), 89–101. doi:10.1300/J082v42n01_05

McHugh, M. C. (2005). Understanding gender and intimate partner abuse. *Sex Roles*, 52(11–12), 717–724. doi:10.1007/s11199–11005–4194–4198

Merrill, G. (1996). Ruling the exception: Same-sex battering and domestic violence theory. In Renzetti, C. & Miley, C. (Ed.) *Violence in gay and lesbian domestic partnerships* (pp. 9–21). New York: Harrington Park Press

Merrill, G. S. & Wolfe, V. A. (2000). Battered gay men: An exploration of abuse, help seeking, and why they stay. *Journal of Homosexuality*, 39(2), 1–30.

Morin, C. (2014). Re-traumatised: How gendered laws exacerbate the harm for same-sex victims of intimate partner violence. *New England Journal on Criminal & Civil Confinement*, 40(2). 477–497.

Nuttbrock, L., Bockting, W., Rosenblum, A., Hwahng, S., Mason, M., Macri, M., & Becker, J. (2015). Transgender community involvement and the psychological impact of abuse among transgender women. *Psychology of Sexual Orientation and Gender Diversity*, 2(4), 386–390. doi:10.1037/sgd0000126

Pagelow, M. D. (1981). Factors affecting women's decisions to leave violent relationships. *Journal of Family Issues*, 2(4), 391–414.

Pattavina, A., Hirschel, D., Buzawa, E., Faggiani, D., & Bentley, H. (2007). A comparison of the police response to heterosexual versus same-sex intimate partner violence. *Violence Against Women*, 13(4), 374–394. doi:10.1177/1077801207299206

Poindexter, C. C. (1997). Sociopolitical antecedents to Stonewall: Analysis of the origins of the gay rights movement in the United States. *Social Work*, 42(6), 607–615.

Próspero, M. & Kim, M. (2009) Mutual partner violence: Mental health symptoms among female and male victims in four racial/ethnic groups. *Journal of Interpersonal Violence*, 24(12) 2039–2056. doi:10.1177/0886260508327705.

Raymond, J. (1994). *The transsexual empire: The making of the she-male*. New York: Teachers College Press.

Renzetti, C. M. (1989). Building a second closet: Third party responses to victims of lesbian partner abuse. *Family Relations*, 157–163.

Renzetti, C. M. (1992). *Violent betrayal: Partner abuse in lesbian relationships*. Thousand Oaks, CA: Sage Publications.

Roberts, T. & Fantz, C. (2014). Barriers to quality health care for the transgender population. *Clinical Biochemistry*, 47, 983–987. doi:10.1016/j.clinbiochem.2014.02.009

Shires, D. & Jaffee, K. (2015). Factors associated with health care discrimination experiences among a national sample of female-to-male transgender individuals. *Health & Social Work*, 40(2), 134–141. doi:10.1093/hsw/hlr025

Shuster, M., Reisner, S., & Onorato, S. (2016). Beyond bathrooms – meeting the health needs of transgender people. *The New England Journal of Medicine*, 375(2), 101–103.

Simmons, C. A., Farrar, M., Frazer, K., & Thompson, M. J. (2011). From the voices of women: Facilitating survivor access to IPV services. *Violence against Women*, 17(10), 1226–1243.

Stotzer, R. (2009). Violence against transgender people: A review of United States data. *Aggression and Violent Behaviour*, 14, 170–179. doi:10.1016/j.avb.2009.01.006

Stotzer, R. (2014). Law enforcement and criminal justice personnel interactions with transgender people in the United States: A literature review. *Aggression and Violent Behaviour*, 19, 263–277. doi:10.1016/j.avb.2014.04.012

Telesco, G. A. (2001). Sex role identity and relationship factors as correlates of abusive behavior in lesbian relationships. *ProQuest Dissertations and Theses*, 8, 173–173. doi:10.1300/J137v08n02_10

The Scottish Trans Alliance. (2010). Out of sight, out of mind? Transgender people's experiences of domestic abuse. Retrieved from: www.scottishtrans.org/resources/research-evidence/ (Accessed on 2 June, 2017).

Turell, S. C. (2000). A descriptive analysis of same-sex relationship violence for a diverse sample. *Journal of Family Violence*, 15(3), 281–293.

Turell, S. C. & Cornell-Swanson, L. V. (2005). Not all alike: Within-group differences in seeking help for same-sex relationship abuses. *Journal of Gay & Lesbian Social Services*, 18(1), 71–88.

Walker, J. (2015). Investigating trans people's vulnerabilities to intimate partner violence/abuse . *Partner Abuse*, 6(1), 107–125. doi:10.1891/1946–6560.6.1.107

West, C. M. (1998). Leaving a second closet: Outing partner violence in same-sex couples. In Jasinski, J. L. & Williams, L. M. (Eds) *Partner violence: A comprehensive review of 20 years of research* (pp. 163–183). Thousand Oaks, CA: Sage Publications, Inc.

Whitton, S., Newcomb, M., Messinger, A., Byck, G., & Mustanski, B. (2016). A longitudinal study of IPV victimisation among sexual minority youth. *Journal of Interpersonal Violence*, 1–34. doi:10.1177/0886260516646093

Winter, S., Diamond, M., Green, J., Karasic, D., Reed, T., Whitter, S., & Wylie, K. (2016). Transgender people: Health at the margins of society. *The Lancet*, 388, 390–400. doi:10.1016/S0140–6736(16)00683–00688

Yerke, A. & DeFeo, J. (2016). Redefining intimate partner violence beyond the binary to include transgender people. *Journal of Family Violence*, 31, 975–979. doi:10.1007/s10896–10016–9887-y

PART II
Practice

7

THE EVOLUTION OF EVIDENCE-BASED TREATMENT FOR DOMESTIC VIOLENCE PERPETRATORS

John Hamel

My initial training in the area of intimate partner violence (IPV) treatment drew almost exclusively from the "Duluth" Model (Pence & Paymar, 1993). According to this model, abuse between intimate partners – whether physical, emotional, or sexual – is perpetrated by men against their women with motivations rooted in patriarchy and male privilege (e.g. Dobash & Dobash, 1979). It soon became evident that my training had not adequately prepared me for the work I was doing. These men certainly had some misconceptions about women and struggled to understand and communicate with their female partners. However, few evidenced outright misogyny or insisted on rigid adherence to gender roles; although the interpersonal abuse perpetrated by these men was sometimes instrumental, out of a desire to exercise power and control, it was more often reactive, arising within the context of mutually escalated conflict. These conflicts seemed to arise less from the female partner's resistance to the man's attempts to maintain "male privilege" than typical marital differences in such matters as parenting or what to spend their money on, and perceived inadequacies in the other's way of relating and communicating.

Over time, I observed that my clients were a heterogeneous group. Many were emotionally abusive, but this type of abuse mostly consisted of verbal abuse in contrast to a persistent pattern of isolating and threatening behaviours characteristic of batterers. Some showed no signs of psychopathology; the rest suffered from an anxiety or mood disorder, or evidenced signs of Post-Traumatic Stress Disorder or Borderline Personality Disorder. Many had problems with drugs and alcohol. What most of these clients appeared to need was help with impulse control, as well as more effective ways of communicating and resolving their relationship conflicts.

A recurring complaint from these men was that their partners were as physically abusive and domineering as they were, but not being held accountable for their behaviour. Although my initial training taught me to dismiss such allegations as examples of blame and denial, lest I unwittingly allow myself to "collude" with these manipulative clients, many appeared to be highly credible. To resolve the discrepancies between my initial training and my clinical experience, and to enhance by therapeutic skills with this population, I began attending nearby domestic violence seminars and events. Unfortunately, the sole therapeutic tools made available were the Power and Control "Wheel," a visual depiction of the ways men abuse and control women (Pence & Paymar, 1993); and the 3-phase battering cycle first proposed by Walker (1983), consisting of tension-building, an acute battering incident, and then contrition during which the batterer professes regret and seeks to remain in the relationship. The Wheel, however, did not address the types of abuse and control tactics my clients alleged of their partners (e.g. withdrawing sex and affection, threatening to take the children). Furthermore, the violence perpetrated by many of my clients did not fit the Walker model; I later learned this model depicts a pattern of unilateral abuse by someone with Borderline Personality Disorder (Dutton, 1998), but does not account for violence perpetrated by psychopaths and other instrumental batterers, which consists only of an acute battering event, without a build-up or contrition phase. It also does not account for the conflict-driven, mutual abuse cycles reported by many of my clients.

Evidence-based practice

According to the American Psychological Association (APA Presidential Task Force on Evidence-Based Practice, 2006), "evidence-based practice in psychology (EBPP) is the integration of the best available research with clinical expertise on the context of patient characteristics, culture, and preferences" (p. 273). Given the paucity of useful and reliable domestic treatment models at my disposal, it was necessary, in the beginning, to rely on my clinical experience. The men enrolled on my programmes, I observed, exhibited greater motivation to change and take responsibility for their behaviour when I maintained a safe and productive group environment and showed them respect. Using principles of established client-centred and non-judgemental therapies (e.g. Miller & Rollnick, 2002; Rogers, 1951), I sought to empower my clients to address their needs, rather than lecture them on their abusive and controlling behaviours (Maslow, 1970). But these approaches were not always sufficient in dealing with such a heterogeneous and challenging population. For my work to be truly evidence-based, I realised, it would need to draw upon research specific to IPV – its characteristics, causes, and consequences.

A new treatment model

Evidence for a gender-inclusive approach

The National Family Violence Surveys (NFVS) revealed that about 6 million men and 6 million women were physically assaulted by their partner, and an equal number of men and women were verbally abused (Straus & Gelles, 1990). These findings were confirmed in a later meta-analysis by Archer (2000). These studies also found that the physical and emotional consequences of IPV, including experienced physical injuries and symptoms of depression, anxiety, and PTSD, were higher for female victims compared to males.

Evidence for the heterogeneity of partner abuse

Meta-analyses of studies on patriarchy and partner violence found correlations between physical abuse and attitudes condoning such violence; however, traditional gender role attitudes did not differentiate non-violent men from those who abuse their partners (Sugarman & Frankel, 1996). Indeed, within the IPV literature, many risk factors have been identified for IPV perpetration. Among the first to recognise the heterogeneity of men's IPV were Hamberger and Hastings (1986), who categorised this population on the basis of distinct personality characteristics. Subsequently, Dutton (1998) proposed a two-dimensional model: impulsive versus instrumental on one axis, and under-controlled versus over-controlled on the other. The far more robust typology proposed by Amy Holtzworth-Munroe and her colleagues (Holtzworth-Munroe & Stuart, 1994) has found much greater acceptance within the academic community, and among clinicians. Their meta-analytic review of the literature yielded a threefold typology of male batterers distinguishing, *Family-Only* types, from the *Dysphoric/Borderline* category and the *Generally-Violent/Antisocial* men

Additionally, other typologies have attempted to capture the bidirectional nature of IPV. Johnson (2000) proposed the term *Intimate Terrorism*, as the frequent use by one party of physical violence together with a pattern of abuse and control. *Common Couple Violence* (or *Situational Violence*) described the mutual use of lower-level non-controlling physical violence in relationships characterised by high conflict and poor communication. Johnson regarded this as the most common type of violence among intimate partners and claimed that men accounted for 97% of intimate terrorists, however his hypotheses about his typology and gender have received inconsistent support.

Evidence for the systemic nature of partner abuse

According to the National Family Violence Surveys (Straus, 1993), in at least 50% of abusive relationships both partners are violent. The characteristics of abusive relationships were explored by various researchers in a number of well-designed laboratory studies with high conflict couples in the 1990s (e.g. Burman, John, & Margolin, 1992), which identified a variety of abusive relational dynamics in which *both* partners negatively contributed. Specific abuse cycles were identified, such as approach-avoid and attack-defend, involving various degrees of negative reciprocity (aggression or negative communication is met with aggression or negative communication by the partner, rather than attempts to defuse, redirect, or end the conflict). Because violence can emerge from interactive processes involving contributions from both partners, rather than driven solely by the actions of one pathological individual, these findings suggest that treatment for violent couples requires interventions that target relationship dynamics in addition to individual personality factors. Furthermore, other findings, including significant correlations between rates of child abuse and inter-parental violence, provided support for a model of IPV as a systemic and family problem.

Evidence for alternative treatment modalities

My research also led me to a small but convincing body of evidence for alternative treatment options to the standard psychoeducational group model (Hamel & Nicholls, 2007). The use of family therapy has never been empirically tested for IPV cases, although this modality has been found to be the most effective in the treatment of substance abusers, an acting-out population that shares many characteristics with part-ner-violent individuals (Stanton & Shadish, 1997). However, empirical support was subsequently found for couples therapy in IPV cases involving common couple vio-lence (O'Leary, Heyman, & Neidig, 1999). Stith, Rosen, and McCollum (2004) also reported successful outcomes for couples therapy, with the lowest recidivism rates among participants in the multi-couples format. Despite its demonstrated efficacy, and its endorsement by a number of feminist theorists and clinicians (e.g. Goldner, 1998), couples therapy continues to be prohibited in a majority of states for individuals mandated to batterer intervention (Babcock et al., 2016).

Treatment implications

Assessment

An important consideration in IPV assessments, especially in cases involving what appears to be mutual combat, is the extent to which one partner may initiate the abuse, and the other react in either self-defence or in retaliation. Identifying *the dominant aggressor*, when there is one, can be part of a systemic intervention approach in which all parties are held responsible for their actions, but help in the allocation of clinical resources (Hamel, 2011). Another consideration is whether the abuse is perpetrated primarily for coercive, or instrumental, purposes (that is, to dominate and control), or expressively (that is, due to poor impulse control or lack of communication and conflict resolution skills; Hamel, Desmarais, & Nicholls, 2007). The recommended assessment procedure presented in Hamel (2005) consists of an oral interview, conducted in the vein of Motivational Interviewing (Miller & Rollnick, 2002), necessary for overcoming resistance and developing a strong client-therapist alliance, and the administration of various questionnaires suggested in the literature: Conflict Tactics Scales (Straus, 1979), to measure rates of verbal and physical abuse; the Controlling and Abusive Tactics Questionnaire, useful in measuring emotional abuse and control; and the Experiences in Close Relationships Questionnaire (Fraley, Waller, & Brennan, 2000), focused on a client's attachment style and dependency needs (see Hamel, 2005, for a further review on the needs of ethnic minority and LGBT clients, personality-disordered perpetrators, and individuals with a history of substance abuse).

Treatment

The core elements of perpetrator treatment, to be included regardless of the modality in which services are delivered, include: overcome stress, challenge irrational and pro-violent beliefs, identify unhealthy and abusive interaction patterns, acquire pro-social interpersonal skills, and overcome emotional/mental disorders and childhood trauma. An important consideration is how to maintain the physical and emotional safety of victims when conducting treatment within the modalities of couples or family therapy (e.g. Geffner, Barrett, & Rossman, 1995). This can be achieved with a three-phase approach, which focuses on trust-building and basic emotion management and behaviour change in the first phase; proceeds to the teaching of pro-social communication and conflict resolution skills (with practice exercises limited to minor conflicts) followed by an exploration of core issues and the freer expression of affect. The phased approach has been successfully used in the fields of chemical dependency and trauma work, and has found support from studies on partner-violent couples (e.g. Ronan, Dreer, Dollard, & Ronan, 2004). Given that changes in one part of the system affects other parts of the system, the full range of modalities must be considered (e.g. Lane & Russell, 1989). In Hamel (2005), various treatment options are offered to clinicians working with members of the family unit. Information is given on the way systems tend to resist change, and how to best address this problem. Special attention is paid to insecure attachment dynamics, and how they can lead to violence (Sonkin & Dutton, 2003). Additional suggestions are presented for conducting effective case management (e.g. referrals to substance abuse treatment, mental health resources), helping clients establish personal goals, and how to benefit for the use of Cognitive Behaviour Therapy (CBT) progress logs.

Hamel (2005) proposes a 26–52 session domestic violence perpetrator group programme, including guidelines for facilitators, and the client workbook exercises. The educational topics were selected based largely on what research indicates are the most significant risk factors for domestic violence. The sessions on anger management, for example, target aggressive impulses, and the communication and conflict resolution sections address the needs of clients in high-conflict relationships.

The pervasiveness of misinformation

Unfortunately, most of the previously cited research has been unavailable to frontline treatment providers. The perseverance of the dominant policy and treatment model, the "*gender paradigm*" (e.g. Dutton & Nicholls, 2005), has been explained according to cultural and historical factors, such as the appropriation of the domestic violence shelter movement by ideological feminists, and the unwillingness of policy makers to challenge a worthwhile social movement despite its flaws (e.g. Straus, 2010). It has also been explained as the failure of clinicians to properly identify and overcome cognitive errors such as confirmation bias (Nicholls, Desmarais, Douglas, & Kropp, 2006).

Results of a domestic violence knowledge assessment

Over the years, a significant number of clients referred to one of the batterer intervention programmes in the San Francisco Bay Area have been referred by the family court, following allegations of IPV by the other parent in a disputed custody case. Although fathers accounted for most of these referrals, the mothers often admitted, in separate interviews, of having perpetrated intimate partner abuse at levels comparable to, or higher than, the fathers. When I brought up these findings at various county-wide family violence community meetings, or at professional meetings with family court professionals, I was greeted with indifference or out-right resistance. My guess was that this resistance was not simply due to political reasons, because among those professionals were attorneys whose loyalties were for their clients rather than feminist advocacy groups, and that perhaps it was at least partly due to a lack of accurate information.

I therefore constructed a ten-item assessment of basic domestic violence knowledge, and administered it to child custody mediators, evaluators, therapists, attorneys, and judges throughout the United States, as well as to victim advocates and a comparison group of undergraduate university students (Hamel, Desmarais, Nicholls, Malley-Morrison, & Aaronson, 2009). The correct answers were based on the review I conducted of the extant social science literature; incorrect answers were meant to be consistent with the patriarchal paradigm. We hypothesised that the family court professionals would answer less than 50% of the items correctly. Given the focus of victim advocates on battered women, we hypothesised that this group would have the lowest scores. The university students, we thought, would score better than the advocates and not significantly worse than the family court professionals. Of the 410 respondents who completed the knowledge assessment, about a quarter (24%) identified themselves as child custody mediators or evaluators, 15% as family law attorneys, 3% as family law judges, 4% as victim advocates or domestic violence shelter workers, and 32% as university students. The remaining 22% indicated they were either health professionals, court administrators, or researchers.

Rates of correct responding were very low overall. On average, respondents answered well below 50%, only 2.80 out of ten items correctly (SD = 1.92). Chi-square analyses revealed that, with the exception of some items, respondents answered incorrectly significantly more often than correctly. Furthermore, response rates for each item were highly consistent with the gender paradigm (the man is usually the perpetrator), as the contrary answer (that the woman is usually the perpetrator) was never selected by a majority of respondents. It is notable that the "I don't know" option was infrequently selected, on average about 20% of the time, indicating that incorrect answers were due to prevailing beliefs (the paradigm) rather than lack of knowledge per se.

Results supported our other predictions as well. Family court professionals scored significantly better (M = 3.11; SD = 2.01) than did shelter workers and victim advocates (M = 1.93; SD = 1.00; t (11) = 2.16, p < .05). As hypothesised, the student group scored higher on average than did the shelter/victim advocacy group (M = 2.66; SD = 1.65), and not significantly lower than the family court professionals, including judges and attorneys. This was a remarkable finding, given the students' far lesser amount of education and training. Results from this study informed a paper I co-authored, Dutton, Hamel, and Aaronson (2010), which challenged prevailing assumptions among family court researchers and professionals, in particular regarding the relative distribution of controlling-coercive violence across gender. In the Hamel et al. (2009) study, 44% of the knowledge assessment respondents wrongly assumed that verbal and emotional abuse and controlling behaviours are perpetrated almost always by the man and sometimes by the woman; and 39% indicated, incorrectly, that the percentage of battering perpetrated by men is 80–95% of the total.

Perceptions of motives

Since the publication of Archer's (2000) meta-analysis there has been a notable increase in the number of studies finding equal rates of physical abuse perpetration across gender (Desmarais, Reeves, Nicholls, Telford, & Fiebert, 2012). Today, scholars who identify as "feminist" are likely to acknowledge these findings; however, there remains continued resistance to the possibility that comparable numbers of men and women use IPV in order to dominate and control their partners (e.g. Stark, 2007). Because the motive to dominate and control has traditionally been associated with patriarchal structures, and these conditions benefit men, female-perpetrated violence is presumed to be driven by other motives, mostly self-defence, and being expressive rather than instrumental in nature (e.g. Dragiewicz, 2008).

In fact, male and female perpetrators assault intimate partners for essentially the same reasons. When asked, survey respondents describe a variety of motives: to express anger, to control, in self-defence, in retaliation, or simply in an attempt to communicate (e.g. Langhinrichsen-Rohling & McCullars, 2012). Many of these studies were published in the 1990s (e.g. Follingstad, Wright, Lloyd, & Sebastian, 1991). Why, then, were these studies generally ignored, and why are some of the gender paradigm-consistent conclusions reached in the IPV motivation literature unsupported even by the researchers' own data (Feder & Henning, 2005).

I set out to answer these questions in Hamel et al. (2007). We cited research from national and community surveys that find significantly greater acceptance of female-perpetrated partner violence than male-perpetrated violence including among mental health professionals. For example, in a study involving case vignettes, male and female psychologists judged emotional abuse as more severe when perpetrated by men (Follingstad, DeHart, & Green, 2004); and in several other studies the potential danger posed by violent female psychiatric patients was grossly underestimated, especially by female clinicians (e.g. Elbogen, Williams, Kim, Tomkins, & Scalora, 2001). From these findings, it was theorised that mental health professionals would be more likely to ascribe expressive motives to female abusers and coercive motives to male abusers.

Short IPV vignettes were constructed, from which expressive and coercive motives could reasonably be assumed on the basis of the behaviours depicted, with the lowest degree of coercion in vignette number one, increasing in severity up to number three. They were included in two questionnaires, which we distributed to 128 male and 273 female respondents. Half of them were family violence professionals, including therapists and victim advocates, and 42% undergraduate university students. In one questionnaire, the perpetrators depicted in the three vignettes were male; in the other, they were female. The respondents were asked to provide demographic information, and to indicate on a five-point Likert scale the extent to which they thought the abuse depicted was primarily expressive, primarily coercive, or somewhere in between. Given their connections with shelters, who tend to represent the most gendered views of domestic violence, and their familiarity with mostly female victims, we hypothesised that, as a group, the victim advocates would be the most likely to ascribe expressive motives in the vignettes involving female-perpetrated abuse and coercive motives in those depicting male aggression. Based on previous research (e.g. Elbogen et al., 2001), we expected similar responses from the female respondents.

Overall, respondents understood the vignettes as we constructed them – intended to depict increasing degrees of coercion. The aggression in vignette number one was deemed to be the most expressive, by a majority of respondents ($M = 2.09$, SD = 0.99) and most coercive in vignette number three ($M = 3.74$, SD = 1.20). Ratings of vignette two fell between these two ($M = 3.28$, SD = 1.05). Respondents were not confused about the motives for the behaviours depicted, which strengthens the following findings.

A significant main effect of perpetrator gender on severity ratings was found for vignette number one, with ratings of male-perpetrated aggression significantly greater ($M = 2.22$, SD = .99) than those of female-perpetrated aggression ($M = 1.94$, SD = .75). Additionally, for vignette number two, male-perpetrated aggression was significantly greater (M =3.46, SD = 1.05) than female-perpetrated aggression ($M = 3.09$, SD = .98). We did not find a significant main effect of perpetrator gender on ratings for vignette number three. We also did not find a main effect for respondent gender for vignettes one and three, but did observe a significant main effect of respondent gender on ratings in vignette number two, with ratings of male respondents significantly higher ($M = 3.47$, SD = .94) than those of female respondents ($M = 3.19$, SD = 1.06). Finally, results supported our hypothesis that victim advocates would ascribe the most coercive intentions to men, and the most expressive intentions to women. Across the three vignettes, those who identified themselves as victim advocates (including shelter workers) gave higher ratings for male-perpetrated aggression than female-perpetrated aggression. We concluded:

> The argument that the focus on male-perpetrated IPV is warranted because of significant differences between genders was negated by this study's design, which presented hypothetical scenarios involving identical behaviors by male and female perpetrators. That is, given the same set of facts, domestic violence professionals rated male-perpetrated violence as more coercive and intentional

and female-perpetrated violence as more expressive. To the extent that expressive motives are supposed to indicate a lesser threat, female-perpetrated IPV is therefore assumed to be less serious than male-perpetrated IPV.

(Hamel et al. 2007, p. 571)

Gender and emotional abuse and control

The belief that women's violence is expressive rather than coercive underlies many current IPV policies, which are disproportionately responsive to the needs of female victims, and it extends beyond motives for physical violence perpetration to perpetration involving nonphysical abuse. For example, Hamel (2011) examined the California law enforcement officers' manual on IPV arrest procedures and found no mention and no case vignettes of a female "dominant aggressor" in the section on mutual abuse cases; unsurprising given that among the main criterion for determining the dominant aggressor is which partner has a history of power and control behaviours. This study was cited by Leisring (2011) to support her contention that female-perpetrated violence is minimised by law enforcement.

However, aside from sexual abuse, the empirical evidence refutes the notion that men are significantly more likely than women to engage in those so-called "power and control" behaviours, which also include stalking, threats, and attempts to restrict a partner's movement or diminish their self-esteem (e.g. Maiuro, 2001). In intimate relationships, men have consistently been found to physically stalk and sexually abuse partners at significantly higher rates than women. However, verbal abuse, threats, possessive behaviours, and attempts to degrade and control one's partner are perpetrated, overall, far more often than physical assault, stalking, or sexual abuse (Carney & Barner, 2012); and there is convincing evidence that these other power and control behaviours are perpetrated at comparable rates across gender (e.g. Follingstad & Rogers, 2014; Kasian & Painter, 1992). Furthermore, research indicates that non-physical forms of abuse predict physical abuse perpetration (e.g. Stets, 1991; White, Merrill, & Koss, 2001). Indeed, based on Johnson's definition of intimate terrorism as the combination of physical and emotional abuse and control, the reanalysis of data from the National Violence Against Women Survey by Jasinski, Blumenstein, and Morgan (2014) found rates of intimate terrorism to be comparable across gender.

Aware that few studies have addressed these issues with individuals court-mandated to a batterer intervention programme (Feder & Henning, 2005), I decided to conduct research into such programmes in California, using what would become known as the Controlling and Abusive Tactics Questionnaire (CAT), both to measure rates of emotional abuse and control across gender and to create a reliable, validated instrument for assessing this particular population in clinical practice (Hamel, Jones, Dutton, & Graham-Kevan, 2015). Most previous measures of non-physical types of abuse had been based on samples of male perpetrators and/or female victims (Follingstad, Hause, Rutledge, & Polek, 1992), with Tolman's (1989, 1999) 58-item Psychological Maltreatment of Women Inventory (PMWI), the most widely known and utilised (see O'Leary, 2001; Graham-Kevan, 2007 for a full review). Whilst other measures (e.g. see Kasian & Painter, 1992; Graham-Kevan & Archer, 2003; Murphy & Hoover, 2001; Follingstad, 2011) have been developed, none of these previous instruments were field tested with both male and female offenders in perpetrator programmes. However, previous research with court-mandated male offenders found high rates of emotional abuse and control by their non-adjudicated female partners, who were legally regarded as the "victims" in the relationship (Capaldi et al., 2009).

The items used in the CAT research were derived from these instruments and supplemented with clinical observations. To make the instrument truly gender-inclusive, additional items were derived from reports by male victims (Hines, Brown, & Dunning, 2007) and a treatment manual for female batterers (Koonin, Cabarcas, & Geffner, 2003), yielding behaviours normally associated with females such as, "makes fun of partner's sexual performance," "excludes partner from child rearing decisions." The original CAT instrument featured 62 items with high face value, arranged in the following ten categories: threats and intimidation, isolation and jealousy, economic abuse, diminishment of self-esteem, general control, obsessive relational intrusion (e.g. stalking), passive-aggressiveness and withdrawal, using children, legal system abuse, and sexual coercion. The instrument, which asked about behaviours perpetrated as well as received, was administered in person to 240 male and 188 female participants in 15 urban and rural California counties.

Items that were not sufficiently endorsed were subsequently dropped. An initial factor analysis was then conducted. For abuse perpetrated, no significant differences were found across gender for 47 items. Women reported significantly more perpetration for nine items (e.g. "searches partner's purse/wallet/cell phone calls," "withholds affection or sex"); men reported significantly more perpetration for six items (e.g. "controls the money and excludes partner from financial decisions," "pressures partner to have sex when he/she doesn't want to"). As part of our overall study (Hamel et al., 2015), we subsequently conducted a confirmatory factor analysis online with 177 men and 200 women. This yielded four distinct categories for men (derogation and control, jealous hypervigilance, threats/control of space, sexual derogation) and four for women (derogation and control, jealous hypervigilance, threats, control of space). For the sake of simplicity when working with clinical populations, I have created a combined version, the CAT-2 (C).

We then administered the CAT-2 to another online sample of adults, so we could compare the CAT items to those on the Follingstad (2011) questionnaire, and we correlated its items to the Buss-Perry Aggression Scale (Buss & Perry, 1992) as well as to an assessment of malevolent personalities, known as the Dark Triad (Paulhus & Williams, 2002). CAT-2 was significantly and positively correlated with the Follingstad measure (IPV; men: $r = .93$, $p < .001$; women: $r = .93$, $p < .001$), the Buss-Perry measure (men: $r = .35$, $p < .001$; women: $r = .27$, $p < .001$), and the psychopathy subscale of the Dark Triad measure (men: $r = .51$, $p < .001$; women: $r .34$, $p < .001$). The CAT-2 therefore has been shown to have good construct and convergent validity. Since its creation, the CAT has been administered to hundreds of court-mandated IPV perpetrators in my clinical practice.

Towards evidence-based practice

The second edition of *Gender-Inclusive Treatment of Intimate Partner Abuse* (Hamel, 2014) builds on the gender-inclusive and systemic model of treatment introduced in the first edition with additional research evidence from sources such as the *Partner Abuse State of Knowledge Project* (PASK).

The revised book retains the essential elements from the original interview protocol, plus two added instruments. The first is the Safe at Home Questionnaire – Revised, based on the Transtheoretical Stages of Change theory, which measures a client's likelihood of taking responsibility for their abuse. I administer the instrument to both men and women, because my recent research field tested with court-mandated perpetrators of both sexes found comparable motivation levels for men and women (Sielski, Begun, & Hamel, 2015). The second is the Reasons for My Violence Scale, which gauges motivation. I also use this with clients of both sexes, based on a further study I conducted examining 177 male and female clients enrolled in a Batterer Intervention Programme (BIP) showing similar motivations across gender (Elmquist et al., 2014). This study was later cited in a paper by Cannon and Buttell (2015) on heteronormative bias towards domestic violence perpetrators in the LGBT community. The version of the CAT in the second edition reflects the final changes as reported in Hamel (2005), with slightly differing versions for males and females.

Given the significant amount of misinformation prevalent among family court professionals, discussed previously, I added a new chapter to focus on partner abuse in disputed child custody cases, to capture my research that commented on how parents are motivated to minimise, distort, and lie in order to maintain custody of their children (Dutton et al., 2010). Some allege IPV or child abuse by the other parent; others, who have minimal visitation rights, charge that the parent with primary custody has been deliberately trying to alienate that child. Both sets of allegations can be true, and should therefore be taken seriously. The impact of IPV on children is well-known, but alienation is a form of emotional child abuse, with serious lifetime consequences. The real possibility, however, of false or exaggerated charges renders the assessment process difficult at best. Echoing concerns raised (e.g. Hamel et al., 2009; Dutton et al., 2010) cautioning family court mediators and evaluators about "the perceived notion from the family court side that advocates believe research supporting the overwhelming prevalence of males as perpetrators in classic battering should be considered probative" (Hamel, 2014, p. 446). To avoid the predisposition to automatically view the father as the dominant aggressor and, therefore, not fit to have custody of the children, therapists are advised to consider assessment protocols that help to substantiate abuse, and to differentiate between true alienation of a child and his/her estrangement due to the effects of the abuse, or due to poor parenting or other reasons.

The Alternative Behavior Choices perpetrator programme

The most current version of the group intervention programme for perpetrators, *Alternative Behavior Choices*, can be found in Hamel (2017), and reflects findings from the PASK literature reviews, including the review of risk factor research by Capaldi, Knoble, Shortt, and Kim (2012), as well as recent research conducted with colleagues on evidence-based perpetrator programme standards (Babcock et al., 2016). According to this research, a Motivational Interviewing (MI) style and a strong client-facilitator alliance are among the most robust predictors of successful treatment outcomes. I have retained its non-confrontational, client-centred approach. The programme curriculum for female offenders continues to remain the same as for the men, given the similarities across gender for this population (see Babcock et al., 2016), and we have kept the client progress logs in light of BIP outcome research finding homework compliance to predict diminished levels of psychological abuse.

Based on feedback from clients and my group facilitators, and in accordance with the research literature (e.g. Babcock et al., 2016; Buttell, Hamel, Ferreira, & Cannon, 2016), I have simplified the original psychoeducational curriculum. Alternative Behavior Choices now consists of 16 core lessons, divided into three sections; overall, the curriculum emphasises emotion management and relationship-building skills. All clients are exposed to the same educational material, adapted to meet the particular needs of each client through a careful assessment, personal client goals, group discussions, and, when necessary, referrals to outside agencies.

According to the research I conducted (Buttell et al., 2016), nearly a third of those currently enrolled in BIPs (perpetrator programmes) are unemployed, and the programmes found to be the most successful in reducing rates of recidivism include a stress reduction component in their curriculum (Babcock et al., 2016). Lesson nine therefore includes relaxation and meditation exercises. Poor impulse control is targeted in several lessons, given research finding lowered rates of relationship violence by men who have learned to lower their anger levels (e.g. Hamberger & Hastings, 1988). In lessons four and five, we teach participants about the function of emotions, including the positive functions of anger. Relevant neuropsychological findings are outlined in lesson six, and essential anger management strategies are then explained in lesson seven. Interventions that specifically target emotional dependency and insecure attachment styles have yet to be empirically tested; however, their role in IPV dynamics has been well-documented, as previously discussed. Accordingly, lesson 11 discusses the various ways that insecure attachment can lead to escalated conflict and violence.

Given that pro-violent attitudes and a need to dominate predict the use of physical IPV, and that successful domestic violence interventions based on CBT models target cognitive distortions and irrational beliefs, the intervention helps clients examine their irrational, sexist, and anti-social attitudes in session eight. Jealousy, a major motive for interpersonal aggression (Langhinrichsen-Rohling & McCullars, 2012), is the focus of lesson four, and one of its primary antidotes, empathy, is discussed in lesson 12. The first three lessons address the various causes of IPV, with exercises devoted to exploring the role that developmental and family of origin factors have on one's current personality and behaviour. Within a primarily psychoeducational approach, we provide the group structure, support, acceptance, and skills found to be highly effective with Dysphoric-Borderline types (Fruzzetti & Levensky, 2000). In lesson 14, we also teach them the positive parenting practices needed to understand the consequences of their behaviours on their children, and the intergenerational cycle of abuse.

The final factor, being in a high conflict relationship, is addressed in lessons 10 through 16 and the exercises on communication, conflict containment, and conflict resolution. Participants review the abuse dynamics outlined in chapters 10 and 11 (involving negative reciprocity and insecure attachment, fear, retribution, and mind reading and self-fulfilling prophesies), and are helped to understand how these contribute to relationship conflict and violence. According to my research work with Babcock et al. (2016), improved communication skills have been shown to reduce relationship violence by men and among couples, and lower recidivism rates have been reported for CBT programmes that incorporate communication and conflict resolution skills.

Future directions

To move forward, evidence-based practice will need to further separate from the gender paradigm. To do so, scholars will need to replicate current findings (see Hamel et al., 2007; Hamel et al., 2009; Hamel et al., 2015) and investigate additional ways that the gender paradigm unduly influences IPV intervention policies. A preponderance of research reports on rates of IPV risk factors, but far less on contextual factors, and the data base upon which evidence-based practice depends will need to grow substantially to include findings from well-designed experimental outcome studies. Additionally, most IPV research has been conducted in the United States, the United Kingdom, and Canada, and the findings presented here may not all meet the treatment needs of all perpetrators. Very little has been published about IPV relationship dynamics in highly patriarchal countries, where gender roles are a greater risk factor than in the West (Esquivel-Santoveña, Lambert, & Hamel, 2013). How gender interacts with personality, stress, relationship conflict, substance abuse, and other factors should provide valuable insights in maximising treatment efficacy. Already, many agencies throughout Africa and South America combine feminist theory with CBT and other psychological approaches (Esquivel-Santoveña & da Silva, 2016).

Most clinicians do not have access to peer-reviewed journal articles, and "fact sheets" on IPV are notoriously unreliable (Hines, 2014). Still, results from 238 BIP directors who completed the North American Domestic Violence Intervention Program Survey (Buttell et al., 2016) are noteworthy; only about a third of all programmes continue to identify primarily as Duluth, down from the 53% reported in a previous national survey by Price and Rosenbaum (2009). Group facilitators are on the whole well-trained, with a majority of agencies requiring a Master's degree or higher and the average facilitator having eight years of clinical experience and 30 hours of annual training. The large majority of programmes, including many ostensibly identified as Duluth, teach the emotion management and communication and conflict resolution skills found to be effective in reducing rates of recidivism. Although most programmes approve of their state standards, two-thirds at least "sometimes" supplement them. Assessments appear to be very thorough (average intake is 90–120 minutes), and 63.9% reported to adapting their programme to meet client needs.

Ultimately, there will need to be a great deal more communication and cooperation among research scholars and clinicians. Currently, treatment providers can access the Partner Abuse State of Knowledge manuscripts for free, (see www.dom esticviolenceresearch.org). They may also contact the Association of Domestic Violence Intervention Programs (ADVIP; www.domesticviolenceintervention.net), a web-based organisation that brings together intervention provider and research scholars from around the world, providing them with up-to-date research and recommendations for evidence-based standards (Babcock et al., 2016) and online forums with which to exchange IPV-related news and information.

References

APA Presidential Task Force on Evidence-Based Practice. (2006). Evidence based practice in psychology. *American Psychologist*, 61(4), 271–285. doi:10.1037/0003–066X.61.4.271

Archer, J. (2000). Sex differences in aggression between heterosexual partners: A meta-analytic review. *Psychological Bulletin*, 126(5), 651–680. doi:10.1037/0033–2909.126.5.651

Babcock, J., Armenti, N., Cannon, C., Lauve-Moon, K., Buttell, F., Ferreira, R., Cantos, A., Hamel, J., Kelly, D., Jordan, C., Lehmann, P., Leisring, P., Murphy, C., O'Leary, K. D., Bannon, S., Salis, K. L., & Solano, I., (2016). Domestic violence perpetrator programs: A proposal for evidence-based standards in the United States. *Partner Abuse*, 7(4). doi:10.1891/1946–6560.7.4.355

Burman, B., John, R., & Margolin, G. (1992). Observed patterns of conflict in violent, nonviolent, and nondistressed couples. *Behavioral Assessment*, 14, 15–37.

Buss, A. H. & Perry, M. (1992). The aggression questionnaire. *Journal of Personality and Social Psychology*, 63(3), 452. doi:10.1037/0022–3514.63.3.452

Buttell, F. P., Hamel, J., Ferreira, R. J., & Cannon, C. (2016). A survey of domestic violence perpetrator programs in the U.S. and Canada: Findings and implications for policy intervention. *Partner Abuse*, 7(3), 226–276. doi:10.1891/1946–6560.7.3.226

Cannon, C. & Buttell, F. (2015). Illusion of inclusion: The failure of the gender paradigm to account for intimate partner violence in LGBT relationships . *Partner Abuse*, 6(1), 65–77. doi:10.1891/1946–6560.6.1.65

Capaldi, D. M., Knoble, N. B., Shortt, J. W., & Kim, H. K. (2012). A systematic review of risk factors for intimate partner violence. *Partner Abuse*, 3, 231–280. doi:10.1891/1946–6560.3.2.231

Capaldi, D., Shortt, J., Kim, H., Wilson, J., Crosby, L., & Tucci, S. (2009). Official incidents of domestic violence: Types, injury, and associations with nonofficial couple aggression. *Violence and Victims*, 24(4), 502–519.

Carney, M. & Barner, J. (2012). Prevalence of partner abuse: Rates of emotional abuse and control. *Partner Abuse*, 3(3), 286–335. doi:10.1891/1946–6560.3.3.286

Desmarais, S. L., Reeves, K. A., Nicholls, T. L., Telford, R., & Fiebert, M. S. (2012). Prevalence of physical violence in intimate relationships – Part 2: Rates of male and female perpetration. *Partner Abuse*, 3(2), 170–198. doi:10.1891/1946–6560.3.2.170

Dobash, R. P. & Dobash, R. E. (1979). *Violence against wives: A case against the patriarchy.* New York: The Free Press.

Dragiewicz, M. (2008). Patriarchy reasserted: Fathers' rights and anti-VAWA activism. *Feminist Criminology*, 3(2), 121–144. doi:10.1177/1557085108316731

Dutton, D. (1998). *The abusive personality.* New York: Guilford.

Dutton, D. G., Hamel, J., & Aaronson, J. (2010). The gender paradigm in family court processes: Re-balancing the scales of justice from biased social science. *Journal of Child Custody*, 7(1), 1–31. doi:10.1080/15379410903554816

Dutton, D. & Nicholls, T. (2005). The gender paradigm in domestic violence research and theory: The conflict of theory and data. *Aggression and Violent Behavior*, 10, 680–714. doi:10.1016/j.avb.2005.02.001

Elbogen, E. B., Williams, A. L., Kim, D., Tomkins, A. J., & Scalora, M. J. (2001). Gender and Perceptions of dangerousness in civil psychiatric patients. *Legal and Criminological Psychology*, 6, 215–228. doi:10.1348/135532501168299

Elmquist, J., Hamel, J., Shorey, R. C., Labrecque, L., Ninnemann, A., & Stuart, G. L. (2014). Motivations for intimate partner violence in men arrested for domestic violence and court referred to batterer intervention programs. *Partner Abuse*, 5(4), 359–374. doi:10.1891/1946–6560.5.4.359

Esquivel-Santoveña, E. E. & da Silva, T. (2016). Domestic violence intervention programs for perpetrators in Latin America and the Caribbean. *Partner Abuse*, 7(3), 316–352. doi:10.1891/1946–6560.7.3.316

Esquivel-Santoveña, E. E., Lambert, T. L., & Hamel, J. (2013). Partner abuse worldwide. *Partner Abuse*, 4(1), 6–75. doi:10.1891/1946–6560.4.1.6

Feder, L. & Henning, K. (2005). A comparison of male and female dually arrested domestic violence offenders. *Violence and Victims*, 20(2), 153–171.

Follingstad, D. R. (2011). A measure of severe psychological abuse normed on a nationally representative sample of adults. *Journal of Interpersonal Violence*, 26, 1194–1214. doi:10.1177/0886260510368157

Follingstad, D., DeHart, D., & Green, E. (2004). Psychologists' judgments of psychologically aggressive actions when perpetrated by a husband versus a wife. *Violence and Victims*, 19, 435–452.

Follingstad, D. R., Hause, E. S., Rutledge, L. L., & Polek, D. S. (1992). Effects of battered women's early responses on later abuse patterns. *Violence and Victims*, 7(2), 109–128.

Follingstad, D. R. & Rogers, M. J. (2014). The nature and prevalence of partner psychological abuse in a national sample of adults. *Violence and Victims*, 29(1), 3–23.

Follingstad, D., Wright, S., Lloyd, S., & Sebastian, J. (1991). Sex differences in motivations and effects in dating relationships. *Family Relations*, 40, 51–57.

Fraley, R. C., Waller, N. G., & Brennan, K. A. (2000). An item-response theory analysis of self-report measures of adult attachment. *Journal of Personality and Social Psychology*, 78, 350–365. doi:10.1037/0022–3514.78.2.350

Fruzzetti, A. & Levensky, E. (2000). Dialectical behavior therapy for domestic violence: Rationale and procedures. *Cognitive and Behavioral Practice*, 7, 435–447. doi:10.1016/S1077–7229(00)80055–80053

Geffner, R., Barrett, M., & Rossman, R. (1995). Domestic violence and sexual abuse: Multiple systems perspectives. In Mikesell, R., McDaniels, S., & Lusterman, D. (Eds) *Integrating family therapy: Handbook of psychology and systems theory* (pp. 501–517. Washington, DC: American Psychological Association.

Goldner, V. (1998). The treatment of violence and victimization in intimate relationships. *Family Process*, 37(3), 263–286. doi:10.1111/j.1545–5300.1998.00263.x

Graham-Kevan, N. (2007). Power and control in relationship aggression. In Hamel, J. & Nicholls, T. (Eds) *Family interventions in domestic violence: A handbook of gender-inclusive theory and treatment* (pp. 87–107). New York, NY: Springer Publishing.

Graham-Kevan, N. & Archer, J. (2003). Patriarchal terrorism and common couple violence: A test of Johnson's predictions in four British samples. *Journal of Interpersonal Violence*, 18, 1247–1270. doi:10.1177/0886260503256656

Hamberger, L. & Hastings, J. (1986). Personality correlates of men who abuse their partners. *Journal of Family Violence*, 1(4), 323–341. doi:10.1007/BF00978276

Hamberger, L. K. & Hastings, J. E. (1988). Skills training for treatment of spouse abusers: An outcome study. *Journal of Family Violence*, 3(2), 121–130. doi:10.1007/BF00994029

Hamel, J. (2005). *Gender-inclusive treatment of intimate partner abuse: A comprehensive approach.* New York: Springer.

Hamel, J. (2011). In dubious battle: The politics of mandatory arrest and dominant aggressor laws. *Partner Abuse*, 2(2), 224–245. doi:10.1891/1946–6560.2.2.224

Hamel, J. (2014). *Gender-inclusive treatment of intimate partner abuse: Evidence-based approaches* (2nd ed.). New York: Springer.

Hamel, J. (2017). Understanding and intervening with partner abuse. In Ireland, J. L., Ireland, C. A., Gredecki, N., & Fisher, M. (Eds) *Routledge International Handbook of Forensic Psychology in Secure Settings* (pp. 362–373). Abingdon, Oxon: Routledge.

Hamel, J., Desmarais, S. L., & Nicholls, T. L. (2007). Perceptions of motives in intimate partner violence: Expressive versus coercive violence. *Violence and Victims*, 22(5), 563–576.

Hamel, J., Desmarais, S. L., Nicholls, T. L., Malley-Morrison, K., & Aaronson, J. (2009, July). Domestic violence and child custody: Are family court professionals' decisions based on erroneous beliefs? *Journal of Aggression, Conflict and Peace Research*, 1(2), 37–52. doi:10.1108/17596599200900011

Hamel, J., Jones, D., Dutton, D., & Graham-Kevan, N. (2015). The CAT: A gender-inclusive measure of abusive and controlling tactics. *Violence and Victims*, 30(4), 547–580.

Hamel, J. & Nicholls, T. (2007). *Family interventions in domestic violence.* New York: Springer.

Hines, D. (2014). Extent and implications of the presentation of false facts by domestic violence agencies in the United States. *Partner Abuse*, 5(1), 69–82. doi:10.1891/1946–6560.5.1.69

Hines, D. A., Brown, J., & Dunning, E. (2007). Characteristics of callers to the domestic abuse helpline for men. *Journal of Family Violence*, 22(2), 63–72. doi:10.1007/s10896–10006–9052–0

Holtzworth-Munroe, A., & Stuart, G. (1994). Typologies of male batterers. *Psychological Bulletin*, 116(3), 476–497. doi:10.1037/0033–2909.116.3.476

Jasinski, J., Blumenstein, L., & Morgan, R. (2014). Testing Johnson's typology: Is there gender symmetry in intimate terrorism? *Violence and Victims*, 29(1), 73–88.

Johnson, M. (2000). Conflict and control: Symmetry and asymmetry in domestic violence. *Paper prepared for the National Institute of Justice Gender Symmetry Workshop, Arlington, VA.* Available by contacting author at mpj@psu.edu

Kasian, M. & Painter, S. (1992). Frequency and severity of psychological abuse in a dating population. *Journal of Interpersonal Violence*, 7(3), 350–364. doi:10.1177/088626092007003005

Koonin, M., Cabarcas, A., & Geffner, R. (2003). Treatment of women arrested for domestic violence: Women ending abusive/violent episodes respectfully (WEAVER) manual. Family Violence & Sexual Assault Institute.

Lane, G. & Russell, T. (1989). Second-order systemic work with violent couples. In Caesar, P. & Hamberger, K. (Eds.), *Treating men who batter* (pp. 134–162). New York: Springer.

Langhinrichsen-Rohling, J. & McCullars, A. (2012). Motivations for men and women's intimate partner violence perpetration: A comprehensive review. *Partner Abuse*, 3(4), 429–468. doi:10.1891/1946–6560.3.4.429

Leisring, P. (2011). Top 10 reasons why women's perpetration of intimate partner violence is an important area of inquiry. *Partner Abuse*, 2(4), 452–467. doi:10.1891/1946–6560.2.4.452

Maiuro, R. D. (2001). Sticks and stones may break my bones, but names will also hurt me: Psychological abuse in domestically violent relationships. In O'Leary, K. D. & Maiuro, R. D. (Eds) *Psychological abuse in violent domestic relations* (pp. ix–xx). New York, NY: Springer Publishing.

Maslow, A. (1970). *Motivation and personality* (3rd ed.). New York, NY: Addison-Wesley.

Miller, W. R. & Rollnick, S. (2002). *Motivational interviewing: Preparing people for change* (2nd ed.). New York: Guilford Press.

Murphy, C. & Hoover, S. (2001). Measuring emotional abuse in dating relationships as a multifactorial construct. In O'Leary, K. D. & Maiuro, R. D. (Eds) *Psychological abuse in violent domestic relations* (pp. 29–46). New York, NY: Springer Publishing.

Nicholls, T., Desmarais, S., Douglas, K., & Kropp, R. (2006). Violence risk assessments with perpetrators of intimate partner abuse. In Hamel, J. & Nicholls, T. (Eds) *Family interventions in domestic violence: A handbook of gender-inclusive theory and treatment* (pp. 275–302). New York: Springer.

O'Leary, K. D. (2001). Psychological abuse: A variable deserving critical attention in domestic violence. In O'Leary, K. D. & Maiuro, R. D. (Eds) *Psychological abuse in violent domestic relations* (pp. 3–28). New York, NY: Springer Publishing.

O'Leary, K., Heyman, R., & Neidig, P. (1999). Treatment of wife abuse: A comparison of gender-specific and conjoint approaches. *Behavior Therapy*, 30, 475–505. doi:10.1016/S0005–7894(99)80021–80025

Paulhus, D. L. & Williams, K. M. (2002). The dark triad of personality: Narcissism, Machiavellianism, and psychopathy . *Journal of Research in Personality*, 36(6), 556–563. doi:10.1016/S0092–6566(02)00505–00506

Pence, E. & Paymar, M. (1993), *Education groups for men who batter: The Duluth model.* New York: Springer.

Price, B. & Rosenbaum, A. (2009). Batterer intervention programs: A report from the field. *Violence and Victims*, 24(6), 757–770.

Rogers, C. (1951). *Client-centered therapy: Its current practice, implications and theory.* London: Constable.

Ronan, G., Dreer, L., Dollard, K., & Ronan, D. (2004). Violent couples: Coping and communication skills. *Journal of Family Violence*, 19(2), 131–137. doi:10.1023/B:JOFV.0000019843.26331.cf

Sielski, C., Begun, A., & Hamel, J. (2015). Expanding knowledge concerning the Safe at Home Instrument for assessing readiness-to-change among perpetrators of intimate partner violence. *Partner Abuse*, 6(3), 255–272. doi:10.1891/1946–6560.6.3.255

Sonkin, D. & Dutton, D. (2003). Treating assaultive men from an attachment perspective. In Dutton, D. & Sonkin, D. (Eds) *Intimate violence: Contemporary treatment innovations* (pp.105–134). Binghampton, NY: Hawworth Maltreatment & Trauma Press.

Stanton, M. & Shadish, W. (1997). Outcome, attrition, and family-couples treatment for drug abuse: A meta-analysis and review of the controlled, comparative studies. *Psychological Bulletin*, 122(2), 170–191. doi:10.1037/0033–2909.122.2.170

Stark, E. (2007). *Coercive control: the entrapment of women in personal life.* Oxford University Press.

Stets, J. (1991). Psychological aggression in dating relationships: The role of interpersonal control. *Journal of Family Violence*, 6, 97–114. doi:10.1007/BF00978528

Stith, S., Rosen, K., & McCollum, E. (2004). Treating intimate partner violence within intact couples relationships: Outcomes of multi-couple versus individual couple therapy. *Journal of Marital and Family Therapy*, 30(6), 305–315. doi:10.1111/j.1752–0606.2004.tb01242.x

Straus, M. (1979). Measuring intrafamily conflict and violence: The Conflict Tactics (CT) Scales. *Journal of Marriage and the Family*, 41, 75–88.

Straus, M. (1993). Physical assaults by wives: A major social problem. In Gelles, R. & Loseke, D. (Eds) *Current controversies on family violence* (pp. 67–87). Sage Publications, Inc.

Straus, M. (2010). Thirty years of denying the evidence on gender symmetry in partner violence: Implications for prevention and treatment. *Partner Abuse*, 1(3), 332–362. doi:10,1891/1 94.6–6560,13.332

Straus, M. & Gelles, R. (1990). *Physical violence in American families*. New Brunswick, NJ: Transaction.

Sugarman, D. & Frankel, S. (1996). Patriarchal ideology and wife-assault: A meta-analytic review. *Journal of Family Violence*, 11(1), 13–39. doi:10.1007/BF02333338

Tolman, R. (1989). The development and validation of a non-physical abuse scale. *Violence and Victims*, 4, 159–177.

Tolman, R. (1999). The validation of the psychological maltreatment of women inventory. *Violence and Victims*, 14(1), 25–35.

Walker, L. (1983). *The battered woman syndrome*. New York: Springer.

White, J., Merrill, L., & Koss, M. (2001). Predictors of courtship violence in a Navy recruit sample. *Journal of Interpersonal Violence*, 5, 61–73. doi:10.1177/088626001016009004

8

USING RESEARCH IN PRACTICE

Up2U an innovative approach to tackling domestic abuse

Amy Ford

Introduction

This chapter takes a practitioner perspective on developing and implementing a pro-gramme (Up2U: Creating Healthy Relationships) for people who use abusive and/or violent behaviours in their intimate partner relationships. Working with people who use domestic abuse (perpetrators) has become an area of increased focus, however there remains a polarisation in the views of why people use domestic abuse, and what approach needs to be taken to tackle this. One view of the etiology of domestic abuse is that it is a gendered crime committed by men against women with the intention to dominate them for reasons of power and control (e.g. Dobash & Dobash, 1979, 2004; Pence & Paymar, 1993). In contrast, other researchers claim that gender is only one risk factor for perpetration (e.g. Daly, Power, & Gondolf, 2001), claiming that there is a more equal distribution across gender in the perpetration of domestic abuse (e.g. Archer, 2000). This in turn can cause confusion for commissioners, service providers, and funders about how to tackle and work with perpetrators of domestic abuse. In this chapter I will outline how I designed a programme and approach to address this debate developing different programme pathways based on risk and need, rather than ideological assumptions.

A second area of debate is whether "perpetrator programmes" work to change behaviour. Many of the perpetrator programme evaluations in the UK (Westmarland, Kelly, & Chalder-Mils, 2010) and the US (Gondolf & Jones, 2001) are either too small to show reliable results, or have shown small effect sizes and no significant reduction in re-assault rates. Furthermore, many meta-analyses of perpetrator programmes have been carried out again showing little or no effect (e.g. Babcock, Green, & Robie, 2004). This has led to an overcautious culture in providing funding for these pro-grammes; commissioners are uncertain what to commission and at times commission nothing for fear of wasting public money on programmes that have shown little success. The result of this is very small-scale projects being implemented, which leads to small-scale evaluations that lack reliable and robust research designs. The gap between research and practice has been highlighted by many researchers (e.g. Gondolf, 2009), questioning how much each is influencing the other. To address this gap Up2U: Creating Healthy Relationships was designed, integral to which is a robust evaluation strategy (see Pearson & Ford, 2017).

Why Portsmouth City Council developed Up2U?

Portsmouth, as with many towns and cities in the UK, has identified domestic violence and abuse (DVA) as a strategic priority. DVA victim services include refuge provision, Independent Domestic Violence Advocates (IDVA) and outreach support. In 2012, Portsmouth completed a Domestic Abuse Review commissioned by the Safer Portsmouth Partnership and the Children's Trust Board, which highlighted a gap in provision for perpetrators. At that time, the only provision available was a court mandated Building Better Relationships (BBR) programme leaving most perpetrators without options. Portsmouth City Council (PCC) Children's Social Care did not recommission a Respect accredited domestic abuse perpetrator programme (UK membership organisation for work with domestic abuse perpetrators) as they did not feel it was offering measurable outcomes. This is where my Up2U journey began. In 2014 I was employed by PCC, on a three-month contract, as their "Domestic Abuse Perpetrator Programme Coordinator" with an initial remit to secure funding for my new position and to find a perpetrator programme to deliver in the city.

When I undertook local informal research, I found that different services had quite different viewpoints around DVA and how to respond. DVA victim services worked to a model of male dominance, power, and control. Working mostly with female victims, they also worked with male victims but men were always assessed as possible perpetrators in initial assessment stages. Children's Social Care reported DVA as a factor in 70% of child protection plans; their observations were more around unhealthy relationships with one or at times both partners using abusive and/or violent behaviours. This pattern was also seen within substance misuse services, whereby "chaotic" relationships were observed. The police reported seeing both patterns with reports of primary perpetrators and reports of couples where both partners have been both the suspect of DVA and the aggrieved. These anecdotal findings highlighted the importance of a programme that would be adaptable to different needs, genders, and levels of risk.

In the UK the predominant type of perpetrator programme is a 26–30-week group work programme delivered by Respect membership organisations. The Respect viewpoint remains rooted in the ideology that men use domestic abuse for reasons of male dominance, power, and control therefore this model did not appear to fit the needs of Portsmouth. The poor fit prompted me to review domestic abuse perpetrator programmes nationally and internationally with a view to identifying best practice. Given the criticisms I was already aware of relating to evaluation and measurable outcomes, I incorporated these criteria into my evaluation. The following is a summary of the main findings.

What is Research telling us about working with perpetrators and how was this implemented in Up2U?

Finding: what is the role of gender in domestic abuse?

One of the key debates underpinning the polarisation around the role of gender is the research used to inform theory. There is research that supports both positions; however the methodology used is often criticised. The gendered model cites extensive research (e.g. Hester, 2009) where men are found to be the main perpetrator and women the victim; the finding here also states that when women perpetrate domestic abuse this is most often the result of self-defence or self-preservation from suffering ongoing abuse (Hester & Westmarland, 2007). In contrast, alternative models often argue that much of the research used to support the gendered model has a gender bias utilising clinical samples of male perpetrators and female victims, thus selecting samples that support this hypothesis (Dixon & Graham-Kevan, 2011). Women's violence and men's victimisation is therefore not explored, and this data is not used or is discounted. Instead this alternative perspective has sought to use research that explores the experiences of men and women in terms of both perpetration and victimisation (Carney, Buttell, & Dutton, 2007; Bates, Graham-Kevan, & Archer, 2014), the findings of which support the view that there is a more equal gender distribution for both DVA perpetrators and victims suggesting that gender is not the main risk factor for DVA.

As a result of this, the gender-based perspective has promoted perpetrator intervention programmes that target male dominance, power, and control following the Duluth Model of psycho-education with some Cognitive Behavioural Therapy (CBT) elements (Gondolf, 2009). In contrast alternative approaches recommend more needs-based interventions, drawing on the wider "what works" principles that are supported by many years of empirical research and evidence (Gilchrist et al., 2003; Miller, Drake, & Nafziger, 2013).

The development of Up2U acknowledged this polarisation, but has taken a neutral stance with regard to this debate. Up2U acknowledges that some DVA is about dominance, power, and control; however, other risk and need factors, alongside female perpetrators, are recognised in the programme design and delivery. Furthermore, to contribute to this debate Up2U is collecting data regarding gender, perpetration, and victimisation for analysis.

Finding: previous methodological flaws and over reliance on police data

Westmarland et al. (2010) suggest that the disagreement about perpetrator programme effectiveness is linked to the over reliance on police data, and the failure to include more qualitative outcome measures, therefore not accurately measuring success. Gondolf (2004) investigated a set of 40 published Duluth-based programme evaluations that showed little or no effect, and followed by conducting a longitudinal four-year follow up evaluation in four areas. The findings were that there had been a de-escalation of re-assault and other DVA for a large percentage of the sample, this was supported by self-reports by partners. He therefore concluded that the question of the effectiveness of perpetrator programmes is linked to methodological shortcomings.

For the delivery of Up2U, police data as well as qualitative and quantitative self-reporting by the perpetrator and their partner/ex-partner are being used to measure success. A full evaluation framework has been set up from the outset capturing progress data and completion data. An independent evaluation is being carried out by the University of Portsmouth.

Finding: importance should be placed on programme dosage and intensity, not length.

Research by Gondolf (2004) found that more importance should be placed on dosage (e.g. number of hours) and intensity, rather than the length of the programme. This is supported by research with other offender types that programme dosage should be matched to risk levels (e.g. Kroner & Takahashi, 2012). This is also one of the major principles of the "what works" literature for offender rehabilitation; the meta-analysis by Andrews et al. (1990) found that higher risk clients had less recidivism with high intensity and dosage treatments than if they were given low intensity/dosage treatments. Conversely, high intensity treatment actually increased levels of recidivism for lower risk offenders (Bonta & Andrews, 2003).

Rather than having a standard length programme with success requiring full completion, Up2U was developed and is delivered to ensure dosage level is matched to the assessed and changing level of risk. For example, if someone is assessed as a medium-risk they may not need as much intervention time as a high-risk perpetrator. For the highest risk perpetrators, the programme is delivered at greater intensity with two or more intervention sessions per week. In addition, some perpetrators may not be assessed as appropriate for group delivery therefore the programme would be delivered one-to-one.

Finding: not all domestic abuse is about power and control; programmes should be responsive to risk and need

Many researchers recognise that men may be domestically abusive for reasons of power and control, however growing evidence suggests that DVA is a more complex issue with no one cause or pattern that fits all situations (e.g. Gilchrist et al., 2003). Daly et al. (2001) suggest that pre-existing risk factors include higher exposure to violence as a child, low education, substance misuse, and history of general violence, and that these risk factors are more prevalent for men who drop out of programmes.

Many existing programmes have been designed around the Duluth Model, but as a plethora of research suggests a variety of risk factors for DVA perpetrators, it is suggested that programmes should be more responsive to need (e.g. Graham-Kevan, 2007). Furthermore, some researchers (e.g. Kelly & Johnson, 2008) have argued that the mixed outcomes for the effectiveness of these programmes might be due to programmes, in general, not distinguishing between types of abusers, and the delivery of power and control models to perpetrators who abuse with different risk factors.

The National Offender Management Service (NOMS) reviewed its DVA programme content and redeveloped its perpetrator programme to launch "Building Better Relationships"; this is developed using the "Good Lives" model (Ward & Brown, 2004) that is strength rather than deficit focused. To overcome issues of motivation and defensiveness, intervention is delivered to build on existing skills, assets, and resources (Langlands, Ward, & Gilchrist, 2009).

Up2U is designed to respond to this research by completing a full assessment of risk/need associated with offending. Up2U is designed with integral assessment of risk/need/responsivity to ensure the programme can respond to the assessed level of risk and the associated needs of the perpetrator. For example, for a high-risk violent perpetrator their individual programme would be high in intensity and dosage, whereas for a medium-risk perpetrator the dosage would be lower.

Finding: high levels of dropout rates between assessment to session transitions, and due to the length of the programmes

Many evaluations of perpetrator programmes, including the evaluation of "Strength to Change" programme in Hull, found a high level of dropout rates after assessment whilst on a waiting list for a group, and between the transitions from one-to-one sessions to group work. This was also found in the evaluation of the Tyneside Domestic Abuse Perpetrator Programme. The recommendation in the "Strength to Change" report was to increase the frequency of one-to-one work; it was suggested that this would also be therapeutically beneficial (Stanley, Borthwick, Graham-Kevan, & Chamberlain, 2011). Although there is currently little research exploring this suggestion, many high-risk clients have previous dropped out of group situations, (e.g. school), therefore Up2U has the flexibility to deliver both one-to-one and group sessions with the intention of promoting better retention for higher risk clients.

After reviewing this research, alongside the anecdotal local findings, it became apparent that a new approach was needed to work with people who use DVA in their intimate partner relationships. Therefore, the decision of PCC was to develop its own programme.

What can we learn from other fields to use with perpetrators?

Offender rehabilitation

Over a number of years researchers in the reducing reoffending field (e.g. Forensic Psychology, prison and probation) have developed an extensive body of evidence through the evaluation of approaches and interventions most linked with reducing recidivism; this is known as the "what works" principles (Andrews & Bonta, 1994;

Gendreau, Little, & Goggin, 1996; Craig, Gannon, & Dixon, 2013). The risk, need, responsivity (RNR) model (Andrews, Bonta, & Wormith, 2008) is very influential, whereby any intervention is targeted to match an individual's level of risk, criminogenic needs, and is responsive to other needs such as level of motivation and learning style. This model was developed through extensive research which additionally supports the notion that dosage (number of hours and intensity of intervention) should be matched to the level of risk and that the type of intervention delivered should be matched to need (Smith, Gendreau, & Swartz, 2009). A further "what works" principle has been the success of true CBT in reducing recidivism (see also Wilson, Bouffard, & MacKenzie, 2005).

This body of evidence is now being recognised as being a useful approach to adopt with DVA perpetrators (e.g. Polaschek, 2012; Dutton & Corvo, 2006). Many in the field recognise that research has shown that a large proportion of perpetrators have pre-existing risk factors such as high exposure to violence as a child, low education, substance misuse, attachment disorders, mental ill health, poor emotional regulation, learnt ways of resolving conflict, and non-domestic violence (Daly et al., 2001). This has been found to be the case for female perpetrators as well as male (Graham-Kevan & Archer, 2009), although it should be noted that the research base for female perpetrators is currently smaller.

Furthermore, a growing body of literature has identified the similarities in risk and criminogenic need between DVA perpetrators and violent offenders (e.g. Bates, Archer, & Graham-Kevan, 2017); providing support for using RNR and the "what works" principles with these clients. Currently, interventions for violent offenders consist of CBT with a focus on emotional regulation, problem solving, cognitive self-talk, and the link to feeling and behaviour, moral reasoning, and offence analysis. Although DVA perpetrator programmes do touch on these, opportunities for experiential learning and consolidating new CBT skills is limited as the larger focus of these programme is on psycho-education.

As a responsive programme, Up2U assesses all perpetrators for risk of re-offending, risk of serious harm, and criminogenic need. Their intervention is individually tailored to their identified needs. The number of hours and frequency of delivery (dosage) is matched to their assessed level of risk. To deliver a true CBT programme, these skills are delivered over a period of time to ensure that perpetrators can practice and embed them into their lives. In contrast to other violent offenders it is recognised that DVA is of a more intimate nature, therefore Up2U also focuses on the perpetrator's thinking, feeling, and behaviour within their relationship.

Strength-based approach and Motivational Interviewing

Perpetrator engagement and motivation to change have been key themes in the research reviewed, with high attrition rates within many programmes. It has been suggested that this may be due to the use of a "deficit"-based approach outlining to a perpetrator all that is wrong with them and their behaviour (Lehmann & Simmons, 2009). Many researchers both within the DVA field and in the wider offender literature have proposed that a strength-based approach will enable greater motivation resulting in more positive outcomes (e.g. Ward & Brown, 2004). This approach is now used within sexual offending programmes, and NOMS has developed a new domestic abuse programme, "Building Better Relationships", which uses principles from the strength-based "Good Lives Model", demonstrating the shift to this approach.

Motivational interviewing (MI; Miller & Rollnick, 1991) is widely regarded as a successful intervention to engage clients, and is widely used in substance misuse services and work with offenders. It enables programme facilitators to work with a client to establish at what stage of readiness to change they are and to identify their intrinsic motivation. Additionally, MI gives an opportunity to build a therapeutic alliance, which in most fields is considered as important, if not more important, to successful outcomes as the content of a programme. Up2U has a six-week module at the start of the programme to engage and assess perpetrators which uses MI; a strength-based approach is used throughout the programme. All programme facilitators receive training in MI and pro-social modelling.

Trauma informed approach

Many researchers now advocate for a trauma informed approach (e.g. Dixon & Graham-Kevan, 2011) in recognition that many DVA perpetrators may have experienced previous trauma, including adverse childhood experiences (ACEs). Findings from the ACE literature (see Dube, Anda, Felitti, Edwards, & Williamson, 2002) showed a link between adult DVA perpetrators and a high number of ACEs; the link was more complicated as many of these adults also exhibited many other complex adult problems (e.g. substance misuse, mental health, and physical health). Up2U is designed to avoid any assumption about why a person may use DVA, and recognises that many clients who use abusive behaviours were themselves victims of DVA in childhood. As a behaviour change programme Up2U does not offer trauma therapy or counselling, but has the capacity to work on coping strategies and offers referral pathways for trauma, where appropriate.

Research from these fields has been fully utilised in the design of Up2U; all clients are assessed and offered intervention pathways based on their own individual needs therefore making Up2U a true RNR model for perpetrators of domestic abuse.

A different way of looking at domestic violence and abuse

The focus on DVA is helpful in that it clearly identifies this important issue and encourages focus on intervention; this has primarily been on the victim, but more recently there has been a greater focus on perpetrators, although there remains a significant lack of evidence-based practice within this field. However, this focus can detract from the overall quality of the relationship, and may miss many healthy aspects of the relationship which can be strengthened. In response to this Up2U was designed to help clients identify their behaviours across the spectrum of "healthy–unhealthy–abusive" therefore giving a clearer overview of all aspects of the relationship.

This has led to a reframing of DVA, rather than to assume that a man, or woman, who uses abusive and/or violent behaviours towards their intimate partner does so for reasons of power and control. Up2U enables clients to identify healthy behaviours to keep, and unhealthy/abusive behaviours to change. This reframing has also enabled more therapeutic work with non-abusive partners offering them the relationship element of the programme.

A further strategy used by Up2U is to avoid the use of judgemental language. For example, the use of the word "perpetrator" can be loaded with negative connotations and can demotivate a client. Therefore, all programme delivery and marketing materials use the phrase "people who use abusive and/ or violent behaviours in their intimate partner relationships". In addition, Up2U recognises that clients may use minimisations and justifications, and see this as part of the programme; as a therapeutic alliance is developed the expectation is that this will reduce.

As the Up2U programme and project has further developed we have seen an increase in referrals for both partners in the relationship as co-abusive. To address this, we have developed Up2U: Family Intervention to work within Children's Social Care. This project works with both partners where DVA is identified as an issue. By analysing and assessing each partner and their behaviours, we have developed a process to identify different patterns within the relationship for partner A and partner B. These include: abusive–non-abusive; abusive–non-abusive/ unhealthy; abusive–abusive; unhealthy–unhealthy. This is a new innovative approach and enables us to work with both unhealthy and abusive behaviours within a relationship.

The design and development of Up2U: Creating Healthy Relationships Programme

The Up2U: Creating Healthy Relationships Programme was developed in 2014 in response to the criticisms and recommendations from previous evaluations into perpetrator programmes in both the UK and US. Up2U utilises the principles of risk, need, and responsivity (Andrews, Bonta, & Wormith, 2008) offering a gender neutral, tailored response based on individual need, rather than an ideological model based on male dominance, power, and control (e.g. Pence & Paymar, 1993). As this design was a step away from the usual approaches to DVA, a multi-agency quality assurance group was established to create awareness of the programme and to gather multi-agency support. The quality assurance group had representatives from victim services, mental health, substance misuse, children's social care, police, criminal justice, and health. PCC also commissioned consultancy support from the Cognitive Centre who has the lead for the Level of Service assessments in the UK.

As previously discussed, Up2U recognises that people use DVA for different underlying reasons ranging from childhood trauma and emotional dysregulation, learned behaviour, attitudes that support gender differentials, and poor conflict resolution, as well as for reasons of power and control. Up2U was designed as an assessment-led intervention programme responding to individual need, risk, and responsivity by offering tailored pathways.

The programme length can range from six to 40 sessions, with the option of extended sessions where risk and need indicate. This is a departure from the "one size fits all" delivery in this field, enabling the "dosage" of the programme to be higher for high-risk clients and avoiding over delivery to lower risk clients. This is further supported by a flexible intensity of delivery; very high-risk individuals can have sessions delivered two times per week. Up2U can be delivered one-to-one or in groups, therefore being responsive to clients' needs and learning styles.

To ensure that the programme is both responsive to different clients' needs and can be evaluated, the programme was designed as a series of modules: 1) Engagement and Assessment; 2) Thinking, Feeling, and Behaviour; 3) Relationships; 4) Skills for Change; 5) Targeted Sessions – Stalking Behaviours; 6) Targeted Sessions – Unhealthy Sexualised Behaviours; 7) Targeted Sessions – Skills for Change 2; 8)Targeted Sessions – Abuse and Substance Misuse; and 9) Moving On. These modules are designed to be matched to a client's identified needs. Module 3 "Relationships" is the core module that all clients will receive; this can also be delivered to non-abusive partners as the focus is on healthy and unhealthy behaviours within a relationship.

To address the high level of dropout rates and low completion rates of many Domestic Abuse Perpetrator Programmes, Up2U uses motivational interviewing techniques to engage individuals, working with their resistance to build strong therapeutic relationships to optimise their commitment to the programme. As Up2U is a needs-based intervention, the programme can be tailored to work with both men and women from the age of 16, and can be delivered to people who use DVA behaviours in same-sex relationships.

The importance of assessment

The quality of the assessment of a client's risk and need underpins the whole delivery of Up2U, therefore when designing the programme it was essential that we could offer a thorough assessment to tailor the programme pathway. As Up2U is a new approach it was also important that we implemented evidence-based assessments to counter any potential criticism and to ensure robust assessment. The further benefit of these assessments is their importance in the evaluation of Up2U to measure risk reduction and patterns of risk and need.

The assessment tools selected for Up2U are:

- LS/RNR (Level of Service/Risk, Need, Responsivity) to identify target areas for change that may be linked with future abusive behaviours. It also provides an assessment of future risk of offending or rule breaking behaviours and assesses responsivity factors. This assessment has also been validated for the use with women (Vose, Lowenkamp, Smith, & Cullen, 2009).

- SARA (Spousal Assault Risk Assessment) – provides an assessment of the risk of domestic violence.
- DASH RIC Perpetrator Version identifies abusive behaviours that have been or are being used within the relationship. This can also be cross-checked with the assessment used for victims to assess levels of minimisation and denial.
- CRAIQ, a self-assessment psychometric questionnaire to assess conflict resolution, impulsivity, and aggression.

These assessments enable Up2U to work with the client to produce an assessment report that identifies: risk of domestic abuse; risk of domestic violence; risk of offending; patterns of domestic abuse; target areas for intervention for risk reduction; and the elements of the Up2U programme that will be delivered (which modules and sessions) and the delivery order, mode of delivery (i.e. one-to-one or group), the length of delivery, and the intensity of delivery (i.e. number of sessions per week).

Up2U aims to be an inclusive programme and tries to avoid exclusion of clients; all clients are asked if they admit to using abusive behaviour and want to change prior to being accepted onto assessment. The main reasons for exclusion would be severe learning difficulties resulting in a person not being able to access the programme content; unstable mental health; or substance misuse (we will work with this when a client is stable enough to access the programme); and false compliance, when a client is going through the motions but is resisting change. Up2U will, and does, work with very high-risk clients.

Implementation of Up2U in Portsmouth – challenges and successes

The delivery of Up2U went live in May 2014. Initially I was the only member of staff on the project and due to managing the programme, writing the programme, and liaising with other professionals' capacity, delivery was limited. Capacity and funding has been one of the biggest challenges in setting up and delivering the programme. A small amount of additional funding was secured for delivery of Up2U in year one giving slightly increased capacity of an additional full-time member of delivery staff. In year two (April 2015–March 2016) PCC secured a one-year Department of Communities and Local Government (DCLG) "Transformation Challenge Award" funding, which enabled greater delivery capacity as well as full-time dedicated support for non-abusive partners and support for children. This enabled us to take on more referrals to contribute to the overall evaluation, and to develop a more therapeutic approach for non-abusive partners. However, this funding was only for one year and did not give stability to delivery, or the team. Funding issues have been an ongoing issue for Up2U, and a delivery problem faced by service providers nationally. Commissioners mainly invest in DVA victims' services and appear to be reluctant to fund programmes for perpetrators. This is often due to the lack of knowledge and agreement about "what works" for perpetrators of domestic abuse, but also many commissioners feel that reallocating funding from victims' services to perpetrator programmes is politically sensitive.

To overcome the year-to-year funding issues, PCC in partnership with Southern Domestic Abuse Service (SDAS) applied for Big Lottery Reaching Communities funding and was successfully awarded £500,000 for delivery of Up2U in Portsmouth and South East Hampshire to start in July 2017. This has enabled us to expand the delivery of Up2U and for the first time the project delivery is committed for a three-year period.

A further challenge for the implementation was to establish with other services and referrers, as the underpinning theory of Up2U was not based on the Duluth Model. All initial referrals were for men; however, by delivering awareness training to other professional teams (e.g. Social Work, Substance Misuse), Up2U then saw a more diverse referral group including women and people in same-sex relationships. This remains an ongoing challenge for Up2U with ongoing training for Social Workers in DVA awareness to include the identification of female perpetrators and bidirectional DVA.

As the programme delivery has grown, it has become important that all programme facilitators adhere to programme integrity. All Up2U Facilitators have to successfully complete ten days Up2U assessment and programme training, and annual refresher training to maintain their programme certification. In addition, all facilitators have monthly programme observations to ensure they are delivering the programme as designed, Up2U clinical supervision, and monthly file audits. More recently PCC in Partnership with SDAS has successfully been awarded £300,000 Violence against Women and Girls (VAWG) funding for Up2U: Family Intervention and £300,000 Covenant Funding for Up2U: Armed Forces.

Evaluation

As Up2U was designed based on evidence-based practice used in other fields (e.g. "what works" in offender rehabilitation) it was important to develop an evaluation that tested this evidence base as used in the Up2U programme, and in the field of DVA. We hope that this will contribute to evidence-based practice and "what works" with people who use abusive and/or violent behaviours towards their intimate partner at both a national and international level. As the LS/RNR and SARA are both integral to the Up2U assessment, these were also useful research tools to measure risk reduction before and after the programme. This research design as well as access to police and Children's Social Care data was built into the design and development of the programme and delivery from the outset.

To develop an independent evaluation, PCC partnered up with Dr Dominic Pearson and Dr Claire Nee, University of Portsmouth (UoP), to design and implement the research and evaluation of the Up2U: Creating Healthy Relationships programme. One of the initial challenges faced, as outlined with other DVA evaluations, was the potentially small sample group therefore risking a less robust and significant research base. However, to address the research gap within the sector a Random Control Trial (RCT) design was agreed. The evaluation design is discussed in more detail elsewhere (see Pearson & Ford, 2017). To implement research on this scale it was both important and necessary for us to secure additional delivery funding to randomise 400+ clients. However, to date no research funding has been secured, bringing about challenges in terms of resource and capacity for both the research and delivery teams. Although challenging, the importance and significance of this research has maintained high levels of involvement and input from the university since their initial involvement.

To develop an evidenced approach a pragmatic RCT was selected comparing Up2U to current provision. Both groups receive an initial assessment, which includes baseline assessments and business as usual pathways. Data for both cohorts will be collected at six-monthly intervals before, during, and after programme completion. The evaluation will complete in 2020 with an interim evaluation expected in 2019.

One of the ambitions of the PCC and UoP partnership was to bridge the gap between research and practice, and explore how each can, and should, influence the other. This can often cause frustrations as research designs can be quite restrictive and real-life research environments can be messy, with clients not always adhering to follow up assessments. The strength of the partnership has enabled us to learn and adapt to this environment. I find this is worthy of mentioning as many service providers and commissioners do not commit to robust evaluations due to some of these issues, however these partnerships need to be developed to enable an evidence base to develop in this field.

Who has Up2U worked with?

As of January 2018 there had been 181 referrals to Up2U, 146 men and 35 women. Of interest 33% (n = 59) of these referrals were identified as co-abuse, where both partners had used violent or abusive behaviours. The assessed risk profile (using LS/RNR) of these referrals is 6% very high, 30% high, 35% medium, and 23% low. An outcome snapshot at the end of 2016/17 identified 33 clients who had completed the Up2U programme; 22 of these clients had completed the Up2U programme and were followed up at 12 months after completion. Key findings include:

- There were 44 children with open cases with children's social care prior to the Up2U programme, 37 on Child Protection (CP) Plans, six in local authority care (LAC), and one on a Child in Need (CiN) plan. Twelve months after clients had completed the Up2U programme only 16 children remained open to children's services and 28 cases had been closed.
- In the 12 months prior to starting the Up2U programme there were 22 incidents where clients were suspects of DVA, 18 arrests, and nine convictions for

DVA. In the 12 months after completion this was reduced to one incident where clients were suspected of DVA, one arrest, and no convictions for DVA.

- In the 12 months prior to starting the Up2U programme the clients were MARAC (Multi Agency Risk Assessment Conference) offenders 22 times; in the 12 months after completion this was reduced to twice.

As the evaluation continues robust data will be available. Please see the following for further illustration with a more in-depth client case study.

Up2U: an early case study

Client A was referred to Up2U in 2014, his children were in Local Authority Care and he had previous arrests for domestic abuse. Initially he agreed to the referral to Up2U as he was trying to prevent his children going up for adoption. He admitted some domestic abuse, but used some minimisation as he felt it would go against him, and his children would be at risk of adoption. He was assessed as high-risk on the LS/RNR and high-risk on SARA which would indicate a high-risk pathway of 28 Up2U sessions. It was agreed he would attend one-to-one sessions as he struggled with attending groups.

Client A had been in Local Authority care as a child and had suffered a number of ACEs, including neglect, witnessing DVA, and being a victim in a fire. As an adult he had been diagnosed with Post-Traumatic Stress Disorder (PTSD), and had a history of poor employment. Client A attended his sessions every week, demonstrated learning, and was able to evidence how he had changed his behaviour in previously high-risk situations. At about week 18 of the programme his children were put into adoption, unfortunately this process had begun prior to his engagement with the programme. Many professionals expected him to leave the programme and return to his previous behaviours; however, he continued and completed the Up2U programme.

Twelve months after completing he had no contact with the police, had been promoted and won an award at work, and was enrolled in a course to further his education. He had split up from his previous partner and reported that he did not want a relationship until he knew how to use healthy relationship behaviours; he did not ever want any children to witness domestic abuse again.

Conclusion

The Up2U: Creating Healthy Relationships programme has been an innovative step away from more Duluth-based interventions for "perpetrators" of domestic abuse. The programme is now also delivered in Poole, Dorset, Rotherham, and in the Renfrewshire Criminal Justice area. Early indications show positive results for clients with the results of the evaluation due in 2020. The project has also expanded in the Portsmouth area, and we have begun to specialise more with co-abusive and unhealthy relationships. Many other areas have expressed an interest in the

Up2U programme and we have been highlighted as developing an innovative approach to domestic abuse and violence. As an approach, and a programme, it represents an important step forward towards the goal of true evidence-based practice in domestic abuse interventions.

References

Andrews, D. A. & Bonta, J. (1994). *The psychology of criminal conduct*. Cincinnati: Anderson.

Andrews, D. A., Bonta, J. L., & Wormith, J. S. (2008). *Levels of Service/Case Management Inventory (LS/CMI). Supplement: A gender-informed risk/need/responsivity assessment*. Toronto: Multi-Health Systems Inc.

Andrews, D. A., Zinger, I., Hoge, R. D., Bonta, J., Gendreau, P., & Cullen, F. T. (1990). Does correctional treatment work? A clinically relevant and psychologically informed meta-analysis. *Criminology*, 28, 369–404. doi:10.1111/j.1745–9125.1990.tb01330.x

Archer, J. (2000). Sex differences in aggression between heterosexual partners: A meta-analytic review. *Psychological Bulletin, 126*, 651–680. doi:10.1037MJ033-2909.I26. 5. 651

Babcock, J. C., Green, C. E., & Robie, C. (2004). Does batterers' treatment work? A meta-analytic review of domestic violence treatment. *Clinical Psychology Review*, 23(8), 1023–1053. doi:10.1016/j.cpr.2002.07.001

Bates, E. A., Archer, J., & Graham-Kevan, N. (2017). Do the same risk and protective factors influence aggression toward partners and same-sex others? *Aggressive Behavior*, 43(2), 163–175. doi:10.1002/ab.21672

Bates, E. A., Graham-Kevan, N., & Archer, J. (2014). Testing predictions from the male control theory of men's partner violence. *Aggressive Behavior*, 40(1), 42–55. doi:10.1002/ab.21499

Bonta, J. & Andrews, D. A. (2003). A commentary on Ward and Stewart's model of human needs. *Psychology Crime and Law, 9*(3), 215–218. doi:10.1080/10683/16031000112115

Carney, M., Buttell, F., & Dutton, D. (2007). Women who perpetrate intimate partner violence: A review of the literature with recommendations for treatment. *Aggression and Violent Behavior*, 12, 108–115. doi:10.1016/j.avb.2006.05.002

Craig, L. A., Gannon, T. A., & Dixon, L. (Eds) (2013). *What works in offender rehabilitation: An evidence-based approach to assessment and treatment*. Chichester: John Wiley & Sons.

Daly, J. E., Power, T. G., & Gondolf, E. W. (2001). Predictors of batterer program attendance. *Journal of Interpersonal Violence*, 16, 971–991.

Dixon, L. & Graham-Kevan, N. (2011). Understanding the nature and aetiology of intimate partner-violence and implications for practice: A review of the evidence base. *Clinical Psychology Review*, 31, 1145–1155. doi:10.1016/j.cpr.2011.07.001

Dobash, R. E. & Dobash, R. (1979). *Violence against wives: A case against the patriarchy*. New York: Free Press.

Dobash, R. P. & Dobash, R. E. (2004). Women's violence to men in intimate relationships: Working on a puzzle. *British Journal of Criminology*, 44(3), 324–349. doi:10.1093/bjc/azh026

Dube, S. R., Anda, R. F., Felitti, V. J., Edwards, V. J., & Williamson, D. F. (2002). Exposure to abuse, neglect and household dysfunction among adults who witnessed intimate partner violence as children. *Violence and Victims*, 17, 3–17.

Dutton, D. & Corvo, K. (2006). Transforming a flawed policy: A call to revive psychology and science in domestic violence research and practice. *Aggression and Violent Behaviour*, 11, 457–483. doi:10.1016/j.avb.2006.01.007

Gendreau, P., Little, T., & Goggin, C. (1996). A meta-analysis of the predictors of adult offender recidivism: What works! *Criminology*, 34(4), 575–608. doi:10.1111/j.1745–9125.1996.tb01220.x

Gilchrist, E., Johnson, R., Takriti, R., Weston, S., Beech, A., & Kebbell, M. (2003). Domestic Violence Offender: Characteristics and Offending Related Needs. Home Office Findings 217. Retrieved from: http://webarchive.nationalarchives.gov.uk/20110218135832/http://rds.homeoffice.gov.uk/rds/pdfs2/r217.pdf

Gondolf, E. W. (2004). Evaluating batterer counseling programs: A difficult task showing some effects and implications. *Aggression and Violent Behavior*, 9(6), 605–631. doi:10.1016/j.avb.2003.06.001

Gondolf, E. W. (2009). The survival of batterer programs? Responding to "evidence-based practice" and improving program operation. Paper Presented to Batterer Intervention: Doing the Work and Measuring the Progress, 3–4 December, 2009.

Gondolf, E. W. & Jones, A. S. (2001). The program effect of batterer programs in three cities. *Violence and Victims*, 16(6), 693–704.

Graham-Kevan, N. (2007). Domestic violence: Research and implications for batterer programmes in Europe. *European Journal on Criminal Policy and Research*, 13(3–4), 213–225. doi:10.1007/s10610–10007–9045–9044

Graham-Kevan, N. & Archer, J. (2009). Control tactics and partner violence in heterosexual relationships. *Evolution and Human Behaviour*, 30, 445–452. doi:10.1016/j.evolhumanbehav.2009.06.007

Hester, M. & Westmarland, N. (2007). Domestic violence perpetrators. *Criminal Justice Matters*, 66, 34–39. doi:10.1080/09627250608553400

Hester, M. (2009). *Who does what to whom? Gender and domestic violence perpetrators.* Bristol: University of Bristol in association with the Northern Rock Foundation.

Kelly, J. B. & Johnson, M. P. (2008). Differentiation among types of intimate partner violence for interventions. *Family Court Review*, 46(3), 476–499. doi:10.1111/j.1744–1617.2008.00215

Kroner, D. G. & Takahashi, M. (2012). Every session counts: The differential impact of previous programmes and current programme dosage on offender recidivism. *Legal and Criminological Psychology*, 17(1), 136–150. doi:10.1111/j.2044–8333.2010.02001.x

Langlands, R. L., Ward, T., & Gilchrist, E. (2009). Applying the Good Lives Model to male perpetrators of domestic violence. *Behaviour Change*, 26, 113–129. doi:10.1375/bech.26.2.113

Lehmann, P. & Simmons, C. A. (2009). The state of batterer intervention programs: An analytical discussion. In Lehmann, P. & Simmons, C. A. (Eds) *Strengths based batterer intervention: A new paradigm in ending family violence* (pp. 3–37). New York: Springer Publishing Company.

Miller, M., Drake, E., & Nafziger, M. (2013). *What works to reduce recidivism by domestic violence offenders?* (Document No. 13-01-1201). Olympia: Washington State Institute for Public Policy.

Miller, W. R. & Rollnick, S. (1991). *Motivational interviewing.* New York, NY: The Guilford Press

Pearson, D. A. S. & Ford, A. (2017). Design of the Up2U domestic abuse perpetrator programme. *Journal of Aggression, Conflict and Peace Research*, 10(3), 189–201. doi:10.1108/JACPR-04-2017-0280

Pence, E. & Paymar, M. (1993). *Education groups for men who batter: The Duluth model.* New York: Springer Publishing Company.

Polaschek, D. L. L. (2012). An appraisal of the Risk-Need-Responsivity (RNR) Model of offender rehabilitation and its application in correctional treatment. *Legal and Criminological Psychology*, 17(1), 1–17. doi:10.1111/j.2044-8333.2011.02038.

Smith, P., Gendreau, P., & Swartz, K. (2009). Validating the principles of effective intervention: A systematic review of the contributions of meta-analysis in the field of corrections. *Victims & Offenders*, 4, 148–169. doi:10.1080/15564880802612581

Stanley, N., Borthwick, R., Graham-Kevan, N., & Chamberlain, R. (2011). Strength to change: An evaluation of a new initiative for male perpetrators of domestic abuse. Retrieved from: http://clok.uclan.ac.uk/2973/1/STCfinal_report_31-5-11_pdf.pdf

Vose, B., Lowenkamp, C. T., Smith, P., & Cullen, F. T. (2009). Gender and the predictive validity of the LSI-R: A study of parolees and probationers. *Journal of Contemporary Criminal Justice*, 25(4), 459–471. doi:10.1177/1043986209344797

Ward, T. & Brown, M. (2004). The Good Lives Model and the conceptual issues in offender rehabilitation. *Psychology, Crime & Law*, 10(3), 243–257. doi:10.1080/10683160410001662744

Westmarland, N., Kelly, L., & Chalder-Mills, J. (2010). *What counts as success?* (Briefing note). London: Respect.

Wilson, D. B., Bouffard, L. A., & MacKenzie, D. L. (2005). A quantitative review of structured, group-oriented, cognitive-behavioral programs for offenders. *Criminal Justice and Behavior*, 32(2), 172–204. doi:10.1177/0093854804272889

9

TOWARDS EVIDENCE-BASED TREATMENT OF FEMALE PERPETRATED INTIMATE PARTNER VIOLENCE AND ABUSE

Erica Bowen & Jenny Mackay

In recent decades, there has been a plethora of research activity in the field of intimate partner violence and abuse (IPVA) perpetration, as psychologists, criminologists, and sociologists have tried to understand why some individuals are violent in intimate relationships. This originated from the determined work of feminist groups around the 1970s, who advocated for an increased awareness of domestic violence and for focussed funding and support for victims. This work has been vital in raising public awareness of the problem and changing policy in the area, although this has resulted in a dominant narrative about IPVA; that it is perpetrated by men against women.

More recently, research has explored whether, and how, women perpetrate IPVA. This began with explorations of family violence and the development of scales which aimed to measure its prevalence (Hines & Douglas, 2009), specifically the Conflict Tactics Scale (CTS; Straus, 1979). Over time, the use of these act-based, general population measures highlighted the unexpected finding that women were admitting to perpetrating aggressive behaviours in intimate relationships at a rate similar to, or even greater than, men (Straus, 2004). What followed were criticisms of the CTS (e.g. Kimmel, 2002), adaptations of the measure (CTS2; Straus, Hamby, Boney-McCoy, & Sugarman, 1996) and eventually the oft-quoted meta-analysis by Archer (2000), demonstrating that when using act-based, self-report measures, women were significantly more likely than men to perpetrate physical violence. Whilst many researchers argued that the figures likely reflected the use of self-defence by women in abusive relationships (e.g. White, Smith, Koss, & Figueredo, 2000), there is now more research suggesting that this is not reflective of all violence by women (Dutton, Nicholls, & Spidel, 2005).

Although some women use aggressive behaviours in relationships as a means of self-defence, this is not always the case, meaning that some women are violent and abusive in intimate relationships with the result of causing harm to victims in both heterosexual and same-sex relationships (Dutton et al., 2005; Rohrbaugh, 2006). This indicates that there are women who, as primary perpetrators, would benefit from receiving intervention to reduce the risk of perpetrating violence in future intimate relationships. It follows that understanding more about the nature of women's IPVA perpetration, and the risk and need factors of women perpetrators, is crucial to understanding the types of intervention that would be effective. This chapter will discuss what is known about the nature and prevalence of IPVA perpetrated by women and then explore the evidence of the associated risk and need factors. The implications for potential treatments are then presented.

Nature and prevalence of IPVA perpetrated by women

IPVA may be perpetrated by women in either heterosexual or same-sex relationships. Women engage in a range of violent behaviour not dissimilar to men (Hines & Douglas, 2009), although there is some dispute about the comparable seriousness of the injuries caused, with evidence that women are more likely to be more seriously injured (Archer, 2000). In a study exploring the characteristics of men who called a domestic violence helpline, it was found that men reported experiencing controlling behaviours and physical violence that was similar to that which is often described by women who are victims (Hines, Brown, & Dunning, 2007).

In empirical studies, women are often asked about their motivations for perpetrating IPVA, interestingly, more often than men (Langhinrichsen-Rohling, McCullars, & Misra, 2012). This suggests that researchers want to explain women's use of IPVA, perhaps being more willing to understand and sympathise with women compared to men. Whilst it is important to understand the motivation behind behaviour, the danger of explaining only women's use of IPVA is that this establishes the view that it is unavoidable, with the opposite being true for men, and detracts from understanding what to target in interventions. A review of studies investigating the motives of women and men who perpetrated IPVA found that common themes were those of self-defence, power/control, anger/ expression of negative emotion and retaliation, with some support for the notion that self-defence is more likely to be a motive for women than men (Langhinrichsen-Rohling et al., 2012). This demonstrates that there are a range of motives reported by women, and gives some indication as to the nature of the violence that is used by women in relationships.

Research exploring the prevalence of IPVA perpetration by women reveals rates not dissimilar to men. In a systematic review of longitudinal studies, self-reported rates of perpetrating IPVA within heterosexual relationships by both sexes ranged from 19% reporting physical aggression to 70% reporting psychological aggression (Costa et al., 2015). International research investigating university students' self-reported IPVA perpetration across 32 countries reveals that 31.6% of women report perpetrating minor physical violence and 10.6% report perpetrating severe physical violence (Straus, 2008).

A review of research exploring victimisation of men in heterosexual relationships showed that men reporting that they have experienced IPVA (of any form) ranged between 0.6% and 32% (Nowinski & Bowen, 2012). The Crime Survey for England and Wales also reports on IPVA victimisation, and the latest survey showed that 10.3% of men reported experiencing any type of partner abuse since the age of 16, which is an estimated 1.6 million men (Office for National Statistics, 2016). Although it is unknown in these victimisation figures whether the perpetrators were women or men, in previous Home Office figures, 17% of women identifying as lesbian or bisexual stated that they had experienced domestic abuse within the last year (Smith et al., 2010), possibly indicating the prevalence of IPVA perpetrated by women as reported in crime surveys. However, crime survey figures may underestimate the numbers of victims, as respondents may not recognise themselves as victims of crime because they may not perceive the behaviours they experience from partners as a criminal act (Hines & Douglas, 2009).

Further research on the prevalence of IPVA perpetrated against women identifying as lesbians reported rates of 43.8% of physical violence, rape, and/or stalking, and rates of 29.4% for severe physical violence (Walters, Chen, & Breiding, 2013). In a review of IPVA in self-identified lesbians, Badenes-Ribera, Frias-Navarro, Bonilla-Campos, Pons-Salvador, and Monterde-i-Bort (2015) reported a mean life-time victimisation prevalence of 48% and perpetration prevalence of 43%. These figures suggest substantial numbers of women are perpetrating IPVA, particularly within same-sex relationships, and demonstrate that there is a cause for concern regarding violent behaviour used by women in intimate relationships. What is not clear from these figures is whether they reflect the conclusions of some researchers, that this behaviour is self-defence, or whether there are particular risk and need factors that make some women more vulnerable to perpetrating IPVA, and that if targeted by interventions, could reduce the likelihood of them becoming violent in the future.

Considerations of risk

The Risk-Need-Responsivity model (RNR; Andrews & Bonta, 2010) is an influential model in the development of offending behaviour interventions. Based on the three principles of risk, need, and responsivity, the model states that matching the right offender with the right intervention is likely to produce the most effective means of reducing reoffending. This targeted approach to delivering offending behaviour interventions requires a strong understanding of the risk factors associated with a particular set of behaviours. The RNR model refers to such factors as criminogenic needs (Andrews & Bonta, 2010).

Risk factors have also been defined by Kraemer et al. (1997) as those factors which are correlated with a behaviour of interest but also precede that behaviour. They further add causal risk factors as those which meet the definition but that can be changed and in doing so, alter the behaviour of interest; for example, improving anger management skills leading to a change in the perpetration of IPVA. Causal risk factors as defined here are arguably similar to the criminogenic need principle of the RNR model. Without knowing the risk factors associated with IPVA perpetration by women, this means intervention may not be targeted correctly, resulting in potentially wasted resources and the possibility of not impacting the behaviour. Not impacting behaviour change means that problem behaviours are maintained and possibly could become worse, resulting in further violence.

What do we know about the risk factors of women who perpetrate IPVA?

One of the difficulties in seeking causal risk factors is that to be most confident about the time-based association between exposure (risk factor) and outcome (IPVA) longitudinal studies which assess factors and the outcome behaviour at various time points are needed. However, the majority of studies in this area use retrospective or cross-sectional methods, often relying solely on self-report data. A small number of reviews synthesise what is known about the risk factors of women who perpetrate IPVA, although most of these explore the risk factors of both women and men.

One such paper reviewed 228 empirical studies that had a clear statistical association between risk factors and partner violence and found a long list of associated factors (Capaldi, Knoble, Shortt, & Kim, 2012). These included: deprivation; minority group membership (with income as a mediator); substance abuse; being separated from partner; low relationship satisfaction and high discord/conflict; stress related to acculturation, finances, and work; exposure to violence between parents and experience of child abuse (low to moderate significant associations, possibly mediated by an individual's anti-social behaviour and adult adjustment); involvement with aggressive peers in adolescence; conduct problems and anti-social behaviour (both often mediators of early factors such as harsh parental treatment). The only differences found between women and men were that there were stronger associations found between alcohol use, depression, and IPVA perpetration for women than for men. However, precedence of these factors was not established in the empirical studies, therefore it is not clear if these have a causal or comorbid relationship with IPVA perpetration. Similar factors were found to be associated with IPVA perpetration in a review that examined only longitudinal studies (Costa et al., 2015). This review found that the most consistent predictors of IPVA perpetration were childhood and adolescent problems and having experienced abuse, with other significant predictors being other behaviour problems reported in childhood including: being withdrawn, aggressive behaviour, conduct disorder, and adolescent alcohol and substance use. Again, this review explored both women and men, and only heterosexual relationships, but gives some indication of the factors that might be associated with IPVA perpetration in women.

There have been very few reviews exploring factors associated with women only. One review has synthesised the knowledge of women's motivations for using IPVA, reporting that they were associated with self-defence in 87% of the studies, expression of feelings in 70%, and coercive control in 61% (Bair-Merritt et al., 2010). Although it is important to know about motivations when considering designing treatment programmes for women, as it gives an insight into the context of women's use of violence, exploring motivations does not tell us about the criminogenic need of this population, and what it is that needs to change to reduce the likelihood of IPVA being perpetrated in the future. Laskey (2016) reviewed papers that investigated the characteristics of women who perpetrated IPVA, finding that common correlates were emotional dysregulation, substance misuse, trauma symptoms, interpersonal dependency, unstable mood, and attachment issues. Again, whilst these characteristics cannot yet be said to be causal risk factors of IPVA perpetrated by women, they suggest areas of commonality amongst this complex population.

One very recent review has specifically sought studies examining causal risk factors as defined by Kraemer et al. (1997) amongst women perpetrators who are situated within criminal justice settings (Mackay, Bowen, Walker, & O'Doherty, 2018). Amongst the studies found in this review, there were no causal risk factors identified, largely due to the design and analyses carried out in the studies. However, there were several factors that appeared to be correlated with IPVA perpetration, which included having experienced child abuse, substance use, borderline personality traits and attachment issues, and having experienced trauma. The results of the review suggest that, despite the methodological shortcomings of the studies investigating factors associated with IPVA perpetration, there is a very complex interaction of factors at play for women who are violent in relationships.

Whilst the empirical evidence to date is still largely inconclusive regarding what the risk factors for IPVA perpetration by women are, there is some indication about the types of factors that may need to be incorporated into interventions. Although it is also still unclear as to whether women would require interventions that looked substantially different to those currently offered to men, there may be elements of current provision for men that would be beneficial.

What do we know about effective approaches to the treatment of IPVA perpetrators?

Interventions for IPVA perpetrators most often adopt a group-based approach whereby small groups of (typically) men engage in a number of educational and therapeutic activities that are designed to a) raise awareness of the problematic nature and costs in terms of damage to victims of IPVA, b) educate concerning the range of abusive behaviours that comprise IPVA, c) re-train problem thinking and self-talk, d) examine how socialisation leads to pro-violence attitudes and abusive behaviours, and e) teach and rehearse a range of non-violent non-abusive communication, listening, and emotion management skills (Bowen, 2011). Group interventions differ in terms of their length (number and duration of sessions), how they are theoretically described, referral criteria (self-referral, court-mandated), operating context (community or corrections), and links with victim support services (Bowen & Day, 2019). Despite these operational variations, however, there is often little difference between models that are described as psychoeducational or cognitive behavioural in approach (Babcock, Green, & Robie, 2004). Moreover, few treatment models that are not described as psychoeducation or cognitive behavioural are detailed in the literature, due to the implementation by North American authorities of state standards that mandate these approaches over alternatives, and which specifically prohibit the use of couples counselling, and individual one-to-one approaches are viewed as a last resort (Maiuro & Eberle, 2008). Similar standards have existed in the UK for a number of years although there is some movement towards making these less rigid.

It might be expected that the existence of such standards reflected the empirical evidence concerning the effectiveness of group-based approaches over and above other non-psychoeducational or cognitive behavioural approaches, and other non-group approaches. However, one artefact of the existence of state standards has been the suppression of alternative models, and consequently questions concerning the relative effectiveness of these versus alternative models remain unanswered (Babcock et al., 2016). When we examine the empirical data concerning the efficacy of these widely endorsed models, it is clear that notwithstanding the methodological challenges of evaluating interventions, the empirical evidence does not support the use of one model over and above another, and that the average treatment effects of these interventions are typically small and non-significant (see Babcock et al., 2004 and Feder & Wilson, 2005 for relevant meta-analyses). Babcock et al. (2004) in their meta-analysis report that on average, interventions lead to a 5% reduction in recidivism, with no discernible differences between CBT and Duluth-informed men's programmes.

The effectiveness of men's IPVA perpetrator programmes is of relevance here as traditionally women arrested for IPVA have been referred to the interventions designed for their male counterparts. The number of published studies that have examined the impact of tertiary interventions on women perpetrators of IPVA is very small indeed. Buttell (2002) examined the impact of completing a 12-week CBT perpetrator programme on levels of moral reasoning in women and found no significant impact of the intervention. Carney and Buttell (2004, 2006) adopted a pre-post-test design to examine the impact of a 12-week psychoeducational (feminist-informed, cognitive-behavioural) intervention on the psychological outcomes of women perpetrators. Women who completed the group intervention showed decreases in passive-aggressive behaviour towards their partners, reductions in controlling behaviours towards partners, and reductions in propensity towards physical violence. However, the impact of the intervention on actual physical violence is unknown, and the lack of control group precludes the ability to confer these effects to the intervention.

Tutty, Babins-Wagner, and Rothery (2006, 2009) evaluated the Responsible Choices for Women programme in Alberta, Canada. The 15-week programme includes both unstructured and structured psychotherapeutic and psychoeducational content. The 2006 evaluation found that non-physical abuse towards a partner, depression, and stress reduced, and self-esteem increased after the intervention, although scores remained in a clinical level post-intervention. Perhaps surprisingly, self-reported physical abuse was not significantly different at the end of the intervention than it had been beforehand. In 2009 the team conducted an evaluation with a larger sample size of 269 women, of which 101 had been court-mandated to attend. Again, using a pre-post-test design it was found that depression stress and non-physical abuse improved as a consequence of intervention, and that in contrast to the earlier study the scores were in the normal range post-intervention. In addition, both physical and non-physical victimisation by partners decreased. In contrast to expectations though, self-reported physical aggression towards a partner increased post-intervention, for both court-mandated and non-court-mandated participants.

Although these five studies provide mixed, poor quality evidence of the effectiveness of interventions with women who perpetrate IPVA, Babcock et al. (2016) note that more promising, better quality evidence comes surprisingly from studies of interventions designed to meet the needs of women as victims of IPVA, as mothers at high risk of child maltreatment, or as mental health patients. For example, Macy, Rizo, Guo, and Ermentrout (2013) evaluated using a pre-post design (no-control group), a 13-week IPV safety and parenting programme for mothers mandated to services. Participants were victims of IPVA but were excluded if they were assessed as being primary abusers in their relationship. It was found that the social cognitive, empowerment model reduced both psychological and physical victimisation and perpetration significantly between pre- and 3-month post intervention follow-up. In a more stringent randomised controlled trial (RCT) design, Bair-Merritt and colleagues (2010) evaluated a three-year home visitation programme for mothers who were at risk of child maltreatment. The findings showed significant reductions in mothers' physical IPVA perpetration and victimisation. Although the programme had little specific IPVA content, it was suggested to impact on it through lowering parenting stress, increasing parenting efficacy, and also support. Another RCT design was adopted by Zarling, Lawrence, and Marchman (2015) in their evaluation of a community (not court-mandated) 12-week mixed-gender group of Acceptance and Commitment Therapy (ACT) compared to a support and discussion control group. Participants had been referred from mental health clinicians and reported perpetrating at least two physically aggressive acts towards current or former partners in the previous six months, although couples were not referred. Those in the ACT group reported reduced perpetration of psychological and physical aggression at two points: end and six months post intervention.

Taken together these outcome studies suggest that intervention models developed for men who perpetrate IPVA have limited impact on women. However, it is not known whether this impact is more negligible than that identified for men, and consequently there is insufficient evidence to determine whether existing models are, or are not, appropriate for, and effective with, women.

Working with women who perpetrate IPVA

In order to increase the likelihood that behaviour will change, research evidence shows that several things have to happen. First, clients need to realise that they may benefit from intervention. Second, they need to attend an intervention. Third, they need to engage with the content, and fourth, they need to complete the intervention. There is also a requirement that the content and methods of intervention appropriately address the underlying causes of IPVA. In lieu of clear empirical evidence from clinical work with women IPVA perpetrators, some potential evidence-based methods of intervention can be suggested when we look to the broader psychotherapy and corrections literatures.

Identifying a need to change

It is widely acknowledged that individuals identified as perpetrators of IPVA, regardless of gender, are likely to be resistant to engaging with an intervention and many may deny or minimise their behaviours (Bowen, 2011). Only one study has compared readiness to change in men and women IPVA perpetrators; Babcock, Canady, Senior, and Eckhardt (2005) recruited 120 IPVA perpetrators (52 women) from a programme in Houston, Texas. These two groups were compared on the URICA-DV (University of Rhode Island Change Assessment Inventory for Domestic Violence; Levesque, Gelles, & Velicer, 2000) stage of change assessment, the Process of Change Scale (Eckhardt, Babcock, & Homack, 2004), self-reported IPVA and emotional abuse. Comparison on URICA-DV subscale scores yielded no significant differences between men and women. Women were more likely than men to report physical IPVA perpetration. Cluster analysis of these scores resulted in three clusters: Immotive (69% men); Preparticipation (52% men), and Decision Making (61% men). The Immotive group scored higher than average on Precontemplation and lower on contemplation and action subscales suggesting that they were more likely to deny the existence of problem behaviours and were poorly engaged in the change process. The Preparticipation cluster exhibited average scores on all URICA-DV subscales suggesting that they may acknowledge problem behaviour and have become moderately engaged in the change process. The Decision Making group scored higher than average on Contemplation, Action, and Maintenance URICA-DV subscales and Precontemplation scores were lower than average suggesting that these individuals are engaged in action to reduce problem behaviour. When the processes of change were compared across these three groups it was confirmed that individuals in the Preparticipation and Decision Making group used more behavioural processes of change than those in the Immotive group. No reliable gender differences were found in the processes of change used.

The findings from this study, although tentative due to the sample size and number of comparative analyses conducted, suggest that men and women who have been arrested for IPVA do not differ in their readiness to change or the processes of change used. The findings do suggest, however, that interventions which adopt an "action" perspective, that is, which assume that the clients referred to intervention are ready to change their behaviour, may be inappropriate and that motivational enhancement may be required for women who perpetrate IPVA.

One approach to increasing a client's ability to determine for themselves that intervention may be warranted, and for which there is mounting evidence of its effectiveness, is motivational interviewing (MI: Miller & Rollnick, 2012). MI is a client-centred directive therapeutic style that enables individuals to identify a need for change through identifying and challenging ambivalence. This is achieved through helping the individual identify their own motivations for change and increasing intrinsic motivation through the identification of self-determined goals.

A small selection of papers identifies evidence of the potential efficacy of MI-informed interventions improving treatment adherence, completion, and outcomes in heterosexual men. For example, Musser, Semiatin, Taft, and Murphy (2008) found that attendance of a two-session MI intake programme resulted in more constructive in-session behaviour during the early phase of the programme, greater compliance with homework assignments, higher late session therapist ratings of the working alliance, and more help seeking outside of the domestic violence programme. Kistenmacher and Weiss (2008) conducted a small study in which 33 male perpetrators were randomly assigned to a MI or control condition before attending the programme. Consistent with predictions, the MI group demonstrated generally more improvement on stages of change subscales than the control group. Further, the MI group demonstrated a significantly greater decrease in the extent to which they blamed their violence on external factors. More recently, Crane, Eckhardt, and Schlauch (2015) found that a one-day MI add-on to standard domestic violence treatment significantly increased attendance and completion among perpetrators who were binge drinkers. Increasing evidence also illustrates that MI is most effective with clients who, pre-intervention, are most reluctant to change (e.g. Murphy, Linehan, Reyner, Musser, & Taft, 2012).

Intervention content

Babcock et al. (2016) have conducted a considerable literature review upon which recommendations for evidence-based state standards have been made. Within this review, six treatment targets are identified as having the most consistent evidence for their role in IPVA perpetration among samples of men who are perpetrators. These are summarised in Table 9.1 and cross referred with the findings of the systematic reviews described previously.

Table 9.1 shows that only some of the evidence-based treatment targets identified by Babcock et al. are consistently identified in the existing syntheses concerning women IPVA perpetrators. Specifically, there is no direct evidence for the role of impulsivity. However, the syntheses of studies including women IPVA perpetrators also more readily identified trauma, childhood experiences of abuse, and borderline personality traits as of potential relevance to women's IPVA perpetration, which are not directly represented in the factors identified by Babcock et al. as having the most evidence for their association with IPVA perpetration in men.

TABLE 9.1 Summary of evidence-based risk factors for IPVA across research syntheses

Treatment targets identified by Babcock et al. (2016)	Presence/absence of treatment targets identified in syntheses including female IPVA perpetrators			
	Capaldi et al. (2012)	Costa et al. (2015)	Laskey (2016)	Mackay et al. (2018)
Stress	Y			
Aggressive personality		Y		
Poor impulse control				
Depression	Y			
Emotional insecurity			Y	Y
Alcohol/Drug dependency	Y	Y	Y	Y
Childhood interparental violence	Y	Y		
High conflict relationships	Y			

Dowd and Leisring (2008) provide a useful overview of treatment considerations and approaches for working with women IPVA perpetrators, which reflect those issues identified here. Specifically, they suggest that there may be a core set of treatment issues to be addressed with all women who perpetrate IPVA, and other more bespoke issues that might need to be addressed for a minority of this client group. The core issues and methods are summarised in Table 9.2.

Other potential modules or interventions required by women IPVA perpetrators identified by Dowd and Leisring include treatment for conditions that might undermine emotional and behavioural control. These might also be identified as responsivity issues as they are likely to impact on the ability, if left untreated, of a client to engage effectively in any form of intervention. Such factors include mood disorders, hormonal and medical conditions, post-traumatic stress disorder, and substance use.

Borrowing from the corrections literature, considerable evidence indicates that behaviour change interventions for offenders that: incorporate multi-modal approaches; have a skills orientation; adopt a cognitive-behavioural focus; and have a clear theoretical framework and rationale for the application of specific methods are most effective (McGuire, 2000). The results of existing meta-analyses, however, challenge this view when working with IPVA perpetrators, at least on the face of it. We have previously noted the findings of systematic literature reviews that have identified borderline personality traits as consistent predictors of women's IPVA perpetration (Laskey, 2016; Mackay et al., 2018). Within the heterosexual IPVA treatment literature only one study reports on attempts to align treatment modality to personality pathology. Saunders (1996) found that male IPVA perpetrators who were characterised by anti-social personality disorder traits responded better to the most often provided psychoeducational programmes, whereas those with borderline

TABLE 9.2 Summary of global intervention methods for women IPVA perpetrators (summarised from Dowd & Leisring, 2008)

Intervention focus	Description
Safety planning	Based on an assumption that most women IPVA perpetrators will be in a bidirectionally violent relationship. Safety planning is recommended to enable her to make herself safe should she be threatened by her partner. Alongside this, women need to develop insight into their own risky behaviours.
Managing conflict	Time out technique recommended in early stages of treatment to prevent escalation of violence, and to enable her to tolerate her partner's use of time out without trying to prevent him leaving.
Consequences of aggression	Women should be encouraged to understand the costs and consequences of their behaviour on their partner, on children, and on others. In addition, the negative impact on their own lives in the short, medium and long terms should be examined.
Emotional education	Psychoeducational components concerning the survival value of emotions; the links between emotions, thoughts, and behaviour, and the identification and labelling of emotions. Exercises in empathy are used to highlight and practice empathy for the emotional responses of others.
Familiarity with emotion arousal	Examination and identification of triggers and situational cues for emotional arousal, as well as understanding how her own behaviour may trigger emotions in others. Recognising and disrupting arousal early on are the main goals.
Socialisation	The focus is on understanding how emotional reactions and management are learned within family and cultural environments. Gender role expectations are examined, and women are encouraged to understand how they and men are placed under pressure to conform to societal expectations.
Cognitive restructuring	The reduction of cognitive distortions is central to improving emotional regulation, and so the role of thinking errors in the escalation of conflict is explained. Women are shown how to challenge and modify their reactions. An important adjunct to this is challenging attitudes and assumptions about men which can be the foundation of some thinking errors.
Communication skills	Communication skills are taught using role play methods to increase the use of active listening strategies, as well as the use of "I" statements, paraphrasing and reflecting.
Negotiation of power and control and assertiveness skills	On the assumption that aggressive women find it difficult to share power and control in their relationships, the intervention focuses on negotiation skills. Given concerns that increased assertiveness may increase risk of victimisation, such work is conducted within the context of safety planning.
Characteristics of healthy and unhealthy relationships	The focus is on reducing psychologically abusive behaviour, and increasing awareness of positive relationship characteristics such as trust, intimacy, lack of jealousy, positive communication, lack of violence.

Intervention focus	Description
Stress management	The consequences of excessive and prolonged stress on emotion regulation, behaviour, and health are explored. Sources of stress are identified and methods of managing stress considered.
Problem solving and coping	Improved problem solving should increase positive coping strategies and reduce stress. Women learn how to define problems, brainstorm and evaluate alternatives, and select and implement solutions.
Relaxation skills	Linked to stress management and coping strategies, women are taught a range of relaxation techniques. In addition, women are encouraged to consider other methods of relaxation.

traits responded better to process psychodynamic treatment models. These findings indicate that prior to intervention work, a thorough assessment is required which accounts for personality presentation, psychopathology, learning styles, the function of IPVA behaviours, attitudes and beliefs that may maintain and reward IPVA behaviours, and that interventions should be tailored to account for, and address, these issues of risk and need.

Facilitating engagement and completion

Existing interventions for heterosexual men who perpetrate IPVA have been characterised as engaging in the shaming of clients, by directly challenging them and focusing on problem behaviour at the exclusion of alternatives or solutions to problem behaviours, and have been identified as anti-therapeutic (Dutton & Corvo, 2007). It is widely accepted that in all therapeutic contexts, including those within corrections systems, developing and maintaining a high quality therapeutic or working alliance is key to facilitating client engagement with the intervention content (Holdsworth, Bowen, Brown, & Howat, 2014), and also increases the likelihood of client completion and non-violence post intervention (Taft, Murphy, King, Musser, & DeDeyn, 2003). Indeed, when studies have examined the common factors that contribute to client change, it has been identified that 40% of change variance can be attributed to extra-therapeutic factors (e.g. motivation, strengths, resources, coping skills, social support); 30% of change variance is attributed to the client/therapist relationship (and the quality of the individual's participation in that relationship); 15% is attributed to the therapist's attitude in conveying a sense of hope for the future in the client, and 15% is attributable directly to the techniques or models of intervention adopted (Lehman & Simmons, 2009). Moreover, the responsivity principle asserts that interventions should be tailored to cater for individual differences in client groups in order to maximise the likelihood that individuals will benefit (Andrews & Bonta, 2010).

Recently, Holdsworth et al. (2014) developed the Program Engagement Theory (PET) which accounts for both facilitators' and offenders' engagement in group offending behaviour programmes, which are argued to be mutually contingent. The PET emphasises the importance of considering change during treatment as a process, not just an outcome, and solution-focused programmes were found to be more conducive to fostering engagement and the change process than were offence-focused programmes (Holdsworth et al., 2014). Indeed, Babcock et al. (2016) endorse the use of strengths-based philosophies with IPVA perpetrators in general, due to their emphasis on developing a respectful and collaborative working relationship between facilitator/therapist and client.

Conclusion

The empirical evidence shows that IPVA is perpetrated and experienced by women at rates similar to, or higher than, those reported by men. What the limited empirical research suggests is that in many ways the IPVA used and experienced is similar in nature to that perpetrated by men. Moreover, where research has been conducted into potential correlates, this too points to situational, individual, and relationship level risk factors that are also associated with men who perpetrate IPVA, possibly due to the likelihood that violence perpetrated by women occurs within a bidirectionally violent relationship. In lieu of clear evidence concerning effective intervention approaches for women IPVA perpetrators, the research examined suggests that the basis of effective intervention is a well-informed assessment of the individual's risk and needs, and that responsivity issues are of primary concern. Adopting a collaborative, supportive, and accepting therapeutic style will also ensure that when interventions are offered, female clients are more likely to engage with and complete them. Moreover, all work in this area should be guided by detailed safety planning.

References

Andrews, D. A. & Bonta, J. (2010). *The psychology of criminal conduct* (5th ed.). Oxford: Routledge

Archer, J. (2000). Sex differences in aggression between heterosexual partners: A meta-analytic review. *Psychological Bulletin*, 126(5), 651–680. doi:10.1037/0033–2909.126.5.651

Babcock, J., Armenti, N., Cannon, C., Lauve-Moon, K., Buttell, F., Ferreira, R., ... & Lehmann, P. (2016). Domestic violence perpetrator programs: A proposal for evidence-based standards in the United States. *Partner Abuse*, 7(4), 355–460. doi:10.1891/1946-6560.7.4.355

Babcock, J. C., Canady, B. E., Senior, A., & Eckhardt, C. I. (2005). Applying the transtheoretical model to female and male perpetrators of intimate partner violence: Gender differences in stages and processes of change. *Violence and Victims*, 20(2), 235–250.

Babcock, J. C., Green, C. E., & Robie, C. (2004). Does batterers' treatment work? A meta-analytic review of domestic violence treatment. *Clinical Psychology Review*, 23, 1023–1053. doi:10.1016/j.cpr.2002.07.001

Badenes-Ribera, L., Frias-Navarro, D., Bonilla-Campos, A., Pons-Salvador, G., & Monterde-i-Bort, H. (2015). Intimate partner violence in self-identified lesbians: A meta-analysis of its prevalence. *Sexuality Research and Social Policy*, 12(1), 47–59. doi:10.1007/s13178–13014–0164–0167

Bair-Merritt, M. H., Crowne, S. S., Thompson, D. A., Sibinga, E., Trent, M., & Campbell, J. (2010). Why do women use intimate partner violence? A systematic review of women's motivations. *Trauma, Violence & Abuse*, 11(4), 178–189. doi:10.1177/1524838010379003

Bowen, E. (2011). *The rehabilitation of partner-violent men*. Chichester: Wiley-Blackwell.

Bowen, E. & Day, A. (2019). Treating intimate partner violence and abuse. In Polascheck, D., Day, A., & Hollin, C. R. *The Wiley international handbook of correctional psychology (pp. 529–542)*. Chichester: Wiley-Blackwell.

Buttell, F. P. (2002). Levels of moral reasoning among female domestic violence offenders: Evaluating the impact of treatment. *Research on Social Work Practice*, 12(3), 349–363. doi:10.1177/1049731502012003001

Capaldi, D. M., Knoble, N. B., Shortt, J. W., & Kim, H. K. (2012). A systematic review of risk factors for intimate partner violence. *Partner Abuse*, 3(2), 231–280. doi:10.1891/1946–6560.3.2.231

Carney, M. M. & Buttell, F. P. (2004). A multidimensional evaluation of a treatment program for female batterers: A pilot study. *Research on Social Work Practice*, 14(4), 249–258. doi:10.1177/1049731503262223

Carney, M. M. & Buttell, F. P. (2006). An evaluation of a court-mandated batterer intervention program: Investigating differential program effect for African American and white women. *Research on Social Work Practice*, 16(6), 571–581. doi:10.1177/1049731506289115

Costa, B. M., Kaestle, C. E., Walker, A., Curtis, A., Day, A., Toumbourou, J. W., & Miller, P. (2015). Longitudinal predictors of domestic violence perpetration and victimization: A systematic review. *Aggression and Violent Behavior*, 24, 261–272. doi:10.1016/j.avb.2015.06.001

Crane, C. A., Eckhardt, C. I., & Schlauch, R. C. (2015). Motivational enhancement mitigates the effects of problematic alcohol use on treatment compliance among partner violent offenders: Results of a randomized clinical trial. *Journal of Consulting and Clinical Psychology*, 83, 689–695. doi:10.1037/a0039345

Dowd, L. & Leisring, P. A. (2008). A framework for treating partner aggressive women. *Violence and Victims*, 23(2), 249–263.

Dutton, D. G. & Corvo, K. (2007). The Duluth model: A data-impervious paradigm and a failed strategy. *Aggression and Violent Behavior*, 12, 658–667. doi:10.1016/j.avb.2007.03.002

Dutton, D. G., Nicholls, T. L., & Spidel, A. (2005). Female perpetrators of intimate abuse. *Journal of Offender Rehabilitation*, 41(4), 1–31. doi:10.1300/J076v41n04_01

Eckhardt, C. I., Babcock, J., & Homack, S. (2004). Partner assaultive men and the stages and processes of change. *Journal of Family Violence*, 19(2), 81–93. doi:10.1023/B:JOFV.0000019839.98858.5c

Feder, L. & Wilson, D. B. (2005). A meta-analytic review of court-mandated batterer intervention programs: Can courts affect abusers' behavior? *Journal of Experimental Criminology*, 1, 239–262. doi:10.1007/s11292–11005–1179–0

Hines, D. A., Brown, J., & Dunning, E. (2007). Characteristics of callers to the domestic abuse helpline for men. *Journal of Family Violence*, 22(2), 63–72. doi:10.1007/s10896–10006–9052–0

Hines, D. A. & Douglas, E. M. (2009). Women's use of intimate partner violence against men: Prevalence, implications, and consequences. *Journal of Aggression, Maltreatment & Trauma*, 18(6), 572–586. doi:10.1080/10926770903103099

Holdsworth, E., Bowen, E., Brown, S., & Howat, D. (2014). Client engagement in psychotherapeutic treatment and associations with client characteristics, therapist characteristics, and treatment factors. *Clinical Psychology Review*, 34, 428–450. doi:10.1016/j.cpr.2014.06.004

Kimmel, M. S. (2002). 'Gender Symmetry' in domestic violence: A substantive and methodological research review. *Violence Against Women*, 8(11), 1332–1363. doi:10.1177/107780102237407

Kistenmacher, B. R. & Weiss, R. L. (2008). Motivational interviewing as a mechanism for change in men who batter: A randomized controlled trial. *Violence and Victims*, 23, 558–570.

Kraemer, H. C., Kazdin, A. E., Offord, D. R., Kessler, R. C., Jensen, P. S., & Kupfer, D. J. (1997). Coming to terms with the terms of risk. *Archives of General Psychiatry*, 54(4), 337–343. doi:10.1001/archpsyc.1997.01830160065009

Langhinrichsen-Rohling, J., McCullars, A., & Misra, T. A. (2012). Motivations for men and women's intimate partner violence perpetration: A comprehensive review. *Partner Abuse*, 3(4), 429–468. doi:10.1891/1946–6560.3.4.429

Laskey, P. (2016). Systematic review of female perpetrators of intimate partner violence and their treatment. *Journal of Applied Psychology and Social Science*, 2(1), 62–88.

Lehmann, C. A. S. P. & Simmons, C. A. (2009). Strength-based batterer intervention: A new direction with a different paradigm. In Lehmann, C. A. S. P. & Simmons, C. A. (Eds) *Strengths-based batterer intervention: A new paradigm in ending family violence* (pp. 39–52). Chicago: Springer.

Levesque, D. A., Gelles, R. J., & Velicer, W. F. (2000). Development and validation of a stages of change measure for men in batterer treatment. *Cognitive Therapy and Research*, 24(2), 175–199. doi:10.1023/A:1005446025201

Mackay, J., Bowen, E., Walker, K., & O'Doherty, L. (2018). Risk factors for female perpetrators of intimate partner violence within criminal justice settings: A systematic review. *Aggression and Violent Behavior*, 41, 128–146

Macy, R. J., Rizo, C. F., Guo, S., & Ermentrout, D. M. (2013). Changes in intimate partner violence among women mandated to community services. *Research on Social Work Practice*, 23(6), 624–638. doi:10.1177/1049731513490810

Maiuro, R. D. & Eberle, J. A. (2008). State standards for domestic violence perpetrator treatment: Current status, trends, and recommendations. *Violence and Victims*, 23(2), 133–155.

McGuire, J. (2000). *Cognitive behavioural approaches: An introduction to theory and research*. London: HMIC/HMIP/Home Office.

Miller, W. R. & Rollnick, S. (2012). *Motivational interviewing: Helping people change*. Guilford Press.

Murphy, C. M., Linehan, E. L., Reyner, J. C., Musser, P. H., & Taft, C. T. (2012). Moderators of response to motivational interviewing for partner-violent men. *Journal of Family Violence*, 27, 671–680. doi:10.1007/s10896–10012–9460–9462

Musser, P. H., Semiatin, J. N., Taft, C. T., & Murphy, C. M. (2008). Motivational interviewing as a pre-group intervention for partner-violent men. *Violence and Victims*, 23, 539–557.

Nowinski, S. N. & Bowen, E. (2012). Partner violence against heterosexual and gay men: Prevalence and correlates. *Aggression and Violent Behavior*, 17(1), 36–52. doi:10.1016/j.avb.2011.09.005

Office for National Statistics. (2016) [Government report]. Retrieved from: www.ons.gov.uk/peoplepopulationandcommunity/crimeandjustice/compendiuc/focusonviolentcrimea ndsexualoffences/yearendingmarch2015/chapter4intimatepersintimatepersonalviolenceand

Rohrbaugh, J. B. (2006). Domestic violence in same-gender relationships. *Family Court Review*, 44(2), 287–299. doi:10.1111/j.1744–1617.2006.00086.x

Saunders, D. G. (1996). Feminist-cognitive-behavioral and process-psychodynamic treatments for men who batter: Interaction of abuser traits and treatment models. *Violence and Victims*, 11, 393–414.

Smith, K., Flatley, J., Coleman, K., Osborne, S., Kaiza, P., & Roe, S. (2010). *Homicides, Firearms Offences and Intimate Violence 2008/09 (Home Office Statistical Bulletin 01/10)*. London: Home Office

Straus, M. A. (1979). Measuring intrafamily conflict and violence: The conflict tactics (CT) scales. *Journal of Marriage and the Family*, 41(1), 75–88.

Straus, M. A. (2004). Women's violence toward men is a serious social problem. In Gelles, R. J. & Loseke, D. E. (Eds) *Current controversies on family violence* (2nd ed., pp. 55–77). Newbury Park: Sage Publications

Straus, M. A. (2008). Dominance and symmetry in partner violence by male and female university students in 32 nations. *Children and Youth Services Review*, 30(3), 252–275. doi:10.1016/j.childyouth.2007.10.004

Straus, M. A., Hamby, S. L., Boney-McCoy, S., & Sugarman, D. B. (1996). The revised conflict tactics scales (CTS2) Development and preliminary psychometric data. *Journal of Family Issues*, 17(3), 283–316. doi:10.1177/019251396017003001

Taft, C. T., Murphy, C. M., King, D. W., Musser, P. H., & DeDeyn, J. M. (2003). Process and treatment adherence factors in group cognitive-behavioral therapy for partner violent men. *Journal of Consulting and Clinical Psychology*, 71, 812–818. doi:10.1037/0022–006X.71.4.812

Tutty, L. M., Babins-Wagner, R., & Rothery, M. A. (2006). Group treatment for aggressive women: An initial evaluation. *Journal of Family Violence*, 21(5), 341–349. doi:10.1007/s10896–10006–9030–9036

Tutty, L. M., Babins-Wagner, R., & Rothery, M. A. (2009). A comparison of women who were mandated and nonmandated to the "responsible choices for women" group. *Journal of Aggression, Maltreatment & Trauma*, 18(7), 770–793. doi:10.1080/10926770903249777

Walters, M. L., ChenJ., & Breiding, M. J. (2013). *The national intimate partner and sexual violence survey (NISVS): 2010 Findings on victimization by sexual orientation.* Atlanta, GA: National Center for Injury Prevention and Control, Centers for Disease Control and Prevention.

White, J. W., Smith, P. H., Koss, M. P., & Figueredo, A. J. (2000). Intimate partner aggression: What have we learned? Comment on Archer (2000). *Psychological Bulletin*, 126 (5), 690–696. doi:10.1037/0033–2909.126.5.690

Zarling, A., Lawrence, E., & Marchman, J. (2015). A randomized controlled trial of acceptance and commitment therapy for aggressive behavior. *Journal of Consulting and Clinical Psychology*, 83(1), 199–212. doi:10.1037/a0037946 10.1037/a0037946

10

RAISING AWARENESS AND IMPROVING SERVICES FOR MALE VICTIMS OF ABUSE

Reflections on a three-year development project in Scotland

Nick Smithers

Introduction

Abused Men in Scotland (AMIS) is a small charity which runs a helpline for men, or women worried about men, in abusive relationships. For three years the Scottish Government funded a development post to raise awareness of men's experience with the hope of improving mainstream service response to the problem. The aim of this chapter is to reflect on those three years in the hope of encouraging wider consideration of changes that might improve approaches to domestic abuse for men, women, and families.

The experience of trying to improve services for men was characterised by frustration at barriers to progress, which at times seemed insurmountable. The organisational barriers, which shall be described in the following, mirrored those faced by men I met and spoke with who were suffering in, at times, acutely dangerous relationships. A common theme that men described was a sense of isolation and a belief that their experience was uniquely unusual. Men tended to believe their situation was not domestic abuse; they often did not realise it could be. The common perception is that domestic abuse is gendered and only women can be victim. A perception fuelled by the rhetoric of domestic abuse identified by Donovan and Hester (2009) that it is a crime perpetrated by heterosexual men against their partners.

While at AMIS I received the following email from one man, John:[1]

> I have also just been on your AMIS website. Sadly my situation seems to tick almost every single box – I find it uncanny to read. I have to use this new email address, and only use the office phone and computer or internet cafe / hotel / airport lounges as my wife checks the webmail server of my normal 2 email addresses, checks all my phone records, my internet history,

my banking – she has all my passwords so can go on line – she will not let me use or carry my mobile phone even at home when out of earshot of her – say letting the dogs out at night ... She word searches my computers at the office and home and she searches my memory sticks.

John was in an abusive relationship of many years standing and embodied the challenges of many male victims who feel similarly trapped. John did not initially approach the organisation of his own volition. His sister had sought help and approached AMIS for advice on her brother's behalf. A meeting was arranged and when I sat down in a café with this proud, ex-military man he described a campaign of control and violence at the hands of his wife which would be familiar to anyone who has studied the dynamics of abusive relationships. He broke down in tears under the weight of telling his story for the first time. Like many men suffering domestic abuse he remains in his marriage counting the days until the next attack. Many may wonder why he does not just leave; the following piece of writing may go some way to explain his difficulty:

> She just got angrier and angrier, called me an effing Dick, marched across room away from me, turning, stamped her feet, pointed at me and then the floor in front of her, and demanded that I come over and tell her I adore her etc... then there was a barrage of hatred from her "I hate you, I hate you...."...[children] pulled blankets over themselves, then [daughter] cried and [son] headed up to his room crying – I quietly told her she had completely disregarded her commitment to me of 48 hours earlier, and now had our stable 14 yr old son crying on his first evening home – I cried too – and went to his room where he and [daughter] were cuddled up together. Three of us blubbed – oh my god. I said to the children that this was so dreadful, I was so sorry – but they told me it was not my fault at all. I said that I could move out and rent somewhere local – to which they pleaded and pleaded for me to stay at home.

The reticence to seek help by many male victims led to involvement of family members, often female, who would phone or email our helpline. On one such occasion, a concerned sister contacted our service in dreadful worry about her brother who she was trying to get help for. When we wrote back after the weekend we were informed, tragically, that the man had killed himself.

There is a double barrier for abused men who need help. First, an inner barrier which is rooted in traditional masculine identity involving suppression of emotional distress, which can lead to self-harm and mental illness (Möller-Leimkühler, 2002). Second, there are external barriers where the situation arises that when men do seek help they find that there is nothing available.

Reflections on project development

My role at AMIS evolved from the presentation of a 15,000-name petition to the Scottish Executive calling for recognition for male victims of domestic abuse. The petition was instigated by men who had experienced abuse, and women who supported their campaign. The petitions committee of the Scottish Government accepted that the issue of domestic abuse against men was of sufficient gravity to require support, and an award of funds was made via the Equalities Unit to AMIS for a National Development Officer.

Equalities was never an easy fit for this project, and certain issues hampered the relationship of the Unit who oversaw the fund and the organisation. Equalities legislation looks to protect people from discrimination based on protective characteristics, one of which is "sex". The Equality Unit framed domestic abuse as Violence Against Women (VAW) or Gender Based Violence. So domestic abuse policy and funds were managed by the Equality Unit, as it was framed by the Government as an issue of gender inequality. The Scottish Government follow the UN line that "Domestic abuse is both a cause and consequence of gender inequality" (United Nations, 1992).

The difficulties that the project faced were highlighted during the early months where there were a number of concerning incidents. An example was brought to our attention at a parliamentary round table event which was hosted on AMIS's behalf by our constituency MSP. Prior to the event the MSP had received an email as follows:

Dear ******

I notice that you are hosting a reception for AMIS tonight and wanted to let you know, on behalf of the Gender-based Violence Network that some of AMIS arguments about male victims misrepresent the evidence. In particular:

*AMIS claim that men are victims of coercive control in the same way as women which is not possible as coercive control is a term coined by our recent visiting Professor Evan Stark to mean control of women by men in the context of gender inequality.

*AMIS claim the numbers reported to policy [sic] show 20% of victims are men, but as outlined in the briefing, the statistics often hide other patterns and indeed some of the men who appear as "victims" are in fact perpetrators of abuse.

*Some men experience abuse in couples where situational violence is common, but the appropriate framing and response to this kind of violence is radically different. It does not require refuge, and counselling approaches which would be dangerous in domestic abuse relationships could be appropriate here.

A link to our briefing which outlines these issues is here http://www.crfr. ac.uk/assets/briefing-69.pdf

Best Wishes,

****

Representing male victims was regarded as a threat to the ideological framing of domestic abuse which dominates policy and spending in Scotland. The national policy approach is well described in this one email – domestic abuse is coercive control, men cannot suffer coercive control ergo men cannot be victims of domestic abuse.

There were other examples of attempts to hinder the work of AMIS and this led to a difficult working environment as, repeatedly, the issue of domestic abuse was reduced to a zero-sum game where any recognition of male victimisation was regarded as a direct threat or attack on women's services. As an organisation, AMIS has always been clear that it does not dispute the higher prevalence of female victimisation, and the need for gender-specific service provision; the position remains that no funding should be drawn from women's services to create services for men. The literature review written by Dr Brian Dempsey (2014), on behalf of the organisation, sets out this position with clarity, but activist academics (as seen earlier) doggedly maintain a false characterisation of the organisational position.

Professor Stark's influence on Scottish Government policy is substantial. Scottish Women's Aid and the Gender Based Violence (GBV) Network proselytised his theories and writings as unchallengeable truth. Theory and research from the field of Forensic Psychology was treated as dangerous if it challenged the orthodox narrative.

Prior to a GBV conference in Edinburgh in 2014, there was a call to the AMIS office from a journalist at a leading daily broadsheet in Scotland. "I am calling to offer you a right to reply" the journalist said. A member of GBV network organising the conference had specifically highlighted the organisation AMIS as a critical reason for the need to maintain a gendered approach to the problem of domestic abuse. It had been argued that AMIS was dangerous because it makes false claims regarding the prevalence and underlying causes of domestic abuse. At the conference, Professor Stark named AMIS as a threat to the progress made by Women's Aid, and more generally the feminist approach to domestic abuse. At the time, with two employees and the only organisation in the country representing male victims, this felt disproportionate and tantamount to bullying.

The conference took a surreal turn when an activist on stage for a panel discussion said to the audience: "We've all had the epiphany, the challenge for us is to communicate that to everyone else out there who have not had the epiphany". This elusive epiphany points to the faith-like, intuitive approach which is taken to domestic abuse rather than a reflective, theoretically rigorous approach. The epiphany, my colleague and I surmised, related to the gendered analysis of domestic abuse and an awareness of "patriarchy" as the organising principle of society.

A final example to illustrate the hostile climate that existed for AMIS relates to a 2015 conference held in Edinburgh as a joint venture between Edinburgh University, AMIS, and Children in Scotland. There were various organisations and individuals presenting at the one-day event including Dr Elly Farmer of the Centre for Social Justice and Dr Nicola Graham-Kevan of University of Central Lancashire. It was Dr Graham-Kevan's keynote in the afternoon which caused some controversy. In a direct challenge to the evidence base of the Caledonian system (Scottish Government, n.d.), which is the Government-funded perpetrator programme in Scotland, Dr Graham-Kevan drew a furious response when she asked one representative for evidence of positive outcomes of the multi-million-pound programme; she was told that "admittedly we don't have a lot of evidence". The depressing aspect of this exchange was that Dr Graham-Kevan had presented evidence of a programme for domestic abuse perpetrators, Inner Strength, which had been designed based on clinically proven interventions, and evaluation of its efficacy was very promising (Forensic Psychological Solutions, n.d.).

This exchange characterised the fickle nature of the domestic abuse service sector. Rather than being encouraged by an example of effective practice, there was a defensive reaction. The aftermath of this was felt for a long time with partner agencies of AMIS being approached by influential members of the GBV network and lobbied to reconsider partnerships with the organisation.

Policy trajectory

To understand why there was such a hostile environment for men's service development it is important to consider the practice and policy context for domestic abuse service provision in Scotland. This context is shaped by the Scottish Executive (2000) definition:

> Domestic abuse (as gender-based abuse), can be perpetrated by partners or ex partners and can include physical abuse (assault and physical attack involving a range of behaviour), sexual abuse (acts which degrade and humiliate women and are perpetrated against their will, including rape) and mental and emotional abuse (such as threats, verbal abuse, racial abuse, withholding money and other types of controlling behaviour such as isolation from family or friends).

This definition is ambiguous, and is embellished in the original document setting out the Executive strategy which makes the case explicitly that while men do suffer domestic abuse the extent is not sufficient to warrant any strategy or related funding. The justification for this position was made by citing research commissioned and carried out by Gadd, Farrall, Dallimore, and Lombard (2002) which has been criticised on methodological grounds, specifically that the sample size was small and men were interviewed in presence of their wives or partners (Dempsey, 2014). The Executive decision to focus solely on domestic abuse as an example of a global phenomenon of Violence Against Women (VAW) is supported by UN directives and strategy. This places domestic abuse in the context of violence against women, alongside other crimes and perceived oppressions, such as commercial sexual exploitation and female genital mutilation. In Scotland, these are grouped together in strategy and policy terms as GBV. The document which followed the initial strategy set out a Prevention agenda and embellished the earlier case for the decision to focus solely on women as victims (Scottish Executive, 2006):

In spite of the wealth of research evidence underlining the gendered nature of domestic abuse/violence against women, there is a **small but vocal** body of research and opinion which argues that women's violence against men is equivalent to, or even greater than, men's violence to women. Research commissioned by the Scottish Executive (published in July 2002), however, found that the incidence of domestic abuse against men in Scotland was at the level suggested by other sources such as the Scottish Police Forces' statistics and the Scottish Crime Survey 2000, ie little more than 6–7% of the total. The research also found that men's experiences of abuse were generally much less severe than women's and that men were less likely to be repeat victims or report feeling fearful in their own homes

The use of statistics here to justify a strategy which ignores male victimisation is undermined by the assertion in the strategy document that "At least a quarter to a third of all women in Scotland will experience domestic abuse at some point in their lives". This approximate estimate of women's experience of domestic abuse in the general population is drawn from the same general population surveys which indicate the higher levels of male victimisation, which the Executive described as "small but vocal". The Executive is effectively using population surveys such as the Scottish Crime and Justice Survey to support its narrative that domestic abuse is a gendered crime while dismissing the same source when it indicates high levels of male victimisation.

Policy and practice development throughout Scotland has continued to follow the pattern set out in 2000, at national and local levels. This is to be expected as the original strategy document places explicit expectations on Local Authorities as well as linking funding to outcomes within the Government policy. The Scottish Government in partnership with the Coalition of Scottish Local Authorities launched an updated strategy to combat domestic abuse within the broader context of Violence Against Women and Girls. The Strategy is titled *Equally Safe: Scotland's Strategy for Preventing and Eradicating Violence Against Women and Girls* (Scottish Government, 2014). As intimated earlier, the strategy goes beyond tackling domestic abuse to address "domestic abuse, rape and sexual assault; sexual harassment and intimidation at work and in public; stalking; commercial sexual exploitation such as prostitution, pornography and human trafficking; dowry-related violence; female genital mutilation (FGM); forced marriage; and so-called 'honour' based violence." Explicitly ambitious in scope, it remains the case that domestic abuse strategy is contained and funded from this workstream shared between the Equalities Unit and Justice Department of the Scottish Government; there are funds adding up to £19 million attached to this strategy which were managed by the VAW fund (£12 million) and £7 million additionally linked to Equally Safe being managed by the Justice Department.

The Equally Safe document cites the following definition:

Gender-based violence is a function of gender inequality, and an abuse of male power and privilege. It takes the form of actions that result in physical, sexual and psychological harm or suffering to women and children, or affront to their human dignity, including threats of such acts, coercion or arbitrary deprivation of liberty, whether occurring in public or private life.

It goes on to emphasise:

This is not to suggest that all men are violent. To be clear, the majority of men are not violent. Nor is it to deny that women use violence or that men use violence against men, including male partners. But evidence shows that men commit the vast majority of violent crimes and sexual offences. During 2012–13 alone, there were 60,080 incidents of domestic abuse recorded by the police in Scotland. Of these, **44,916 (80%) had a female victim and a male perpetrator**.

(Scottish Government, 2014)

While it is heartening that we are reminded that the majority of men are not violent, the statement itself betrays the dominant discourse of patriarchy which implies an inevitability of male violence, and is the core theory which underpins the strategies and services which follow. It is notable that while the GBV definition and scope of the policy relates to a wide range of behaviours, the focus remains on domestic abuse. It is also notable that from the original Scottish Executive document described earlier, the proportion of male victims has risen from 6–7% to 20% of police incidents. The original document used these figures as a justification to focus strategy and funding on services specifically for women and children (or women and girls as the new document specifies). This raises questions about the validity of the Government research data and the decision to dismiss as "small but vocal" a large body of research data which may shed light on a phenomenon which by its nature remains obscured from public view. The rise in numbers of male victims coming to the attention of the police measured against population survey data suggests an uncovering of a hitherto hidden aspect of the phenomenon but also highlights the controversy over gender differences in partner violence. Winstok (2013) suggests the controversy cannot be resolved as "it stems from differing and competing paradigmatic outlooks, which disagree over the identification, definition, and understanding of domestic violence" (p. 399). The apparently competing paradigms are manifest in the policy and practice approach evident in Scotland and through the Scottish Government's framing of the issue, which is able to adapt the rationale despite significant empirical change in data relating to gender of victims. The fact that the number of men identified as victims has continued to increase in the midst of a uniquely gendered approach to the problem is in itself hugely significant.

To emphasise the chosen paradigm of the Scottish Government, Equally Safe goes on to state: "Evidence also shows that the tactics of coercive control – behaviour that seeks to strip away the victim's freedom and sense of self – are rooted in gender inequality, roles and assumptions" (Scottish Government, 2014). The document does not in itself cite the evidence which shows this to be the case, but the two theorists who are commonly cited and have presented their analysis in Scotland are Evan Stark and Michael Johnson. Stark's (2009) framing of domestic abuse as *Coercive Control* is very influential and has been the driving force in legislative developments which have sought to define the crime of domestic abuse as being characterised by a pattern of controlling behaviour. Johnson's typology similarly seeks to distinguish domestic abuse as a pattern of controlling behaviour from discrete incidents. Johnson and Stark both maintain that coercive control is uniquely gendered and a manifestation of societal gender inequality. This analysis is the rationale for a gendered approach to the problem of domestic abuse, and the decision to address domestic abuse as Violence Against Women and co-locate it alongside other distinct crimes or phenomena such as Female Genital Mutilation or commercial sexual exploitation.

Services in Scotland

So, what do services look like on the ground around the country? Following the Scottish Government strategy and associated funding, the Scottish local authority areas' domestic abuse services tend to be led by a VAW officer who coordinates local programmes. These officers form a national VAW network which regularly meets and is overseen by an officer employed by the Scottish Government. This very arrangement created barriers to initiate improvements in the provisions for men at a local level, as the aim of providing targeted services for men is often perceived as either not the role of the VAW partnership, or regarded as being satisfactorily addressed by generic services such as social work, police, housing, or drug and alcohol partnerships. A vicious circle is created whereby the generic services will collectively agree that there is a need to target services for men suffering domestic abuse, but any initiative is by necessity channelled through the VAW partnership which is unwilling or unable to prioritise action. The concern under this arrangement is that any costs attached to a service for men will be taken from services currently allocated to women. The reality is, however, that many of the VAW officers are also responsible for the men in their area; the paradigmatic tension causes a paralysis, and as an organisation providing and campaigning for men's services AMIS was frequently framed in opposition to women's services.

In order to scope services in Scotland, I initially carried out an internet search for domestic abuse services for men in each of 32 local authority areas. The results of this were unsurprising in that there were no targeted services for men available in any area other than Edinburgh, which is the Men's Domestic Abuse Support Service (MDASS), an AMIS project in partnership with Rowan Alba. Otherwise many authorities would direct people either to the AMIS helpline (based in Edinburgh but servicing the country), or the Respect helpline in London. As a follow up, the Women's Aid projects were contacted to explore where they would direct people who were looking for help for men as some local authority websites instructed them as a first contact for men looking for help. Again, understandably most projects in Scotland would direct to AMIS; although one suggested a sexual health clinic, and a number described White Ribbon (a campaign group addressing men's violence against women), some also described the Caledonian Project which is a programme for male domestic abuse perpetrators. Staff members within women's support services are not sure about where men can get support as the reality is that there are typically no services available other than generic support.

Multi-Agency Risk Assessment Conference (MARAC)

In the UK, high risk cases are managed by the MARAC process which is designed to ensure that victims at high risk are not being left without a service. It is a regular meeting of relevant professionals who discuss each referred case, and ensure that the person involved has a coordinated safety plan. Each coordinator was written to and asked the proportion of male victims discussed at MARAC, and any concerns that were held about services for men. Numbers of men being discussed at MARAC are very small and stand at around the 3% mark of the total, despite police incidents recording total male victims at 20%. In England and Wales the figure is slightly higher at around 5%, however the coordinating body Equally Safe are concerned by the low numbers – they estimate that there should be 5–10% of male victims although the method for arriving at this figure is unknown.

At a workshop to explain the development of MARAC in Scotland the development officer described the task of MARAC as "murder prevention". The statistics for intimate partner homicide over a ten-year period from 2004–15 show a total of 140 homicides of which 44 had a male victim, 40 of which were killed by a woman, four by a man. So in Scotland, approximately one in three domestic murder victims over the past ten years are men yet the "murder prevention" services are not working with men.

A number of the MARAC coordinators stated that they felt that targeted services would increase the number of referrals and access to support for men. A person who provides advocacy for MARAC referrals described working with a male victim:

> … to hear a male saying he was in real fear, he was petrified, real fear you know. I'm not sure what we could do as a service to get them through the door apart from maybe letting more people know … because I think it must be awful when you're in that sort of situation and you're seeing all these services for women and even if you could get yourself to a service it's about getting yourself through that door to begin with, which is really so important and if there's no services out there for them or there's a shortage of its very, very difficult …

Elsewhere regional coordinators of MARAC variously expressed the view that men would benefit from tailored services to increase access to support and justice. The Kingdom Abuse Project in Fife receive a limited amount of money to support men affected by domestic abuse who are referred to MARAC, as well as men who may not reach the risk threshold required for referral. In conversation with the manager, she said that there had been a significant rise in men referred since the turn of 2016, but that the project specialises in providing counselling to people who have suffered childhood sexual abuse, and that they do not have the capacity to provide ongoing support to men who are in abusive relationships so tend to try to refer on to other services. Obviously, the lack of specialised services for men is a significant issue. As the respondent there said: "What's offered to men isn't enough". The expectation is that men will be supported by generic services as there is no equivalent to Women's Aid available to support men, and callers to AMIS often reported a sense of helplessness in knowing where and how to get help.

Local funding priorities

In order to collate figures for spend on domestic abuse services broken down by gender, I made Freedom of Information requests in order to assess a range of information related to Government business. Of 32 local authorities which were asked for information, 23 responses were received within the required timeframe of 20 days.

Of the total core local authority funds which are provided to domestic abuse services of £7,998,248, from the 20 authorities that responded there was only £24,191 spent directly on services which supported men experiencing domestic abuse; both of which were Victim Support Scotland services. Some of the local authorities described additional block grants received from the Scottish Government VAWG fund which they distributed; some of these services support men but this only involved directly targeting men by including them on leaflets. Often this inclusion was set with the caveat that women were overwhelmingly the victims, and as such emphasised the rhetoric that could lead to inhibit male victims further.

In summary, there are no services funded by local or central government designed to support men in Scotland. This means that even for men referred to MARAC there are no specialised supports available for long-term support. Men are assumed to be provided for by mainstream services which are evidently deemed unable to meet their needs. As Hine (2017) explains, men have some good reasons not to seek support from generic services because on the rare occasion that they do they are unlikely to be believed or to receive appropriate help. Stereotyped attitudes impede an informed intervention and the prevailing gendered approach to the issue inhibits professionals from understanding the needs of abused men.

Training

Beyond direct support service provision, VAW funding is provided to organisations such as Scottish Women's Aid, Zero Tolerance, White Ribbon, and Engender who provide training and output publicity campaigns to educate and raise awareness about domestic abuse. These organisations present the issue uniformly as a gendered issue perpetrated by men against women.

On three separate occasions, nursing students contacted AMIS to raise concerns about training provided on domestic abuse with one describing their session in university as a "witch hunt against men". When AMIS attempted to follow up and offer to provide training input we were turned down as training provision was centrally provided, by the GBV team.

We were sent the following email by a school pupil from Kilmarnock:

> … as a pupil I see that the female students get a lot more representation for domestic abuse in our school as the school invite people in to speak to the girls/young women about their experiences and support workers to speak to them. This has been noticed by me and my friend Michael who both believe that the male population in our school are not given the same opportunities within our school this is quite clear when you look that the female population have had 5 chats over this year when you compare the male population have had none, when Michael confronted a teacher who he thought could help as she organised the young women's chats she says she was not going to put herself out so Michael and me have decided to do it ourselves.

AMIS provided input to the school pupils and it was enthusiastically received. Sadly, the initiative of the boys in this school was notable, and the opportunity to present a different perspective was the exception.

The feedback loop

A 2015 Scottish Government consultation for a forthcoming domestic abuse legislation highlights a feedback loop between activists, politicians, and practitioners (Scottish Government, 2016). This has the impact of maintaining and strengthening barriers to the development of diverse, evidence-informed services and ultimately to men getting help and also many women getting appropriate help.

The report of the consultation responses described a strong consensus for the legislation to be gendered and reflect the "gendered analysis of domestic abuse". The responses can be understood in the context of a policy-led environment which is biased towards a specific theoretical analysis, while excluding competing theories and research, regardless of the rigour. This can be exemplified by a look at the application form for funds from the Scottish Government VAW fund.

In order to qualify to receive financial support from the fund, organisations must provide evidence of their adherence to the gendered analysis of domestic abuse. The implications of this are that any organisation which may prefer to approach the issue as being characterised or driven by different motives or explanatory factors will not receive funds no matter how successful or well evidenced their approach is shown to be. The result is a service landscape which is forcibly committed to a uni-causal understanding to what is a complex, multi-factorial problem. The organisations who receive Executive funding are networked and coordinated, which may explain the number of responses to the consultation which argued for a gendered law. That is, the law would explicitly be for the crime of violence against women rather than a crime of domestic abuse regardless of the sex or gender of complainant. It is difficult to understand the benefit of creating such a law to explicitly exclude male victims, but the prevalence of the request suggested that there had been strenuous networking going on in order to bring influence to bear on the government; indeed, the consultants who analysed the responses simply noted that there was a high proportion of expert opinion in favour of a specifically gendered law. Thankfully the Justice committee, responsible for scrutinising and introducing the legislation, heeded the evidence provided by AMIS as well as the Victim Support organisation which, in a closed session, had supported male victims to provide testimonials of their experience. The proposed legislation created a domestic abuse offence was not gendered (Domestic Abuse (Scotland) Bill, 2017).

Impact of service scarcity

The Scottish Government Equally Safe strategy was updated in 2018 and now states that: "[Men] are also entitled to support when they experience violence and abuse" (Scottish Government, 2018). While this is a welcome statement from the Government, the previous evidence suggests that there remain significant barriers to men getting help and significant gaps in the service landscape which are preventing men from accessing support.

The prevalence of male victimisation has been contested for many years and is likely to be for years to come, but a combination of data sources provides us with an understanding that this is a problem of sufficient gravity to require a clear and explicit effort to address. The results of an online search indicate how difficult it could be for men to identify that there is support available. The MARAC numbers tell us that the system designed to reduce risk for domestic abuse victims is underrepresented by men. When we look beyond these numbers at the service landscape it is understandable, as there are no bespoke services available for men in any area of Scotland other than MDASS in Edinburgh.

The gender-inclusive services which do exist provide support to male and female domestic abuse victims, but designed as they are for high risk cases and linked to the MARAC process, they are working with similarly low numbers of men. These services are designed for short-term crisis intervention and rely on appropriate support being available to refer clients on for long-term recovery, but a tailored men's service does not exist. This will not change significantly until there are wider efforts made to develop and target services for men.

The experience of men suffering domestic abuse in this context is lonely and traumatic. For such men, there are two barriers to getting help: first, internally in the sense of shame which can inhibit them from seeking help; and second, externally – if a man decides to seek help he either does not know where to look, or is not believed.

As one respondent said

> I was looking for help but didn't know where to go, nobody was able to do anything. I described what was happening to my GP but he said he couldn't do anything unless [the perpetrator] came along herself. I didn't see myself as a victim and the situation escalated. The police, paramedics, GPs, mental health services were all a waste of time – nobody wants to help.

and

> It's difficult for a man to overcome the macho image. But then if he tries to get help he is turned away because he's a man, the other way, for women there's no questions asked. No-one wants to open their eyes to the problem – you just get on with it. It's like how it was for women in the past, you suffer in silence and just put up with it. There's certainly no equality

Conclusion

Felson (2014) argues that the study of gender and violence is characterised by two incompatible activities, science and activism. With a focus on terminology, he emphasises that a scientific approach should avoid activist language which will tend to exaggerate that which one wants to emphasise, rather than portray a more accurate description. It is this activist dominated approach to Violence Against Women which has marginalised consideration of male victims. This approach has been institutionalised and has resulted in a narrow field of inquiry and limitations on theoretical influence on practice development. This is certainly a serious problem for men who suffer abuse but it is also a problem for women as a uni-causal approach is likely to be limited in efficacy.

There is a growing body of evidence which describes coercive control as it is experienced by men whether that be from a male or female partner (e.g. Corbally, 2014; Fjell, 2015). Johnson's control theory has been compellingly challenged at least to raise questions as to its reliability (Bates & Graham-Kevan, 2016). The ever-increasing body of work adds depth to our understanding, but there is a continuing unwillingness to fully accept the extent to which men experience domestic abuse and controlling behaviour which is unethical, and dangerous.

If the suffering of men and boys is to be recognised and addressed it will require a political effort to rethink policy and funding priorities as well as practice developments. There is no good reason to imagine that this would damage current services designed to support women and children; on the contrary, widening the theoretical perspective and applying evidence informed principles can only enhance the sector as a whole.

I have been working for the past year in family social work, and this has provided further insight into the practice of working with families impacted by domestic abuse. This experience has added weight to a conviction that the issue must be addressed as a complex whole, informed by best evidence rather than the activist led approach which currently dominates. The prevalent idea of patriarchal control as uniquely influential in the motivations and context of abuse is intensely limited, and limiting in application. The reality in the practice of social work and policing is family violence taking place influenced by adverse childhood experience, alcohol and/or substance misuse, mental illness, personality disorder, and poverty. While gender roles play a significant part, it is not a definitive one.

Domestic Abuse policy and practice suffers from the reification of one idea, seeing patriarchy as the sole cause of domestic abuse. This reification directly leads to the marginalisation of male victims and an inadequate approach to domestic abuse which cannot succeed in its aim of eradicating the problem. Gender activists deliberately conflate the issue of domestic abuse to be something that "is the cause and the consequence of gender inequality". This catchphrase of the GBV network was oft repeated in public and in the media, and leaves no space for male victims, female perpetrators, or the thousands of children trapped with chaotic abusive parents who do not fit the simplistic model.

A project which at its outset seemed straightforward, in that there are significant numbers of male victims with no service provision, turned out to be anything but. While many individual practitioners and politicians agreed with the principle of improved provision, any progress was bogged down in an ideological and political morass. The Executive decision to treat domestic abuse as an issue caused exclusively by gender inequality has itself created an equality issue for the significant numbers of men suffering abuse. Addressing this situation requires bold, decisive action from politicians to support a theoretically diverse sector; unfortunately the current vicious cycle described here makes this outcome unlikely.

Note

1 Name changed to protect anonymity.

References

Bates, E. A. & Graham-Kevan, N. (2016). Is the presence of control related to help-seeking behavior? A test of Johnson's assumptions regarding sex differences and the role of control in intimate partner violence. *Partner Abuse*, 7(1), 3–25. doi:10.1891/1946-6560.7.1.3

Corbally, M. (2014). Accounting for intimate partner violence: A biographical analysis of narrative strategies used by men experiencing IPV from their female partners. *Journal of Interpersonal Violence*, 30(17), 3112–3132. doi:10.1177/0886260514554429

Dempsey, B. (2014). Men's experience of domestic abuse in Scotland: What we know and how we can know more. Abused Men in Scotland, 2013. Retrieved from: http://tinyurl.com/qaajgng (Accessed 19 April, 2016).

Domestic Abuse (Scotland) Bill [As Introduced]. (2017). Retrieved from: www.parliament.scot/Domestic%20Abuse%20Scotland%20Bill/SPBill08S052017.pdf (Accessed 27 November, 2017).

Donovan, C. & Hester, M. (2009). 'I hate the word "victim"': An exploration of recognition of domestic violence in same sex relationships. *Social Policy and Society*, 9(2), 279–289. doi:10.1017/S1474746409990406

Felson, R. (2014). Back to basics: Gender and the social psychology of aggression. In Gartner, R. & McCarthy, B. (Eds) *The Oxford handbook of gender, sex and crime* (pp. 77–97). Oxford University Press.

Fjell, T. I. (2015). Discrimination of men? Narratives on traditional understanding of gender. *Studia Ethnologica Croatica*, 27, 363–391.

Forensic Psychological Solutions. (n.d.) Retrieved from: www.forensicps.co.uk/ (Accessed on 23 May, 2018).

Gadd, D., Farrall, S., Dallimore, D., & Lombard, N. (2002). *Domestic abuse against men in Scotland*. Scottish Executive Central Research Unit.

Hine, B. (2017). Challenging the gendered discourse of domestic violence: Comments on the Istanbul Convention. Published as part of the 'Gifted Women, Fragile Men' EUROMIND Monographic Series, European Parliament.

Möller-Leimkühler, A. M. (2002). Barriers to help-seeking by men: a review of sociocultural and clinical literature with particular reference to depression. *Journal of Affective Disorders*, 71, 1–9.

Scottish Executive. (2000). Scottish partnership on domestic abuse: National strategy to address domestic abuse in Scotland. Retrieved from: www.gov.scot/resource/doc/158940/0043185.pdf (Accessed 19 April, 2016).

Scottish Executive. (2006). Preventing domestic abuse: A national strategy. Retrieved from: www.gov.scot/Publications/2003/09/18185/26440 (Accessed 25 May, 2018).

Scottish Government. (n.d.). The Caledonian system: An integrated approach to address men's domestic abuse and to improve the lives of women, children and men. Retrieved from: www.gov.scot/Topics/People/Equality/violence-women/CaledonianSystem (Accessed 12 October, 2016).

Scottish Government. (2014). Equally safe: Scotland's strategy for preventing and eradicating violence against women and girls. Retrieved from: www.gov.scot/Resource/0045/00454152.pdf (Accessed 19 April, 2016).

Scottish Government. (2016, 9 September). Criminal offence of domestic abuse analysis of consultation responses. Retrieved from: www.gov.scot/publications/criminal-offence-domestic-abuse-analysis-consultation-responses/

Scottish Government. (2018, 25 April). Equally safe: Scotland's strategy to eradicate violence against women. Retrieved from: www.gov.scot/publications/equally-safe-scotlands-strategy-prevent-eradicate-violence-against-women-girls/pages/3/

Stark, E. (2009). *Coercive control: How men entrap women in personal life*. New York: Oxford University Press.

United Nations. (1992). *Statement on the elimination of violence against women*. Geneva, United Nations.

Winstok, Z. (2013). What can we learn from the controversy over the role of gender in partner violence? *Partner Abuse*, 4(3), 399–412. doi:10.1891/1946–6560.4.3.399

11

CHILDHOOD EXPERIENCES OF DOMESTIC VIOLENCE AND ADULT OUTCOMES

Where are we now: challenges, debates, and interventions?

Julie C. Taylor

Introduction

The impetus for this chapter was a longitudinal study with adult women who had been convicted of an offence and were serving community orders. The research focus was social exclusion, exploring the potential of nature-based work to enhance connectedness. However, as the participants narrated their stories the depressing regularity with which their childhood experiences of domestic violence (DV) were referenced prompted significant reflection on my part. I had already been aware from the criminal justice literature that the rate of childhood adversity in the female "offender" population was high. The body of evidence pointed to an accumulation of disadvantage across a lifetime as opposed to individual pathology or specific deficits (Moffit & Caspi, 2001). Maltreatment and victimisation in their pre-offending lives reportedly serving as the catalyst (Postmus, Severson, Berry, & Yoo, 2009; Severson, Berry, & Postmus, 2007). The evidence suggested that these disadvantages interacted in complex and mutually reinforcing ways (Levitas et al., 2007), ways that served to seriously restrict the women's opportunities to desist from crime (Moffit & Caspi, 2001; Weaver & McNeill, 2010; McNeill, Farrall, Lightowler, & Maruna, 2012).

Despite this, previous studies rarely specified the nature of abuse and victimisation, and so the role of DV had been muted. In gathering the data, hearing how DV had, apparently directly and indirectly, shaped their experiences reinforced my feelings of social injustice. The injustice of a system that can fail to identify a child as a victim but can, with astounding alacrity, apply the offender label when as adults they themselves transgressed. Whilst there is no suggestion here that professionals/services have been remiss in failing to identify victimisation, it seems reasonable to question why this has been the case and what the barriers to identification have been (Turner et al., 2017; Øverlien & Aas, 2016). Particularly when a review of the DV literature revealed a mounting body of evidence to suggest that living in a home where DV and abuse is present can lead to a number of mutually reinforcing negative outcomes (Øverlien, 2010; Callaghan, Fellin, Alexander, Mavrou, & Papathanasiou, 2017), including: difficulties with physical health (Bair-Merritt, Blackstone, & Feudtner, 2006), mental health (Gilbert, et al., 2009), managing emotions (Holt, Buckley, & Whelan, 2008; Peltonen, Ellonen, Larsen, & Helweg-Larsen, 2010), difficulties in social and intimate relationships (Siegel, 2013), problems at school or with education more broadly (Carrell & Hoekstra, 2010), and an increased probability of being convicted of an offence in adolescence or adulthood (Baglivio, Wolff, Piquero, & Epps, 2015; Fox, Perez, Cass, Baglivio, & Epps, 2015). The question arises as to why, given this evidence base, there is such a lag in professional service strategies for identification (Turner et al., 2017) and a corresponding dearth of attention being paid to interventions aimed at ameliorating the negative impacts of DV and abuse on children (Harold & Sellers, 2018).

In seeking answers to these questions, the complexity of the problem quickly became apparent. The child's longstanding obscurity within the system can, at least in part, be explained by the way children have been constructed as passive observers or witnesses to the violence and attributed a corresponding lack of agency by professionals and academics (Callaghan, Alexander, Sixsmith, & Fellin, 2016; Katz, 2015; Kimball, 2016). Whilst recognised by a number of eminent scholars in the field as highly significant, this construction is not the only reason children have been over-looked for such a long time (Callaghan et al., 2017; Øverlien & Aas, 2016). It is clear that researchers have faced challenges at each stage of the investigative process, from defining the problem, accessing participants, measuring the impact, and interpreting the findings (Callaghan et al., 2017; Katz, 2016; Kimball, 2016; Øverlien, 2017). Moreover, very little research has been conducted with the children themselves and so the voice of the child is largely absent (Callaghan et al., 2017; Kimball, 2016). These are significant hurdles and have slowed progress in the field. As a result, it is perhaps only in the last few years that the evidence has begun to mount in a way to suggest that specialised interventions to support children based on research "*with*" children should be a priority (Callaghan, 2015; Harold & Sellers, 2018; Katz, 2015).

In this chapter, I reflect on my experience of working on a project over a three-year period and consider the women's stories in relation to the themes identified in the literature. The experiences related by the participants largely concur with current theorising and evidence. However, unlike much of the literature, the participants in this study offer a retrospective phenomenological perspective on what it was like living in a violent and abusive family home.

Research context and primary themes

The research project that formed the basis for this reflection involved a number of stages and utilised a range of research methods all centred around a community work order and a group of adult women. The women had committed largely acquisitive offences and had been sentenced to attend a community work order.

These orders may be imposed for offences that are serious but not deemed so serious as to warrant custody, meaning the punishment is carried out in a community setting. The length of the order varied across participants depending upon the nature of the offence perpetrated and the number of previous convictions held. Our community work was mainly horticultural with some occasional opportunities to engage in conservation activities. The discussion that follows was largely prompted by conversations in the interview phase of the research but there are some additional elements from field notes recorded post interview. The aim of the interview phase was to find out how the participants made sense of the life events or circumstances that led to their offending behaviour. Seventeen adult women consented to be interviewed, 15 of whom were parents. The interview procedure was mostly unstructured and the subsequent prompts were largely unscripted; the participants were not directly asked about their experiences of DV or their coping styles, yet powerful themes around these issues were identified. The themes have been organised into two clusters: 1. *Barriers to identification:* Silence, secrecy, exclusion, and professionals, and 2. *Intervention needs:* Worthlessness and unrecognised skills. Where direct quotations have been included, pseudonyms have been ascribed.

1. Barriers to identification

Silence, secrecy, and exclusion

Somewhat unexpectedly, early childhood and subsequent adult experiences of DV featured heavily in the women's accounts of their offending. Whilst not narrated as a linear or causal route to offending, participants were reporting behaviours and circumstances that may be predicted to put them at a disadvantage from an early age. These included the use of strategies to avoid revealing their home situation to other people. Participants did not focus on specific incidents of abuse; they referred more frequently to how the abusive environment influenced their lived experiences as children. Reference was made to missing school for bogus reasons, trying to look after their mums or younger siblings, truanting, not being able to have friends home because they could not predict the mood or consequences, trying to avoid conflict, controlling their own feelings and behaviours, and engaging in risky activities such as drug taking and unprotected sex. Most of the behaviours described were intended to serve as coping mechanisms, but appeared to trigger an avalanche of unintended consequences. An example was the use of silence or invisibility; the decision to be very quiet, to go unnoticed at school; according to the participants, being quiet and well behaved was a way to keep the violence at home a secret. One participant explained that her fear of telling led to her isolation at school which, coupled with her anxiety about leaving her mum alone when she was at school, affected her ability to participate in her education. One consequence of this was that she became isolated and felt lonely, she was left out and bullied and fell behind with her work. Ultimately, as soon as she was able, she started to truant to escape from the isolation and bullying.

I just stopped going yeah, so I didn't get no qualifications I was . . . [long pause] . . . scared . . . **THEN** (voice emphasis taken to mean not any more) . . . scared that someone would find out and I would get taken away and put in prison . . . he . . . **he** used to say . . . I'd have to go to prison . . . and it would all be my fault.

[Anna]

Another participant, Ashleigh, described not having friends as easier to manage; she explained that as she got older and saw people going to each other's houses she realised nobody could ever come to her house, so it was easier not to be included. Ashleigh did concede that she wished she had stayed at school and engaged in her education; she could see as an adult what a disadvantage disengaging so early had been: "If I'dve stayed in school and not let home stuff make me feel like . . . you know . . . I was ok at school really, . . . not thick . . ." [Ashleigh].

In another account, a participant explained how her truancy had put her in close proximity to drugs and alcohol. She described how these made her feel better, by feeling less. However, it also led to her engaging in behaviours that put her at risk of exploitation and criminalisation. The account she gave of some of the things she had endured as a young teenager was harrowing to listen to, but from her perspective the emphasis was very much on the relief the drugs and alcohol had brought her. According to the participants' accounts, from an early age they were trying to respond to complex emotional worlds at home but in their effort to do this they found themselves socially isolated and unhappy; the tragedy is that these accounts are not uncommon (e.g. Byrne & Taylor, 2007). One participant went on to say that she could not understand, even now as an adult, how nobody at school had known or guessed what she was going through. This seems a reasonable question to ask but the findings from recent research suggest that professionals are still very poor at identifying domestic abuse despite the visibility of the safeguarding agenda (Turner at al., 2017).

I have several ineffaceable memories from this experience, including listening to the way the women made sense of their worlds: the descriptions of their feelings and behaviours as children when trying to manage their complex family and wider social relationships, and the behaviours they engaged in both within and outside the home to reduce the impact of the abuse on themselves, their mothers and for some, their siblings. Several authors have referred to such behaviours as precocious and attach what could be seen as negative labels and interpretations to them (e.g. premature *parentification*; Holden, 2003). Labels such as these problematise the behaviour and infer deficit.

Katz (2015) explained that in addition to deficits, these labels ascribe passivity to the child, for example, "a child may be **forced** to take on the role of a parent, end up doing the mother's chores, care for siblings and give advice, or comfort her after abuse has taken place" (Little & Kantor, 2002, p. 138). The use of the word *forced* may be true in some circumstances but not all. The women in my sample spoke in terms of their desire to reduce the impact and manage the tension within the home. Whilst it might be fair to say they would have wished for alternative family circumstances, there was no force involved. Perhaps, rather than constructing these behaviours as deficiencies they could just as easily be constructed as assets, signs of sophisticated empathy and care. Callaghan, Alexander, Sixsmith, and Fellin (2018) suggested just this and argued that behaviours such as these could be reframed in the context of strengths rather than weaknesses. They go on to say that the children are not just "damaged" by their experience of DV, the way they learn to navigate and manage the complexity of their developmental niche has the potential to produce a more resilient self.

The explanations of Katz (2015) and Callaghan et al. (2018) are consistent with the accounts shared by my participants. The coping and resilience they showed in the face of so much adversity was humbling, but was unfortunately coupled with an apparent inability to identify their own skills or worth. This is particularly troubling because as parents they appeared to have retained many of the coping strategies and self-beliefs they had developed as children. One example, that troubled me at the time, was a mother who said she never engaged with the school when her children were little, she did not walk them to school or collect them, did not attend parents' evening or any such activities. On prompting, I included a question about safety, she responded that if she went to the school *they* would know her partner hit her and would take the children away. To Jane, her participation in school activities was risky, her reluctance to engage was not a lack of care as it might be construed by others, rather it was precisely because she cared about her children that she could not take the risk of professional intervention:

JANE: I never went to school to get the kids and stuff, I ain't like them other mums right . . . I know it sounds stupid now . . . but I thought they would know like . . . like . . . that he hit me . . .

Jane reported feeling that the risks to the children were greater if she engaged with the school than if she did not. She revealed later that she had similarly tried to avoid talking to anyone outside of the home when she was a child because her father had told her that if anyone "found out" she would be taken away. This lack of engagement was generalised to all professional services and had debilitated her and prevented her from receiving support at several key points. For example, I asked her why she had not explained her circumstances to the magistrate when on a previous occasion the circumstances of her transgression were potentially mitigating, her response again demonstrated her lack of trust in others:

JANE: Then he'd have taken em away wouldn't he, you can't talk to these people Julie, they don't help us, they just take even more . . .

This lack of trust in professional services was not restricted to Jane, I asked Charlie a not dissimilar question and her response was equally as dismissive:

CHARLIE: People like me can't trust people, so like where you say have I talked to my probation officer as if they are there to help me, I don't see it like that, I see them as people you tell nothing, keep quiet keep your head down.

Professionals

The lack of trust in professional services was exemplified by the invocation of a "them" and "us" discourse. The "us" being used to refer to anyone who had similar experiences and were in similar predicaments to their own, the "them" was invoked, often in a derogatory way, to refer to professionals. This "othering", whilst typical across social settings (Barter-Godfrey & Taket, 2009), was a powerful indicator of a lack of belief in support services. A number of the participants reported persistent fears over losing their own children to local authority care if professional services became aware of the violence in their own relationships. It is on this issue that the perceived injustice reached a climax because there is considerable evidence to suggest their concerns may be founded; as children their plight went unnoticed, but as adults and parents themselves they are quite likely to be held responsible (Rhodes, Dichter, Kothari, Marcus, & Cerulli, 2011). Douglas and Walsh (2010) stated that society typically positions the woman as the parent with the responsibility to care for the children. A position that then situates the mother as blameworthy for any DV in the home and any consequent failures to protect the children are hers (Callaghan et al., 2018; Katz, 2015; Powell & Murray, 2008; Radford & Hester, 2006). This narrative produces several concerns including creating biases that may go on to inform professional service responses which in turn may inadvertently perpetuate the intergenerational transmission of abuse. If those charged with supporting families who are experiencing DV hold the mothers in some way responsible, then it may influence their professional response. If mothers believe that this is what professionals think and they have already been indoctrinated to believe it is their fault, then asking for help or reporting the abuse may become even less likely. The women in the sample already held conflicting, and at times paradoxical, beliefs based on their own childhood experiences, and these apparently intractable beliefs served as a significant barrier to help seeking and consequently identification.

The participants' inconsistent beliefs around identification of their abuse in childhood included a belief that the lack of adult intervention was largely attributable to their silence; however, they were simultaneously asserting that adults must have known and elected not to help them. The confusion experienced by participants when recounting their stories was palpable and without exception had left the women resolute in their view that professionals were untrustworthy and did not care. Several participants were clear that adults did know and just elected not to act, but at the same time engaged in behaviour to maintain their "family secret" believing that a failure to do so would have devastating ramifications. The thinking seemed "faulty" at first, but on reflection it was consistent with the incongruous messages they were receiving: the violent member/s of their homes were claiming that they would know if the child disclosed to anyone. For example, Josie said referring to her uncle who was in loco parentis at the time: "he said he would know if I talked . . . and he would kill me."

From an early age, children were being inculcated into believing that adults had a means to know what children were thinking and doing, and in some cases, participants reported that their parent/s were actively forbidding them to tell anyone about what was happening at home or there would be serious consequences. The flaw in the logic is obvious to the outsider; if adults knew everything, why was there such a powerful threat around revealing the secret, the adults would already know. However, as children, the participants who spoke in these terms did not connect the two. It is worth noting that a number of the women (in response to my prompts for further information) reported that both adults (victim and perpetrator) were telling them to keep the violence secret. The adults' motivations were assumed to be different though: the perpetrator to avoid sanction and the adult victim for fear of the child being taken into care. One participant, Camelia, reported that she had been a child victim of DV; when I asked if she had told anyone about her experiences, she said no. Camelia did not connect the lack of help she received with her non-disclosure. Camelia assumed that adults knew and did not care.

The thinking displayed by Camelia and others in the group appeared somewhat childlike on this topic but it is congruent with findings from several Theory of Mind (ToM) studies with maltreated children (Cicchetti, Rogosch, Maughan, Toth, & Bruce, 2003; Pears & Fisher, 2005). ToM is the ability to recognise that other people may hold different views, urges, and beliefs to the ones you are experiencing (Dunn, 1995). More specifically, False Belief understanding, "the ability to make inferences about what other persons believe to be the case in a specific situation" (Cicchetti et al., 2003; p. 1068). ToM is thought to develop in response to attachment style interactions in early childhood and it is argued that in violent and abusive homes the opportunity to engage in these interactions may be compromised (Koizumi, & Takagishi, 2014). If this compromise is coupled with a perpetrator working to inculcate an omnipotent persona, such that the victim believes that they can mind-read, then a disruption to their understanding of what can be known by others may be predicted (Sprung, 2008). This "omnipotent adult" construction may be precisely the image the abuser intends and so, whereas in a non-victimised individual this thinking may appear flawed or immature, it may be reasonable and rational where there have been experiences of DV (Sanderson, 2008). A victim's fear that their abuser will find out if they reveal their experiences to others is known to be a barrier to disclosure (Petersen, Moracco, Goldstein, & Clark, 2005), *believing* that they will *just know* perhaps more so. As children, the participants' understanding of the consequences of intervention by professionals was influenced by the threats made by the abusive adult; for example, the child would be taken away, sent to prison, punished. These powerful emotions had in several cases continued to influence their behaviour as adults and had reportedly affected the way they had gone on to support their own children.

Help seeking

Consistent with current thinking around the child's role in DV situations (e.g. Callaghan, 2015; Katz, 2015; Øverlien & Hyden, 2009), the participants' accounts suggested that as children they had made conscious choices to behave in particular ways in a bid to respond to their situations. They were active not passive. The participants' efforts to respond to the presence of violence in the home had produced short- and long-term, positive and negative effects. "Positive" in the sense that the violence remained secret, which was the participants' overriding priority, but also negative in the sense that many of the consequences made other aspects of their lives difficult. Whilst the participants did not state that the DV they experienced as children led to their current circumstances, it was clear that it had impacted on their engagement with school and had contributed to their exclusion more broadly.

The persistence of childhood coping strategies into adulthood was also noted, with many participants referencing similar strategies to manage violence in subsequent intimate relationships. The entrenchment and habituation of behavioural responses is not atypical (Ehrensaft, et al., 2003), and it may explain why patterns of behaviours that reduce the probability of detection or help-seeking persist. Whilst the experiences of the women explained their resistance as children, and subsequently in adulthood to disclose, it still leaves open the question of why their behaviour and demeanour did not attract attention from others.

Professional concerns

In the main, the participants who discussed their behaviour at school referred to *being quiet, being good, not being noticed,* and *trying to be invisible* as the strategies they used to help them keep the violence at home a secret. Coping strategies in this context are typically referred to as belonging to one of two categories: internalising or externalising strategies. In behavioural terms internalised coping might be displayed as withdrawing, experiencing high levels of anxiety and/or depression; and externalising coping referring to behaving aggressively or engaging in criminal conduct (Moylan et al., 2010). Either coping style can lead to negative outcomes because both can interfere with peer and other relationships, leading to social isolation and as a result inhibit opportunities to learn and develop (Gilliom, Shaw, Beck, Schonberg, & Lukon, 2002). There have been discussions in the literature pointing to a gender divide in coping styles over the years, with girls being more often associated with internalising and boys externalising strategies (Evans, Davies, & DiLillo, 2008; Graham-Bermann & Hughes, 2003) and this account would be consistent with the experiences described by my sample. However, on closer examination the picture is less clear; contemporary studies suggest that factors other than gender appear to mediate this relationship (Sternberg, Baradaran, Abbott, Lamb, & Guterman, 2006; Moylan et al., 2010). The evidence suggests that the age of the child, the type of exposure (Vu, Jouriles, McDonald, & Rosenfield, 2016), and the mother's psychological state and her parenting style (Zarling, et al., 2013) are all important factors when it comes to determining the response style of the child.

Regardless of the coping style adopted, the evidence suggests that internalising and externalising behaviours in childhood present detectable clues to a child's distress that may differ at different stages of development. The fact that they are not detected as frequently as they might be suggests additional barriers, which may reflect a deficiency in training amongst professionals (e.g. teachers, medical practitioners) or it may be even more fundamental than that (Lewis et al., 2017; Turner et al., 2017). A number of researchers and practitioners have argued that one of the major stumbling blocks is the way children have been constructed both within the literature, the policy, and quite possibly the public psyche when it comes to their role in the DV context (CAADA, 2014; Callaghan, 2015; Katz, 2015; Kimball, 2016; Stanley, Miller, & Richardson Foster, 2012).

Constructing the problem: the child's status in a DV context

The problem identified by several scholars and practitioners is two-fold (Callaghan et al., 2018; Katz, 2016; Mullender et al., 2002; Straus, Gelles, & Steinmetz, 2017). Traditionally the child is not positioned in a key role when the dialogue turns to DV, they have been positioned at the margins, neither the victim nor the perpetrator and so largely ignored; or if attended to, attended to alongside the mother as victim (Callaghan et al., 2017; Callaghan et al., 2018; Katz, 2015; Katz, 2016; Øverlien & Hyden, 2009). Whilst at first glance this seems to be a question of semantics, the chosen language perhaps reveals a set of assumptions that have profoundly impacted professional and societal responses to children living in DV contexts. If the differences between the words "victim" and "witness" are considered in the context of the criminal justice system, the problem becomes apparent. In legal situations witnesses tend to be called upon to give a "factual, as they see it account" of what they have observed, they present their account and are then typically released with little after care. The accounts required are typically associated with a specific incident as opposed to providing an account of living within a given context. A victim, by contrast, is considered to have been directly impacted by the events they describe and dependent upon the crime, and may be eligible for support, compensation, and intervention. The relevance of the use of language here is not therefore whimsical, it has quite express meaning and response implications. The work of a small number of scholars has helped to identify this problem and highlight the implications it may have had for children in DV settings. Their work has been highly influential but some inconsistency remains (e.g. Callaghan, 2015; Øverlien & Aas, 2016; Øverlien & Hyden, 2009).

Callaghan et al. (2018) argue that to construct the child as almost peripheral is a poor representation of their lived experience; it fails to acknowledge their role in the family and silences the many and varied ways in which they can and do experience the abuse. A peripheral role also suggests that any support for the children might be secondary to that required by the actual victim, the adult. In response to the concerns raised by academics and practitioners, the term *witness* has largely been replaced by the words *exposed to*, and whilst this may be better, it still constructs the child as passive. It implies that the children participate in the family until there is abuse and then they step aside somehow and wait for it to be over. This construction oversimplifies the violence for many households; the evidence suggests that children in violent homes are often both direct victims of abuse and observers of violence against other family members (Herrenkohl, Sousa, Tajima, Herrenkohl, & Moylan, 2008; Morris, 2009).

Moreover, this frames the violence and abuse as incidental as opposed to a persistent feature of the developmental niche. These complications have prompted a number of scholars to start referring instead to *children who experience* DV (Øverlien, 2010; Callaghan, et al., 2018). These academics argue that the concept of exposure implies that the violence punctuates the developmental niche in discrete episodes and that the child would be passive when it did. Interestingly, this model may represent the external observer's perspective but probably fails to capture the daily lived experience of those within the home. The external observer is only likely to be involved in response to specific events and so their perspective is likely to be created around these pivotal moments. For those living in the family, the abuse is likely to be persistent; it is unlikely to manifest as overt eruptions of violence and abuse on a continuous basis, but the threat presumably remains ubiquitous. Callaghan (2015) explained that when children live in violent contexts, they do not stand outside of the intimate partner dyad, they are triangulated within it, and through this process of triangulation they may be called upon to engage in a number of behaviours or may be used by one parent or the other in a variety of ways, such as to threaten, support perpetration, collude, and/or protect. The accounts given by the participants in my sample suggested they were active in the experience when inside the home by behaving in particular ways to manage the tension or in their responses to the overt abuse, for example, through seeking to protect their siblings or their mothers, and also outside the home in keeping the violence and abuse a secret.

One of the difficulties lies in the system which can only really manage a simple dichotomy of victim and perpetrator. Understandably, in a legal context clarity around roles is required but this binary thinking may cloud the nuances of family dynamics. This dichotomous thinking in police responses is exemplified by Richardson-Foster, Stanley, Miller, and Thomson (2012; p. 230): "Children were not a primary focus for police attention in that they were seen as neither the victim nor the perpetrator but were positioned outside the core dynamic of an incident". Whilst this dichotomy may serve utilitarian needs within the criminal justice, when applied more widely by professionals, it has the potential to minimise the experiences of those not the direct target of the violence in the moments being referred to. It may also serve to misdirect attention from the fact the individual incidences do not represent the lived realities of those living in violent contexts. One of the participants exemplified this when she explained how isolated she had felt as a child and that whilst isolation sometimes felt safe, it could also feel like disconnection or invisibility:

ANNA: I was kinda like invisible, you know, I don't remember anyone asking me if
    I was ok

This final point made by Anna highlights some of the additional problems that situating children at the periphery have produced: where children are positioned at the margins, nobody is necessarily seeing identification as critical to prevent harm, nobody is therefore asking what is happening for them and if identified nobody is factoring their experiences into the interventions offered (Katz, 2016; Munro, 2012; CAADA, 2014).

2. Intervention needs

Worthlessness and the obscurity of skills

The experiences of the small population of participants I was privileged to work with may not represent the most typical life trajectory for those living in violent homes as children, but their stories do resonate with emerging evidence. Their accounts of their childhood experiences and the legacy of these for their adult lives offer a powerful endorsement for demands to prioritise resources for children living in similar circumstances. The beliefs held by the participants consistently suggested they felt others perceived them as worthless: "college ain't for people **like me** I can't even afford to get there" [Camelia]. They also saw themselves as possessing few if any skills: "I aint got no skills, ha, well not one's people **like you** approve of, ha ha" [Ashleigh]l "I ain't good at nothing Julie . . . nothing . . ." [Jane].

However, the resources may not, as much of the literature would suggest (e.g. Bedi & Goddard, 2007; Clements, Oxtoby, & Ogle, 2008; Herrenkohl et al., 2008), necessarily be required to fix a deficit (Callaghan, Alexander, & Fellin, 2016; Katz, 2016). The work with this group of women supports contemporary thinking that children are not passive witnesses to the violence in their homes who only develop harmful behaviours in response to their experiences. The participants also exhibited skills, qualities, and resilience that, had they been identified and harnessed earlier, may have enabled them to make different choices in their adult lives (Katz, 2015; Letourneau, Fedick, & Willms, 2007; Øverlien & Hyden, 2009). The participants' perceptions that they had "no skills" and "little worth" is contrary to my interpretation of their resilience, empathy, capacity to endure, and commitment to their own children. However, the perceptions that they were unworthy of intervention and their lack of opportunities in the workplace (because of their low academic attainment) serves to reinforce their position. Earlier intervention may have enabled some of the skills to be identified and honed. One of the clearest messages from the research and the literature was that many of the strategies the women used to cope as children served to alienate and disconnect them from potentially positive influences and experiences. So, whilst these strategies served to keep them safe at home, they simultaneously detached them from possible sources of support. This disengagement in turn was described as serving to limit their opportunities, resulting in limited choices, often between "a rock and a hard place". The examples given by the participants may augment our understanding of the range of consequences and the nuances that serve to promulgate them.

The literature typically focuses upon the negative behaviours engaged in by the children and in so doing, fails to appreciate the sophistication of many of the behaviours children in these situations display. More recently, scholars have suggested that this deficit approach may serve to influence interventions in ways that are unhelpful in terms of meeting the child's needs. Callaghan (2015) points out that intentionally or otherwise traditional interventions may be guilty of victim blaming. A significant body of literature positions the responsibility of the child's health and well-being with the mother's quality of parenting and psychological functioning (Levendosky & Graham-Bermann, 2001; Levendosky, Leahy, Bogat, Davidson, & von Eye, 2006; Morris, 2009). Consequently, many interventions have historically focused on enhancing the parenting skills of the mother offering little or no support directly to the child (Letourneau et al., 2007; Sturge-Apple, Davies, Cicchetti, & Manning, 2010). Callaghan (2015) further notes that whilst compelling, the research upon which these conclusions have been drawn is largely quantitative and typically based on the victimised parents' reporting. Consequently, how the parent is rating their own and their child's behavioural responses is likely, given the tools available, to be based on incidences of violence as opposed to taking a more lived experience perspective (Kimball, 2016). It is also worth noting that when a victimised parent is reflecting on their own and their child's behaviour they are potentially doing so from a position of complex emotion and so behaviours may appear exaggerated or may be misattributed to the context of violence as opposed to relatively normal behaviours. Moreover, the researchers are positioning themselves as the experts, as opposed to appropriately attributing expertise to those who have experienced the violence. The response: parenting classes, either prescribed or mandated (Rhodes et al., 2011; Austin, Shanahan, Barrios, & Macy, 2017). It is perhaps a professional assumption that the complex relationships that the family members are likely to have negotiated and managed in response to the violence can be remediated by the application of parenting rules – rules developed by professionals whose expectations of behaviour within a family setting are likely to be based on rather different norms. This may account for the limited success of such interventions in ameliorating the negative impacts on children (Austin et al., 2017). It is also worth noting that assumption rather than the engagement with "experts" (e.g. the children) has been argued to be what has held children in the position of witness, or as Callaghan et al. (2018) described, "collateral damage", for decades.

In response to these conceptual and methodological concerns, contemporary researchers are advocating a more strength-based approach to intervention design, with a definitive call for research to be qualitative and focus on the child's experience. It is the child's voice and their experience of living within a context of violence that need to be more thoroughly explored.

Looking forward

In July 2018, the UK Home Office announced their commitment to supporting children who have experienced DV, stating that they were allocating £8 million to fund interventions. This is undeniably a positive step. However, given the estimated size of the problem, the extant challenges around identification and the child's voice being conspicuous by its absence, how best to allocate these funds and for what purpose presents as the next challenge. The Children's Commissioner's report (Longfield, 2018) estimated that in the region of 825,000 children in the UK are living in violent households; this is likely to be a conservative estimate given the role of silence and secrecy in the lives of those affected but it does give some indication of the scale of the problem. The announcement is pivotal; the problem and the extent of it has finally been acknowledged. It is now incumbent upon services and researchers to provide evidence and make a case for who needs what, where, and how.

In responding to this, those working to support children who live in violent and abusive homes may seek to review the way boys are constructed in the literature and responded to by some of the current services available. Callaghan et al. (2018) make a powerful argument for the need to support children better, to recognise their victimisation, to hear their voices, and to respond by providing appropriate support. Callaghan's team also point to the lack of resource and support services currently available to children, and in so doing they do not distinguish between boys and girls. Their treatment of the children is egalitarian; unfortunately, the potential outcomes for children in the current support services does not always follow this practice. Despite a growing body of literature to suggest that gender may obscure rather than facilitate our understanding of DV and abuse, DV is still routinely referred to as a gendered problem and whilst the numbers of those believed to be perpetrating violence and abuse still weigh more heavily towards male perpetrators and female victims (Hague & Malos, 2005; Morris, 2009), the persistence in categorising it in a way that almost infers a causal relationship between gender and violence is arguably unhelpful. It is not just unhelpful to male victims, it is also unhelpful to mothers seeking refuge; women who are unable to use services because male children over 13 years of age may not be welcome. It is unhelpful to boys who are experiencing the violence to be constructed as potential future abusers and more broadly it is unhelpful in a world where the binary of gender is increasingly contested. DV affects both male and female children and whilst they may or may not manage their responses differently, there is no reason to assume that boys are less frightened, shocked, confused, and traumatised than girls; it is highly likely that there are more within than between group differences. Boys in the current construction of the problem appear to be afforded victim status until they reach puberty and then by association are labelled as threats or perpetrators in the waiting (Whitfield, Anda, Dube, & Felitti, 2003). This is a form of discrimination that may be an unintended consequence of the discourse and associated policy, but it is a consequence nonetheless and one that may unwittingly have a part to play in the outcomes for boys. Whilst there is an appetite to start addressing some of the inequalities children have faced over the years in terms of their experiences of living with DV, perhaps now is the time to revisit these policies and reconsider the reasoning behind them. In particular, rethink the message that this exclusion conveys to boys and young men and the barriers it presents to mothers seeking refuge.

Great strides have been made by researchers, practitioners, and policy makers in the field. The profile of the problem has been raised and the children's voice is now actively being sought. There is much to applaud in the dogged determination of those who have been steadfast in their advocacy of children. Researchers and practitioners have gathered a considerable body of robust evidence to alert communities and policy makers to the scale and nature of the problem. Whilst a considerable amount of work remains, the repositioning of children to the centre of the DV debate gives rise to optimism.

References

Austin, A. E., Shanahan, M. E., Barrios, Y. V., & Macy, R. J. (2017). A systematic review of interventions for women parenting in the context of intimate partner violence. *Trauma, Violence, & Abuse*, doi:1524838017719233

Baglivio, M. T., Wolff, K. T., Piquero, A. R., & Epps, N. (2015). The relationship between adverse childhood experiences (ACE) and juvenile offending trajectories in a juvenile offender sample. *Journal of Criminal Justice*, 43(3), 229–241. doi:10.1016/j.jcrimjus.2015.04.012

Bair-Merritt, M. H., Blackstone, M., & Feudtner, C. (2006). Physical health outcomes of childhood exposure to intimate partner violence: a systematic review. *Pediatrics*, 117, e278–290. doi:10.1542/peds.2005-1473

Barter-Godfrey, S. & Taket, A. (2009). Othering, marginalisation and pathways to exclusion in Health. In Taket, A., Crisp, B., Nevill, A., Lamaro, G., Graham, M., & Barter-Godfrey, S. (Eds) *Theorising social exclusion* (pp. 166–172). Abingdon: Routledge.

Bedi, G. & Goddard, C. (2007). Intimate partner violence: What are the impacts on children? *Australian Psychologist*, 42(1), 66–77.

Byrne, D. & Taylor, B. (2007). Children at risk from domestic violence and their educational attainment: Perspectives of education welfare officers, social workers and teachers. *Child Care in Practice*, 13(3), 185–201. doi:10.1080/13575270701353465

CAADA. (2014). In plain sight: Effective help for children exposed to domestic abuse. (Research Report). Cardiff, Wales: Coordinated Action Against Domestic Abuse.

Callaghan, J. (2015). Mothers and children? Representations of mothers in research on children's outcomes in domestic violence. *Psychology of Women Section Review*, 17, 13–20.

Callaghan, J. E., Alexander, J. H., & Fellin, L. C. (2016). Children's embodied experience of living with domestic violence: "I'd go into my panic, and shake, really bad". *Subjectivity*, 9(4), 399–419. doi:10.1057/s41286–41016–0011–0019

Callaghan, J. E., Alexander, J. H., Sixsmith, J., & Fellin, L. C. (2016). Children's experiences of domestic violence and abuse: siblings' accounts of relational coping. *Clinical Child Psychology and Psychiatry*, 21(4), 649–668. doi:10.1177/1359104515620250

Callaghan, J. E. M., Fellin, L. C., Alexander, J. H., Mavrou, S., & Papathanasiou, M. (2017). Children and domestic violence: Emotional competencies in embodied and relational contexts. *Psychology of Violence*, 7(3), 333–342. doi:10.1037/vio0000108

Callaghan, J. E., Alexander, J. H., Sixsmith, J., & Fellin, L. C. (2018). Beyond "witnessing": children's experiences of coercive control in domestic violence and abuse. *Journal of Interpersonal Violence*, 33(10), 1551–1581. doi:10.1177/0886260515618946

Carrell, S. E. & Hoekstra, M. L. (2010). Externalities in the classroom: How children exposed to domestic violence affect everyone's kids. *American Economic Journal: Applied Economics*, 2(1), 211–228.

Cicchetti, D., Rogosch, F. A., Maughan, A., Toth, S. L., & Bruce, J. (2003). False belief understanding in maltreated children. *Development and Psychopathology*, 15(4), 1067–1091. doi:10.1017/S0954579403000440

Clements, C. M., Oxtoby, C., & Ogle, R. L. (2008). Methodological issues in assessing psychological adjustment in child witnesses of intimate partner violence. *Trauma, Violence, & Abuse*, 9(2), 114–127. doi:10.1177/1524838008315870

Douglas, H. & Walsh, T. (2010). Mothers, domestic violence, and child protection. *Violence Against Women*, 16(5), 489–508. doi:10.1177/1077801210365887

Dunn, J. (1995). Children as psychologists: The later correlates of individual differences in understanding of emotions and other minds. *Cognition and Emotion*, 9, 187–201. doi:10.1080/02699939508409008

Ehrensaft, M. K., Cohen, P., Brown, J., Smailes, E., Chen, H., & Johnson, J. G. (2003). Intergenerational transmission of partner violence: A 20-year prospective study. *Journal of Consulting and Clinical Psychology*, 71(4), 741–753. doi:10.1037/0022–006X.71.4.741

Evans, S. E., Davies, C., & DiLillo, D. (2008). Exposure to domestic violence: a meta-analysis of child and adolescent outcomes. *Aggression and Violent Behavior*, 13, 131–140.

Fox, B. H., Perez, N., Cass, E., Baglivio, M. T., & Epps, N. (2015). Trauma changes everything: Examining the relationship between adverse childhood experiences and serious, violent and chronic juvenile offenders. *Child Abuse & Neglect*, 46, 163–173. doi:10.1016/j.chiabu.2015.01.011

Gilbert, R., Kemp, A., Thoburn, J., Sidebotham, P., Radford, L., Glaser, D., & MacMillan, H. L. (2009). Recognising and responding to child maltreatment. *The Lancet*, 373(9658), 167–180. doi:10.1016/S0140–6736(08)61707–61709

Gilliom, M., Shaw, D. S., Beck, J. E., Schonberg, M. A., & Lukon, J. L. (2002). Anger regulation in disadvantaged preschool boys: strategies, antecedents, and the development of self-control. *Developmental Psychology*, 38(2), 222–235. doi:10.1037/0012–1649.38.2.222

Graham-Bermann, S. A. & Hughes, H. M. (2003). Intervention for children exposed to interparental violence (IPV): Assessment of needs and research priorities. *Clinical Child and Family Psychology Review*, 6, 189–204.

Hague, G. & Malos, E. (2005). *Domestic violence: Action for change*. Cheltenham: New Clarion Press.

Harold, G. T. & Sellers, R. (2018). Annual Research Review: Interparental conflict and youth psychopathology: An evidence review and practice focused update. *Journal of Child Psychology and Psychiatry*, 59(4), 374–402. doi:10.1111/jcpp.12893

Herrenkohl, T. I., Sousa, C., Tajima, E. A., Herrenkohl, R. C., & Moylan, C. A. (2008). Intersection of child abuse and children's exposure to domestic violence. *Trauma, Violence, & Abuse*, 9, 84–89.

Holden, G. W. (2003). Children exposed to domestic violence and child abuse: Terminology and taxonomy. *Clinical Child and Family Psychology Review*, 6(3), 151–160. doi:10.1023/A:1024906315255

Holt, S., Buckley, H., & Whelan, S. (2008). The impact of exposure to domestic violence on children and young people: A review of the literature. *Child Abuse & Neglect*, 32(8), 797–810.

Katz, E. (2015). Domestic violence, children's agency and mother–child relationships: Towards a more advanced model. *Children & Society*, 29(1), 69–79. doi:10.1111/chso.12023

Katz, E. (2016). Beyond the physical incident model: how children living with domestic violence are harmed by and resist regimes of coercive control. *Child Abuse Review*, 25(1), 46–59. doi:10.1002/car.2422

Kimball, E. (2016). Edleson revisited: Reviewing children's witnessing of domestic violence 15 years later. *Journal of Family Violence*, 31(5), 625–637. doi:10.1007/s10896–10015–9786–9787

Koizumi, M. & Takagishi, H. (2014). The relationship between child maltreatment and emotion recognition. *PloS One*, 9(1), e86093. doi:10.1371/journal.pone.0086093

Levendosky, A. A. & Graham-Bermann, S. A. (2001). Parenting in battered women: The effects of domestic violence on women and their children. *Journal of Family Violence*, 16(2), 171–192.

Levendosky, A. A., Leahy, K. L., Bogat, G. A., Davidson, W. S., & von Eye, A. (2006). Domestic violence, maternal parenting, maternal mental health, and infant externalizing behavior. *Journal of Family Psychology*, 20(4), 544.

Levitas, R., Pantazis, C., Fahmy, E., Gordon, D., Lloyd, E., & Patsios, D. (2007). The multi-dimensional analysis of social exclusion. Department of Sociology and School for Social Policy, Townsend Centre for the International Study of Poverty and Bristol Institute for Public Affairs, Bristol: University of Bristol.

Letourneau, N. L., Fedick, C. B., & Willms, J. D. (2007). Mothering and domestic violence: A longitudinal analysis. *Journal of Family Violence*, 22, 649–659. doi:10.1007/s10896–10007–9099–9096

Lewis, N. V., Larkins, C., Stanley, N., Szilassy, E., Turner, W., Drinkwater, J., & Feder, G. S. (2017). Training on domestic violence and child safeguarding in general practice: A mixed method evaluation of a pilot intervention. *BMC Family Practice*, 18(1), 33–45. doi:10.1186/s12875–12017–0603–0607

Little, L. & Kantor, G. K. (2002). Using ecological theory to understand intimate partner violence and child maltreatment. *Journal of Community Health Nursing*, 19(3), 133–145.

Longfield, A. (2018). The Children's Commissioner's Vulnerability Report 2018. The children's commissioner for England, London. Retrieved from: www.childrenscomm issioner.gov.uk/wp-content/uploads/2018/07/Childrens-Commissioner-Vulnerability-Rep ort-2018-Overview-Document-1.pdf

McNeill, F., Farrall, S., Lightowler, C., & Maruna, S. (2012). How and why people stop offending: Discovering desistance. Insights Evidence Summary to Support Social Services in Scotland. IRISS.

Moffitt, T. E. & Caspi, A. (2001). Childhood predictors differentiate life-course persistent and adolescence-limited antisocial pathways among males and females. *Development and Psychopathology*, 13(2), 355–375.

Morris, A. (2009). Gendered dynamics of abuse and violence in families: Considering the abusive household gender regime. *Child Abuse Review: Journal of the British Association for the Study and Prevention of Child Abuse and Neglect*, 18(6), 414–427.

Moylan, C. A., Herrenkohl, T. I., Sousa, C., Tajima, E. A., Herrenkohl, R. C., & Russo, M. J. (2010). The effects of child abuse and exposure to domestic violence on adolescent internalizing and externalizing behavior problems. *Journal of Family Violence*, 25(1), 53–63. doi:10.1007/s10896–10009–9269–9269

Mullender, A., Hague, G., Imam, U., Kelly, L., Malos, E., & Regan, L. (2002). *Children's perspectives on domestic violence*. London: Sage.

Munro, E. (2012). The Munro Review of Child Protection: progress report: moving towards a child centred system. London: Department for Education.

Øverlien, C. (2010). Children exposed to domestic violence: Conclusions from the literature and challenges ahead. *Journal of Social Work*, 10(1), 80–97. doi:10.1177/1468017309350663

Øverlien, C. (2017). 'Do you want to do some arm wrestling?': Children's strategies when experiencing domestic violence and the meaning of age. *Child & Family Social Work*, 22(2), 680–688. doi:10.1111/cfs.12283

Øverlien, C. & Aas, G. (2016). The police patrols and children experiencing domestic violence. *Police Practice and Research*, 17(5), 434–447. doi:10.1080/15614263.2015.1086879

Øverlien, C. & Hyden, M. (2009). Children's actions when experiencing domestic violence. *Childhood*, 16, 79–497. doi:10.1177/0907568209343757

Pears, K. C. & Fisher, P. A. (2005). Emotion understanding and theory of mind among maltreated children in foster care: Evidence of deficits. *Development and Psychopathology*, 17(1), 47–65. doi:10.1017/S0954579405050030

Peltonen, K., Ellonen, N., Larsen, H. B., & Helweg-Larsen, K. (2010). Parental violence and adolescent mental health. *European Child & Adolescent Psychiatry*, 19(11), 813–822. doi:10.1007/s00787-010-0130-8

Petersen, R., Moracco, K. E., Goldstein, K. M., & Clark, K. A. (2005). Moving beyond disclosure: Women's perspectives on barriers and motivators to seeking assistance for intimate partner violence. *Women & Health*, 40(3), 63–76. doi:0.1300/J013v40n03_05

Postmus, J. L., Severson, M., Berry, M., & Yoo, J. A. (2009). Women's experiences of violence and seeking help. *Violence Against Women*, 15(7), 852–868. doi:10.1177/1077801209334445

Powell, A. & Murray, S. (2008). Children and domestic violence: Constructing a policy problem in Australia and New Zealand. *Social and Legal Studies*, 17, 453–473.doi:10.1177/0964663908097080

Radford, L. & Hester, M. (2006). *Mothering through domestic violence*. London: Kingsley.

Rhodes, K. V., Dichter, M. E., Kothari, C. L., Marcus, S. C., & Cerulli, C. (2011). The impact of children on legal actions taken by women victims of intimate partner violence. *Journal of Family Violence*, 26(5), 355–364.

Richardson-Foster, H., Stanley, N., Miller, P., & Thomson, G. (2012). Police intervention in domestic violence incidents where children are present: Police and children's perspectives. *Policing and Society*, 22(2), 220–234. doi:10.1080/10439463.2011.636815

Sanderson, C. (2008). *Counselling survivors of domestic abuse*. Jessica Kingsley Publishers.

Severson, M., Berry, M., & Postmus, J. L. (2007). Risks and needs: Factors that predict women's incarceration and inform service planning. In Sheehan, R. (Ed.) *What works with women offenders* (pp. 355–374). Devon, UK: Willan.

Siegel, J. P. (2013). Breaking the links in intergenerational violence: An emotional regulation perspective. *Family Process*, 52(2), 163–178. doi:10.1111/famp.12023

Sprung, M. (2008). Unwanted intrusive thoughts and cognitive functioning and young elementary school children following Hurricane Katrina. *Journal of Clinical Child and Adolescent Psychology*, 37(3), 575–587. doi:10.1080/15374410802148236

Stanley, N., Miller, P., & Richardson Foster, H. (2012). Engaging with children's and parents' perspectives on domestic violence. *Child & Family Social Work*, 17(2), 192–201. doi:10.1111/j.1365–2206.2012.00832.x

Sternberg, K. J., Baradaran, L. P., Abbott, C. B., Lamb, M. E., & Guterman, E. (2006). Type of violence, age, and gender differences in the effects of family violence on children's behavior problems: A mega-analysis. *Developmental Review*, 26(1), 89–112. doi:10.1016/j.dr.2005.12.001

Straus, M. A., Gelles, R. J., & Steinmetz, S. K. (2017). *Behind closed doors: Violence in the American family*. Abingdon: Routledge.

Sturge-Apple, M. L., Davies, P. T., Cicchetti, D., & Manning, L. G. (2010). Mother's parenting practices as explanatory mechanisms in associations between interparental violence and child adjustment. *Partner Abuse*, 1, 45–60. doi:10.1891/1946–6560.1.1.45

Turner, W., Hester, M., Broad, J., Szilassy, E., Feder, G., Drinkwater, J., ... & Stanley, N. (2017). Interventions to improve the response of professionals to children exposed to domestic violence and abuse: A systematic review. *Child Abuse Review*, 26(1), 19–39. doi:10.1002/car.2385

Vu, N. L., Jouriles, E. N., McDonald, R., & Rosenfield, D. (2016). Children's exposure to intimate partner violence: A meta-analysis of longitudinal associations with child adjustment problems. *Clinical Psychology Review*, 46, 25–33. doi:10.1016/j.cpr.2016.04.003

Weaver, B., & McNeill, F. (2010). Travelling hopefully: Desistance research and probation practice. In Brayford, J., Cowe, F., & Deering, J. (Eds) *What else works? Creative work with offenders*. Cullompton: Willan.

Whitfield, C. L., Anda, R. F., Dube, S. R., & Felitti, V. J. (2003). Violent childhood experiences and the risk of intimate partner violence in adults: Assessment in a large health maintenance organization. *Journal of interpersonal violence*, 18(2), 166–185.

Zarling, A. L., Taber-Thomas, S., Murray, A., Knuston, J. F., Lawrence, E., Valles, N. L., … & Bank, L. (2013). Internalizing and externalizing symptoms in young children exposed to intimate partner violence: Examining intervening processes. *Journal of Family Psychology*, 27(6), 945–955. doi:10.1037/a0034804

12

CONCLUSIONS AND RECOMMENDATIONS

Why change current practice?

Julie C. Taylor & Elizabeth A. Bates

In the introduction to the book we stated that there exists a wealth of literature that has developed over the last four decades to show that intimate partner violence (IPV) is a complex, multifarious issue. Despite this evidence base, policy, treatment provision, and practice appear to remain committed to a construction of the problem of IPV that assumes male heterosexual perpetrator and female heterosexual victim. The chapters in this book have presented and reviewed evidence to argue that current constructions of the problem and associated solutions are out of step. They challenge gender as the prevailing explanation of IPV (Dobash & Dobash, 1979, 2004). Proponents of the gendered account suggest that men use violence as one mechanism to control and dominate women, a socially and historically constructed explanation that arose out of gender inequality and male privilege. The emergent framework promulgated a wealth of research and practices designed to work with women as victims, and men (often in prison or mandated to programmes) as perpetrators with the objective of trying to understand the abuse and reduce its impact on women. The evidence discussed in this book suggests that like so many of the issues associated with IPV, the way we construct the problem impacts the response, whether that be research direction or practice. On this issue there seems to have been some reluctance to embrace challenge, or welcome the possibility that some of the underpinning assumptions may be flawed or just one possible account of the phenomenon, representative perhaps of the views of those situated within a specific social strata and potentially zeitgeist dependent.

There is little doubt that gender-based constructions of the problem have had a powerful influence on our responses to it, whether these be in the eye of professionals, policy makers, or the social milieu more broadly. We argue that to maintain a position that situates gender as an almost causal factor in IPV is likely to impede progress, to do more harm than good, particularly in societies where the binary construction of male and female is increasingly contested. We are not suggesting that gender was not once a critically important variable, that this early focus was not helpful in bringing the problem to light and gathering momentum and support for those seeking to eradicate it. We are suggesting that its persistence as an explanation for a social problem that exists in many contemporary societies is, however, problematic because it offers an insufficient and over-simplified account; an account that has not been successful in treating perpetrators or protecting victims. Moreover, rather than encourage equality, it is a model that is in danger of creating or at least prolonging injustices. Each of the chapters in this text examined an area where injustice has been suggested; they reviewed the literature, and either discussed the potential injustice in light of the available evidence or discussed examples of ways of working to ameliorate it. Each chapter culminates with recommendations that seek to widen the scope of the problem and construct it as a behaviour all too common to the species as opposed to trying to attribute it to specific groups.

Elizabeth Bates started the discussion by addressing the problem of gendered models in broad terms, drawing our attention to the data and challenging us to explain the desire to retain a gendered model in light of such poor outcomes for those treated under its auspices. Elizabeth asked whether this desire to persist with a flawed model reflects scientific or political thinking. She further suggested that we look again at prevalence rates, perpetrator demographics, and the over simplified dichotomy of perpetrator-victim, proposing instead that it is time to acknowledge that IPV can be perpetrated by anyone, and that anyone can hold the dual identity of victim and perpetrator, reminding us that these two categories are not mutually exclusive. In Chapter 3 this theme was extended by Jessica McCarrick who drew upon her experiences of working with male victims of IPV. The powerful narratives from male victims led Jessica to lament the lack of support services available to male victims and to question the practices that keep male victims from reporting their experiences. However, she did go on to draw our attention to signs of hope, identifying some localised pockets of good practice. Good practice that could be shared more widely with the right funding and socio-political support.

Benjamin Hine's contribution explored the male perspective further. Benjamin identified the liberal application of stereotypes within the IPV arena and asked us to consider the many and varied ways these stereotypes can influence the way we view and respond to IPV. In particular, our assumptions around victimisation and what a deserving victim "looks" like. He questioned the impact of a myopic lens on how we decide what constitutes violence, using an anecdote to guide us to the crux of the problem. Benjamin questioned why when a woman and a man perform a similar behaviour the perception of it can be so different; he noted that when performed by a woman a hard slap on a man's arm may be construed as vaguely amusing but if performed by a man it may have been assumed to be nefarious and indicative of abuse. This disparity when enculturated through stereotyping is likely to influence not only our interpretation of the behaviour of others but also of our own. Benjamin asserted that for services to be inclusive and victims to be appropriately responded to, these stereotypes have to be challenged, the narratives critically considered, and professionals trained to acknowledge their own assumptions and not be unduly influenced by them. He called for *a dedicated effort to provide "gender-inclusive" as opposed to "gender neutral" training.* Indeed, Benjamin urged academics, practitioners, professionals, and the media to reflect on the pervasive power of stereotypes arguing that it is only through the active rejection of these stereotypes that we will be able to respond equitably and sensitively to IPV victims.

In Chapter 5, Katherine Maurer shifted our attention from the long-held belief that IPV was a form of behaviour primarily associated with adult intimate relationships and discussed instead IPV in adolescent relationships or AIPV. In prompting this redirection of attention, Katherine usefully introduced us to a way of conceptualising IPV that is not constrained by decades of assumptions about gender and sexuality. AIPV is an issue that has become part of popular consciousness only relatively recently and so explanations for it have benefitted from contemporary theorising. Katherine discussed a developmental-ecological-systems (DES) model of IPV and explains how this approach is necessary given the bidirectional nature of the abuse observed in adolescent relationships but also the heterogeneity of the relationship types in which IPV has been reported. Not only is Katherine's work illuminating for the population to which it is intended to apply, it presents significant opportunities to extend our understanding of adult relationship violence. The heterogeneity described by Katherine in adolescent relationship types is, as explained in Philippa and Lauren's chapter, mirrored in the adult world. Indeed, there are also indications in the literature that the traditional assumptions that IPV is uni-directional may present an overly simplistic account for adults as well as adolescents. Bidirectional violence prevalence rates suggest that this pattern of behaviour is more common than previously believed (see Bates 2016; Espinoza & Warner, 2016). The bidirectional nature of the violence discussed in the AIPV literature muddies the water when it comes to offering interventions, the standard perpetrator and victim packages arguably redundant. Katherine discussed an alternative approach, an anti-oppressive practice perspective for interventions which focus on self-regulation, community-based change, and relationship skills. Katherine concluded by suggesting that *advancing the DES model of AIPV in theory, research, and policy has the potential to improve outcomes for all adolescents.* It might also be argued that there are lessons from this work for those currently working in the adult domain as well.

In Chapter 6 Philippa Laskey and Lauren Bolam extended the dialogue further, expressly rejecting the binary of gender and reviewing compelling evidence to refute the dominant belief that IPV is confined to specific groups, highlighting instead the ubiquitous and pernicious nature of IPV and abuse. This chapter offered a critical review of the extant literature and concludes that the data suggests that prevalence rates of IPV in LGBTQ+ relationships are equal, if not significantly higher, than their heterosexual, cisgender counterparts. Not only are the rates apparently higher, the types of abuse identified are in some cases unique, for example, threats to "out" a partner. Whilst the review led Philippa and Lauren to call for further research, they do so in the knowledge that the available assessment tools may not be sufficient to capture the prevalence and nature of abuse being experienced. Disturbingly the evidence suggests that it is not just an understanding of the prevalence and abuse types that is lacking when considering the experiences of individuals from the LGBTQ+ community, there have also been numerous barriers to their reporting of IPV and accessing of support services. Philippa and Lauren concluded that much work is still required to provide services to victims of IPV irrespective of gender and sexuality.

The second half of the book presented a series of commentaries on interventions in IPV alongside practice issues and concerns. John Hamel started the section by identifying the problems associated with attempts to apply a one-size-fits-all theory of perpetrator behaviour, pointing to the heterogeneity of the perpetrator groups he has worked with and the urgent need for programmes to respond to this variation. John guided us through a number of alternative approaches to interventions and commented on their effectiveness. It is clear from the findings discussed that whilst there exists a growing body of evidence for a paradigm shift in intervention design and implementation, there appears to be considerable resistance to a move away from the traditional feminist model. John calls for improved dialogue between researchers and practitioners and more research from across the globe.

Amy Ford's chapter described the development of an intervention programme that has considered many of the points raised and discussed by John. The Up2U programme was developed in response to a county council's decision to make IPV and abuse a strategic priority. Amy described how following a thorough review of literature and extant interventions she became aware of the polarisation of work within the field; gender and its role in IPV being the polarising factor. Amy concluded that whilst there is evidence to support both sides of the argument, constructing her intervention for IPV solely in the context of gender was unlikely to address the heterogeneity observed in the demographics of her perpetrator groups. Amy's response was to develop an intervention that acknowledged that some IPV is as the gendered approach suggests, about dominance, power, and control, but that this alone would be insufficient. Amy explained how her intervention needed to factor in female perpetration and a number of other risk and need factors. The Up2U intervention programme is showing early signs of positive results for clients with the results of the full evaluation due in 2020.

Erica Bowen and Jenny Mackay extended the discussion of female perpetration further and reported that the data so far suggests that IPV is perpetrated and experienced by women at rates on a par with those experienced by men. Moreover, the way the abuse is used appears to bear strong resemblance to the ways it is reportedly used by men. Erica and Jenny examined the limited data on successful interventions for female perpetrators and surmise that in lieu of a robust evidence base they would tentatively recommend interventions predicated on a well-informed assessment of the individual's risk and needs with responsivity as a central focus. Further arguing that engagement and completion may need to be encouraged though the adoption of a collaborative, supportive and accepting therapeutic style. Possibly the critical take home message from their work was that considerably more work needs to be done in the area of female perpetration, from both research and intervention perspectives.

Nick Smithers' chapter has the potential to usefully inform the discussion of female perpetration started by Erica and Jenny. In addition, it makes powerful contributions to our understanding of the power of prejudice and discrimination within this field. Nick's chapter is a hard hitting and moving account of a third sector organisation's attempts to offer support to male victims of domestic violence, and the barriers faced by the organisations in their pursuit of recognition for their work with victims of violence. To those positioned at the margins of the gender debate, the level of resistance described by Nick may seem out of proportion and at times discriminatory. However, those individuals and groups who are most vociferous in their defence of the male perpetrator female victim dichotomy may justifiably feel under siege; funding is scarce, resources limited, and the women and children who gather the courage to seek support are unquestionably in need. So their passionate allegiance to a particular narrative, whilst distressing to those desperately seeking to support victims who do not match their criteria, is in many ways admirable. Their steadfast and dogged determination to support their service users to the very best of their ability makes them powerful advocates and formidable adversaries. However, the support of one group in need ought not be privileged over the needs of others and so it was heartening to read Nick's equally determined account explaining how his organisation seeks to support its service users and raise the profile of male victims. The take home message from this chapter was perhaps epitomised by Nick's report of the school boys who contacted Nick's service asking for some domestic violence education for boys in their school. The boys were aware that the girls were receiving input on domestic violence and abuse and they identified a need amongst the boys. Anecdotal evidence such as this can bring sharp focus to what feels like a perennial problem; both boys and girls are impacted by violence, and this might be as victims, perpetrators, or both. The debate and focus on the prevalence of each category by gender detracts from what should be a focus on individual need; failure to recognise this is likely to exacerbate the problem and create difficulties for the future.

Julie Taylor's chapter continued with the theme of children's experiences of domestic violence and the many and varied ways it can influence development. The chapter drew our attention to a number of assumptions that have influenced the way children have been positioned in the narrative, policy, and practice responses. The discussion of the literature is augmented by reflections from adult women's retrospective phenomenological accounts of their victimisation and the impact this has had on their adult lives. The key message from this chapter is that the failure to achieve a consensus view on children's agency and position within violent families is potentially serving as a barrier to identification and intervention. A consensus has been called for by prominent scholars in the field (e.g. Callaghan, Fellin, Alexander, Mavrou, & Papathanasiou, 2017; Callaghan, Alexander, Sixsmith, & Fellin, 2018; Katz, 2015, 2016; Kimball, 2016; Øverlien, 2017) to help respond more effectively to the needs of children and young people.

This compendium of work is the first of its kind to bring together a critical analysis of a wide breadth of research and practice in the area of IPV. Having highlighted the key findings from each chapter, we wish to conclude this volume with a number of recommendations for the area as we move forward:

1. Both Katherine's and Julie's chapters point to the need to work with children and young people. This preventative narrative responds to claims of intergenerational transmission and the evidence base that suggests experiencing violence in families as children and young people can lead to a range of mutually reinforcing negative outcomes. The impact of IPV on children can have far reaching and significant consequences; evidence is mounting to suggest that the development of unhealthy behaviours in relationships begins in adolescence. By the time the young person reaches early adulthood many of these behaviours have become a repeating and embedded pattern. The research in this book supports this; by working more inclusively and holistically with young people on developing "healthy relationships" we could begin to effectively intervene much earlier. This recommendation involves revisiting how we construct children within the IPV discourse.

2. Several authors call for research and practice to work in a gender inclusive way. Despite some suggestions in the literature, "gender neutral" is not appropriate as it dismisses genuine, ingrained differences that affect men, women, and those not identifying in this binary way. These are ingrained at a level we cannot easily address or undo, so until we can see gender as non-binary and perhaps gender norms differently, we need to respond to gender specific factors in both perpetrator and victim interventions. This allows for women as perpetrators, men as victims, same-sex relationships, non-binary gender identity, and bidirectional abuse.

3. Revisiting the labelling widely adopted in the IPV arena is also recommended; simplistic categorisations belie the complexity of the abuse. Within the literature and indeed in practice, a focus on the "perpetrator" and "victim" label remains. Whilst sometimes appropriate in cases of unilateral violence, it complicates discussion when people fall into both categories. There is a need to shift the language used in the area to allow research and practice to respond without accusations of "victim blaming" or mistakenly overlooking motivations of self-defence. Until we shift from the need to name people as one or other of these categories, we are unlikely to be able to effectively challenge and intervene in particular with bidirectional and mutual IPV.

4. Evidence-based practice and policy is long overdue in this field. Whilst other areas of research and practice see the two working together, barriers exist that have prevented this within the field of IPV. There is fault on both parts of this nexus; academia has not always fostered accessible communication strategies, and practitioners are not always open to changing practice based on new research and evidence. We need to work together to ensure policy and practice are influenced by research, and not by political agendas.

5. Finally, the one-size-fits-all approach needs to be firmly rejected. One of the criticisms of the gendered theory and Duluth Model is that it treats IPV under a one-size-fits-all approach. The work presented in this book eschews this overly simplistic remedy to what the evidence suggests is a complex and heterogeneous phenomenon. Interventions for perpetrators, victims, people who fit into both categories, children, and indeed all those involved, need to be responsive and so tailored to individual need.

References

Bates, E. A. (2016). Current controversies in intimate partner violence: Overlooking bidirectional violence. *Journal of Family Violence*, 31(8), 937–940. doi:10.1007/s10896-016-9862-1023-1053

Callaghan, J. E. M., Fellin, L. C., Alexander, J. H., Mavrou, S., & Papathanasiou, M. (2017). Children and domestic violence: Emotional competencies in embodied and relational contexts. *Psychology of Violence*, 7(3), 333–342. doi:10.1037/vio0000108

Callaghan, J. E., Alexander, J. H., Sixsmith, J., & Fellin, L. C. (2018). Beyond "witnessing": children's experiences of coercive control in domestic violence and abuse. *Journal of Interpersonal Violence*, 33(10), 1551–1581. doi:10.1177/0886260515618946

Dobash, R. E. & Dobash, R. P. (1979). *Violence against wives: A case against the patriarchy*. London: Open Books.

Dobash, R. P. & Dobash, R. E. (2004). Women's violence to men in intimate relationships: Working on a Puzzle. *British Journal of Criminology*, 44, 324–349. doi:10.1093/bjc/azh026

Espinoza, R. C. & Warner, D. (2016). Where do we go from here? Examining intimate partner violence by bringing male victims, female perpetrators, and psychological sciences into the fold. *Journal of Family Violence*, 31(8), 959–966.

Katz, E. (2015). Domestic violence, children's agency and mother–child relationships: Towards a more advanced model. *Children & Society*, 29(1), 69–79. doi:10.1111/chso.12023

Katz, E. (2016). Beyond the physical incident model: How children living with domestic violence are harmed by and resist regimes of coercive control. *Child Abuse Review*, 25(1), 46–59. doi:10.1002/car.2422

Kimball, E. (2016). Edleson revisited: Reviewing children's witnessing of domestic violence 15 years later. *Journal of Family Violence*, 31(5), 625–637. doi:10.1007/s10896-10015-9786-9787

Øverlien, C. (2017). 'Do you want to do some arm wrestling?': Children's strategies when experiencing domestic violence and the meaning of age. *Child & Family Social Work*, 22(2), 680–688. doi:10.1111/cfs.1228z

INDEX

Adolescents 5, 15, 58–68, 126, 174

Alcohol 17, 18, 30, 75, 89, 126, 132, 146, 151, 157

Archer, J. 3, 4, 11, 12, 15, 16, 17, 44, 76, 90, 95, 98, 107, 109, 112, 123, 124

Attitude 5, 12, 14, 28, 36, 40, 47, 52, 54, 66, 67, 76, 91, 100, 115, 127, 133, 134, 148 *see also* Perceptions

Babcock, J. 3, 20, 92, 100, 101, 102, 107, 128, 129, 130, 131–132, 135

Barriers; Help-seeking 47, 140, 150, 166, 175; Internal 47, 150; Interventions 67, 146, 149, 162, 177; LGBTQ+ 73–83; Organisational 139, 176; Victims 5, 26, 139, 154, 156

Batterer 16, 89, 90, 91, 92, 94, 97, 98, 99 *see also* Perpetrator

Bias 16, 27–28, 29, 33, 45, 47, 51, 52, 62–63, 76, 93, 99, 109, 149, 159

Bidirectional 3, 4, 5, 12, 14, 15–16, 20, 44, 60, 62, 68, 75, 76, 89, 90, 91, 92, 97, 117, 133, 135, 174, 177

Blame 5, 28, 47, 89, 131, 159

Britain *see* United Kingdom

Canada 1, 3, 11, 59, 66, 101, 128

Child, 6, 61, 62–63, 65, 92, 94, 98, 99, 108, 110, 112, 118, 119, 126, 127, 129, 154–167

Childhood 4, 17–18, 19, 20, 58, 60, 64, 93, 113, 115, 126, 131, 132, 148, 151, 154–167

Children 6, 13, 17–18, 26, 39, 45, 63, 64, 90, 98, 99, 101, 108, 114, 116, 117, 118, 119, 133, 140, 142, 145, 151, 152, 154–167

Chivalry 13, 17

Coercive control; Controlling 2, 4, 6, 11, 13–15, 18, 19–20, 27, 28, 30, 37, 39, 46, 48, 53, 60, 75, 76, 77, 78, 89, 90, 91, 92, 95, 97–98, 100, 107, 108, 109, 110–111, 114, 115, 124, 127, 128, 132, 133, 140, 141, 142, 143, 145–146, 151, 156, 172, 175

Cognitive Behavioural therapy; CBT, 93, 100, 101, 109, 112, 128

Conflict 3, 16, 17, 18, 48, 66, 89, 90, 91, 92, 93, 100, 101–102, 112, 115, 116, 126, 132, 133, 156

Conflict Tactics Scale; CTS; 12, 15, 62, 92, 123

Control *see* Coercive Control

Couples 1, 5, 12, 14, 15–16, 43, 44, 49, 51, 59–60, 63, 65, 68, 91–92, 93, 101, 108, 128, 129, 141

Criminal Justice System; CJS 4, 26, 27, 28–29, 30, 31, 32–33, 34, 35–36, 37, 38, 40, 47, 48, 62, 77, 78, 162

Dating violence; dating aggression 5, 15, 58–68

Dobash, R.E & Dobash, R.P. 1, 2, 11, 12, 89, 107, 172

Dobash R.P. & Dobash, R. E. 2, 11, 107, 172

Domestic abuse *see* domestic violence

Domestic violence 1, 3, 6, 17, 26, 27, 28, 29, 34, 36, 40, 43, 44–55, 77, 89, 90, 93, 94, 96, 99, 100, 101, 102, 107, 108–120, 123, 124, 125, 130, 131, 139–152, 154–166, 176

Dominate; dominated; domination 2, 11, 13, 20, 64, 92, 95, 100, 107, 172

Duluth 2, 3, 5, 20, 54, 89, 101, 109, 110, 117, 119, 128, 177

Dutton, D. 1, 2, 3, 11, 14, 18, 19, 20, 27, 28, 32, 36, 44, 48, 52, 90, 91, 93, 95, 97, 99, 109, 112, 123, 124, 134

Economic abuse *see* financial abuse

Effective; Effectively; Effectiveness; Evaluations 6; of Group approaches 128; of Interventions 3, 4, 5, 20, 109, 110, 111, 124, 125, 127, 128, 129, 131, 132, 135, 175; of current Models 68, 129; Practice 143; Support 82; Treatment 20, 89, 92, 93, 101; Law and legislation measures 26, 33, 40

Emotion dysregulation *see* emotion regulation

Emotion regulation 3, 17, 19, 112, 115, 127, 133, 134

Emotional aggression; emotional abuse 13, 14, 33, 47, 48, 49, 51, 53, 60, 66, 73, 78, 80, 89, 92, 95, 97–98, 99, 130, 143

Evaluation 3, 6, 13, 20, 107, 108, 109, 110, 111, 114, 115, 116, 117–118, 119, 128, 129, 143, 175

Evidence base 1, 3, 4, 6, 20, 65, 118, 143, 155, 172, 175, 177

Evidence-based; Assessments 115; Practice 4, 90, 99, 101, 113, 117, 120, 130, 149, 151, 177; Programmes 100; Recommendations 3; Risk factors 132; Standards 102, 131; Treatment 5, 131

Evidence informed *see* evidence-based

Family court 28, 94, 95, 99

Family Violence 3, 4, 5, 58, 60, 64, 65, 67, 90, 91, 94, 96, 123, 151

Female perpetrators; female-perpetrated; female perpetration 4, 6, 14, 26, 27, 28, 29, 33, 34, 35, 46, 47, 48, 51, 54, 60, 95, 96, 97, 98, 109, 112, 117, 123–135, 152, 175, 176

Felson, R. B. 13, 16, 17, 151

Feminist 1, 2, 3, 4, 11, 12, 16, 20, 26, 27, 73, 79, 82, 92, 93, 94, 95, 101, 123, 128, 142, 175

Financial abuse 30, 49, 52, 53, 73, 98

Gelles, R. 58, 90, 130, 162

Gendered; Approach 145, 146, 148, 166, 175; Crime 107; Language 26, 40; Model 4, 11–20, 54, 59, 73, 109, 172, 173, 177; Perspectives 96, 139, 144, 148; Practice 3, 40, 142, 149, 150; Stereotypes and beliefs 31, 32, 33, 39, 47

Gender-inclusive 1, 4, 5, 54, 90–91, 98, 99, 150, 174, 177; Gender neutral 12, 54, 114, 174, 177

Gender, sexual and relationship diversities *see* LGBTQ+

Graham-Kevan, N. 3, 11, 12, 14, 17, 73, 76, 97, 98, 109, 110, 111, 112, 113, 142, 143, 151

Hamel, J. 1, 5, 28, 89–102, 175

Help-seeking 47, 161

Hines, D. 73, 98, 111, 123, 124, 125

Homicide 1, 11, 147

Ideology; Ideological 3, 5, 20, 59, 93, 107, 108, 114, 142, 152

Intergenerational; Intergenerational transmission 5, 17, 60, 101, 159, 177

Intervention 1, 2, 20, 27, 49, 61, 66, 100, 124, 125, 127, 130–131, 133, 143, 148, 150, 158, 159, 162, 177; Adolescent 66–68, 174; Children 155, 160, 163, 176; Current 3, 4, 5, 134, 175; Evaluation 128; Group 40, 99, 127, 128; Models 1, 129, 134; Judgements 46, 49, 50–53; Need 125, 126, 132, 156, 164–165; Strategies 5, 59; Therapeutic 6, 135. See also Duluth. See also Perpetrator interventions

Intimate terrorism 14, 16, 37, 53, 91, 97, 37

Jealousy 17, 76, 98, 100, 133

Johnson, M. P. 14, 16, 60, 91, 97, 110, 146, 151

Langhinrichsen-Rohling, J. 3, 4, 15, 16, 44, 47, 48, 53, 59, 60, 68, 95, 100, 124

LGBTQ+; LGBTQI+ 5, 47, 54, 62, 63, 67, 68, 73–83, 92, 99, 174, 175

Marital violence 58, 89

Male privilege 1, 2, 11, 89, 145, 172

Male victimisation; male victimization, Male victims 4, 6, 12, 26–28, 32, 34–36, 39–40, 46–47, 48, 49, 51, 52, 54, 82, 98, 108, 139–152, 166, 173, 176

Masculine; Masculinity 19, 28, 30, 31, 34–35, 38, 45, 51, 140

Mental health; mental illness 18, 31, 53, 54, 76, 77, 79, 82, 93, 95, 112, 113, 114, 116, 129, 140, 150, 151, 155
Motivation 15, 89, 90, 95, 99, 111, 112, 113, 124, 126, 127, 131, 134, 151, 160, 177
Motivational interviewing 92, 100, 112–113, 115, 131
Mutual abuse *see* bidirectional

Narrative 1, 6, 11, 27, 31, 52, 54, 123, 142, 144, 159, 173, 176, 177
National Family Violence Survey 90, 91
Norms 13, 17, 28, 34, 38, 58, 64, 66, 165, 177

Offender 11, 13, 16, 98, 100, 110, 111– 113, 117, 119, 125, 132, 135, 154

Patriarchy: patriarchal 5, 13, 14, 19, 20, 59, 64, 65, 79, 89, 91, 94, 95, 101, 142, 145, 151
Paymar, M. 2, 6, 20, 59, 89, 90, 107, 114
Pence, E. 2, 3, 6, 20, 59, 89, 90, 107, 114
Perceptions 1, 5, 27, 30, 31, 33, 35, 36, 43–55, 65, 77, 95, 139, 164, 173
Perpetrator 2, 3, 12, 15, 30, 34, 37, 61, 62, 68, 75, 78, 94, 97, 107, 112, 114, 124, 131, 135, 160, 163, 166, 172, 176; Adolescent 58, 65; Aetiology 92; Attitudes 5, 28, 29, 34, 43–55; "cast as the perpetrator" 4 30, 31–34; Gender 12, 14, 20, 27, 28, 59, 60, 73, 99, 108, 109, 141, 145; Motivation 95–97; Perpetrator programme; perpetrator treatment 3, 4, 68, 93, 98, 99–101, 107–120, 127–128, 130, 132, 143, 147, 173, 175, 177
Pizzey, E. 1, 11, 17, 27
Police; Arrest 27; Attitudes 36, 47; Data 12, 28, 76, 108, 109–110, 117, 144, 145, 147; Involvement 2, 4, 33, 46, 50, 51, 52, 114, 119; Protection 28; Report 13, 28, 32; Response 28–29, 30, 33, 35, 38, 39, 40, 146, 150, 163; Training 40, 54
Policy 1, 3, 4, 6, 26, 27, 28, 30, 36, 40, 44, 54, 68, 73, 93, 123, 141–142, 144–149, 151, 162, 166, 172, 174, 176, 177
Politics; Political 3, 6, 11, 20, 47, 52, 54, 74, 94, 117, 149, 151, 152, 173, 177
Post-Traumatic Stress Disorder 38, 89, 91, 119, 132
Power 1, 2, 6, 13, 18, 20, 28, 67, 75, 89, 90, 97, 107, 108, 109, 110–111, 114, 115, 124, 133, 145, 174, 175, 176

Practitioner 3, 4, 5, 6, 77, 79, 107, 149, 152, 162, 166, 174, 175, 177
Psychological aggression; psychological abuse (*see also* emotional abuse) 13, 14, 27, 30, 35, 44, 47–48, 49, 51, 53, 60, 61, 62, 63, 75, 100, 124, 129, 133

Queer relationships *see* LBGTQ+

Recommendations 3, 6, 27, 29, 46, 52, 102, 111, 114, 131, 172–177
Renzetti, C. 47, 75, 78
Risk 5, 14, 18, 20, 59, 60, 62, 64, 66, 68, 75, 76, 79, 107, 108, 110, 111, 112, 114, 115, 116, 117, 118, 119, 124, 125–126, 129, 133, 134, 147, 150, 157, 158, 175
Risk assessment 15, 16, 116, 118
Risk factors 4, 15, 16, 63, 65, 67, 91, 93, 100, 101, 107, 109, 110, 111, 112, 126–127, 132, 135, 175

Same-sex relationships 5, 12, 44, 47, 48, 52, 54, 59, 65, 75–78, 115, 117, 124, 125, 177
Scotland 6, 79, 139–152
Self-defence; self-defensive 2, 4, 11, 12, 28, 30, 35, 92, 109, 123, 124, 125, 126, 177
Sex differences 13, 15, 16
Sex parity 4, 12
Situational couple violence 14, 91
Stakeholders 3
Stereotypes 31, 32, 33, 36, 43, 44, 45, 46, 47, 48, 52, 54, 55, 77, 148, 173, 174
Straus, M. 12, 15, 17, 27, 58, 59, 60, 62, 90, 91, 92, 93, 123, 124, 162
Survivors 26–27, 29, 46, 47, 48, 52, 53, 54, 55, 77 *see also* victims

Transgender 5, 59, 74, 77, 79–82
Trauma 4, 5, 14, 17, 18, 19, 20, 29, 30, 31, 93, 113, 115, 127, 131
Trauma informed 113
Treatment; Couples 91; Medical 80; Models 90, 93, 99, 128, 134; Needs or targets 101, 131–134; Outcomes 5, 100, 131; Providers; Provision 1, 93, 102, 172; Sample 16; *see also* perpetrator treatment
Typology 14, 91, 146

Unilateral violence 5, 15, 90, 177
United Kingdom; UK 1, 5, 11, 26, 27, 28, 29, 40, 49, 52, 53, 75, 80, 81, 101, 107, 108, 114, 128, 147, 165
United States 1, 2, 11, 20, 75, 94, 101, 107, 114

Victim; victimisation 12, 18, 19, 29, 30, 37, 58, 61, 62, 65, 75, 109, 119, 123, 125, 127, 129, 133, 160, 163, 165, 166, 174; Assessment 116; Attitudes 5, 13, 27, 28, 43–55, 173; Blaming 164; Children or childhood 113, 154, 160, 162; Groups 5, 20; Intervention, Services or Support 4, 73, 93, 94, 96, 108, 113, 114, 116, 117, 123, 127, 173, 174, 177; LGBTQ+ 73–83, 175; Overlap with perpetration 14, 15, 60, 61, 65, 68, 98, 173; Voices 36, 40; Women 2, 4, 14, 26, 27, 34, 36, 60, 73, 91, 96, 97, 108, 109, 124, 129, 172, 176; *See also* male victims

Vignettes 27, 49, 95, 96, 97

Violence against women 1, 2, 11, 13, 26, 28, 35, 36, 40, 54, 97, 117, 141, 143, 144, 146, 149, 151

Western 3, 53, 54, 59, 74

Women perpetrators *see* female perpetrators